The Institutional Investor Series in Finance

FINANCIAL FUTURES
MARKETS
STRUCTURE, PRICING
AND PRACTICE

John J. Merrick, Jr.

1817

Harper & Row, Publishers, New York
BALLINGER DIVISION

Grand Rapids, Philadelphia, St. Louis, San Francisco
London, Singapore, Sydney, Tokyo, Toronto

International Standard Book Number: 0-88730-338-2

Library of Congress Catalog Card Number: 89-20082

Printed in the United States of America

Library of Congress Cataloging-in-Publication Data

Merrick, John, 1954-
　　Financial futures markets: structure, pricing, and practice / John
J. Merrick, Jr.
　　　　p.　cm. – (The Institutional investor series in finance)
　　Includes bibliographical references.
　　ISBN 0-88730-338-2
　　1. Financial futures.　I. Title.　II. Series.
HG6024.3.M47　1989
332.64'5–dc20   89-20082
                                                                          CIP

90 91 92 93 HC 9 8 7 6 5 4 3 2 1

To John and Mary

Contents

List of Tables and Figures

Acknowledgments

This book draws from experience in both the academic and practitioner's worlds. A good part of the book is based on lectures on financial futures developed for the MBA program at the New York University Graduate School of Business Administration. Other material draws on research focused upon stock index futures markets conducted both as a member of the finance faculty at NYU and as a visiting scholar in the research department of the Federal Reserve Bank of Philadelphia. Finally, an important portion of the book, especially Chapters 4 and 7, draws from work at Shearson Lehman Hutton, Inc.

Special acknowledgments are due to my former evening MBA students, whose input of specific market knowledge greatly speeded my own understanding of the issues; to Stephen Figlewski, with whom I collaborated on a previous futures book; to Kenneth Garbade and William Silber, whose work and discussions helped shape my own interests in the markets; and to Jacques Rolfo for supporting the completion of this project.

Thanks are also due to Burton Cutting, Munir Dauhajre, Masaya Kuramochi, Guy Murray, Tim Quek, and Suresh Sundaresan, for help in production and review of portions of the manuscript. Of course, all of the above are absolved from remaining errors. In particular, the analysis and opinions expressed herein are personal and should not necessarily be construed as reflecting those of Shearson Lehman Hutton, Inc.

Finally, one last apology (this time in writing) is due to Kathy, Andrew and Charlotte for a series of lost weekends.

CHAPTER 1

Introduction and Overview

"Begin at the beginning. . .and go on till you come to the end: then stop.". . . . (Guidance from the King in Lewis Carroll's *Alice's Adventures in Wonderland*)

Exchange-traded financial futures contracts have been among the most important financial innovations of the 1970s and 1980s. With these products, investors can adjust their exposure to fluctuations in securities prices, interest rates, and exchange rates quickly and cheaply. For example:

- A bond dealer caught short in a sudden market rally buys Treasury bond futures to hedge his exposure to further price rises.
- Fearing a rise in interest rates, a corporate treasurer sells a strip of Eurodollar futures contracts to hedge the reset risk on a floating rate liability.
- A fund manager, desiring to shift assets from bonds to stocks quickly, sells Treasury bond futures and buys Standard & Poor's (S&P) 500 index futures, leaving the portfolio itself untouched.
- An equity block desk, temporarily holding a large position in stocks, lays off part of its risk by selling S&P 500 index futures.
- A program trader, seeing S&P 500 index futures trading cheap to the basket of index stocks, buys the futures and sells stocks to capture the mispricing.

These capabilities are extremely important to marketmakers such as banks, bond dealers, and equity block desks, and they are becoming increasingly attractive to insurance companies, pension funds, and other institutional investors charged with managing large securities portfolios.

1

Market Growth

Total trading in futures contracts, both commodities and financials, has grown enormously over the past two decades. Total annual trading volume reached 245.9 million contracts in 1988, up from 228.9 million in 1987 and just 18 million in 1972. This jump in total trading volume represents an annual growth rate of nearly 18% over the 16-year span since 1972.

Even more phenomenal has been the growth of trading in the financial futures sector. The combined contract trading volume of the top three financial contracts—Treasury bonds, Eurodollars, and S&P 500 index futures—accounted for 42% of all U.S. futures contract volume in 1988.

A ranking of the most actively traded United States financial futures contracts is presented in Table 1-1. The Chicago Board of Trade's (CBOT) Treasury bond futures contract is now the most actively traded. In 1988, 70.3 million Treasury bond contracts were traded on the CBOT, up from 66.8 million contracts in 1987 and 52.6 million in 1986. The Chicago Mercantile Exchange's (CME) Eurodollar contract is the most actively traded short-term interest rate futures contract. In 1988, 21.7 million Eurodollar futures contracts were traded on the CME.

An Emerging Industry

Although organized commodity futures trading has existed in the United States for over 100 years, trading in financial futures is relatively new. The first financial futures contracts were the foreign currency futures introduced by the CME's International Monetary Market division in 1972. In that year, trading began in British pound sterling, Canadian dollar, West German mark, Japanese yen, Swiss franc, Mexican peso, Dutch guilder, and French franc contracts. Of these initial eight, the pound, Canadian dollar, mark, yen, and Swiss franc contracts are still actively traded.

The initial success of these contracts led to further innovations by futures exchanges. In 1975, the CBOT introduced a futures contract on Government National Mortgage Association (GNMA) certificates.
In 1976, trading in three-month Treasury bill futures began on the CME. Treasury bond futures were introduced by the CBOT in 1977. Other markets in 10-year Treasury notes (CBOT), Eurodollars (CME), Municipal bonds (CBOT), 5-year Treasury notes (FINEX and CBOT), 2-year Treasury notes (FINEX), and Federal Funds (CBOT) have followed.

Table 1–1.   Contract Volume of Major U.S. Financial Futures Markets.

Contract (Exchange)	Inception	Contract Volume (millions)		
		1988	1987	1986
Treasury Bonds (CBOT)	1977	70.3	66.8	52.6
Eurodollars (CME)	1981	21.7	20.4	10.8
S&P 500 Index (CME)	1982	11.4	19.0	19.5
Japanese Yen (CME)	1972	6.4	5.4	4.0
Deutsche Mark (CME)	1972	5.7	6.0	6.6
Swiss Franc (CME)	1972	5.3	5.3	5.0
Treasury Notes (CBOT)	1982	5.2	5.3	4.4
British Pound (CME)	1972	2.6	2.6	2.7
NYSE Composite (NYFE)	1982	1.7	2.9	3.1
Treasury Bills (CME)	1976	1.4	1.9	1.8
Municipal Bonds (CBOT)	1985	1.3	1.6	0.9
MMI Maxi (CBOT)	1984	1.2	2.6	1.7

CBOT = Chicago Board of Trade; CME = Chicago Mercantile Exchange; NYFE = New York Futures Exchange.

The most successful new futures products of the 1980s were stock index futures. A contract tied to the Value Line Stock Index was introduced by the Kansas City Board of Trade (KCBT) in February 1982, and contracts on the New York Stock Exchange Composite Index at the New York Futures Exchange (NYFE) and on the Standard & Poor's 500 stock index at the CME followed soon after. A more recent entrant to the field by the CBOT is the Major Market Index contract, established in 1984.

The CME's S&P 500 index futures contract assumed the status of the most actively traded stock index contract soon after it was introduced. Until the October 19, 1987 crash of the stock market, the trading volume of the S&P 500 index futures market grew phenomenally. In 1986, about 19.5 million S&P 500 index futures contracts were traded on the CME. In fact, prior to the crash, the dollar value of the S&P 500 futures contracts trading hands on a given day often was more than double the value of actual stock trading on the floor of the New York Stock Exchange. However, S&P 500 index futures trading activity dropped sharply after the October crash, inducing a 2.4% decrease in total S&P 500 contract volume in 1987 (from the 1986 high) and an additional 40.4% decrease in 1988.

Finally, the 1980s witnessed substantial growth in financial contract trading on foreign futures exchanges. For example, the London International Financial Futures Exchange (LIFFE) trades U.S. Treasury bond, Eurodollar, and currency contracts, as well as Eurosterling, Euromark, Short Gilt, Medium Gilt, Long Gilt, German Government Bond (Bund), Japanese Government Bond, and Financial Times Stock Exchange 100 Index futures contracts. The Paris-based Marché à Terme International de France (MATIF) has developed a successful market for French Government debt futures. The Singapore International Monetary Exchange (SIMEX) is an Asian link for trading of Eurodollar, Yen, and Pound contracts (with right of offset against CME contracts). Furthermore, the Tokyo Stock Exchange trades a contract on the Tokyo Stock Price Index (TOPIX) as well as the highly successful Japanese Government Bond futures contract.

Some Contracts Fail

Not all financial futures contracts innovated by futures exchanges succeed. Examples of failed contracts include those based on commercial paper (CBOT), domestic bank certificates of deposit (CME), 2-year Treasury notes (CBOT), 4- to 6-year Treasury notes (CBOT and CME), and the New York Stock Exchange Financial subindex (NYSE). Black's (1986) evidence shows that the existence of a liquid, efficient cross-hedging market is a significant impediment to new contract development.

Ironically, the GNMA contract—the first interest rate contract—has declined dramatically in importance. Attempts to revive this market with redesigned versions of a GNMA contract have not met with much success.[1] Even in the face of such failures, all of the exchanges recognize that continued growth and success depends crucially on experimentation with new contracts. This search is necessary to meet the changing trading needs of securities market participants.[2]

---

1. The latest attempt, a cash settlement version based on the current coupon GNMA, began trading in June 1989.

2. In one of the more novel experiments, the New York Coffee, Sugar and Cocoa Exchange (NYCSC) attempted to develop futures contracts based on different indicators of general economic activity. In fact, the NYCSC commenced trading of a Consumer Price Index futures contract in 1985. However, this CPI futures contract did not generate much interest and has since been delisted.

Why Financial Futures?

The trading volume growth of financial futures over the last two decades is an established fact, as is their increased newsworthiness. But what are the underlying reasons for the spectacular success of these new markets? After all, futures contracts are *derivative* instruments—dependent on the underlying cash markets for their identities. What makes trading financial futures contracts so attractive?

Investors find financial futures useful because they are a convenient and relatively low-cost way either to speculate on or to hedge the uncertain future movements in securities prices, interest rates, or currency values. Speculators, confident in their ability to predict swings in securities prices, find that futures positions are convenient ways to place desired market price bets. Investors who are bullish on the stock market might buy stock index futures as a substitute for buying a portfolio of stocks. Likewise, bearish investors might sell stock index futures as a convenient way to "short" the stock market.

Other, perhaps less confident, investors enter futures positions designed to hedge their current cash market positions. For example, a hedger who owns a portfolio of stocks will sell a properly weighted number of stock index futures contracts to eliminate the net market risk.

Of course, investors could speculate or hedge their risks without resorting to futures market transactions. The would-be bullish stock speculator could simply buy a broad-based portfolio of stocks (or shares in a mutual fund). The would-be stock position hedger could simply sell out the stock portfolio and invest the proceeds in a bank deposit until a less uncertain environment prevailed. However, executing these strategies in the cash market can be cumbersome for the investing public or institutions that are not securities marketmakers themselves. In particular, financial futures markets offer advantages over cash markets in at least two important dimensions: liquidity and direct transactions costs.

Increased Market Liquidity

Market liquidity is loosely defined as the degree to which prices are affected by specific orders. In a liquid market, buy and sell orders can easily be filled without causing "abnormal" price fluctuations. A market where trade is fragmented usually is illiquid. In an illiquid market, corresponding buy and sell orders would cause temporary price distortions around the normal equilibrium price. Moreover, the cost of market-maker services—the bid-ask spread—becomes lower as a market's liquidity increases.

Traditionally, the contribution of a futures market has been the consolidation of order flow and information into a centralized market. Such consolidation obviously is valuable in the context of raw commodity cash markets, such as those for wheat, soybeans, and copper, where trade is fragmented because of both geographic decentralization and quality differences among alternative commodity lots. Exchange trading of standardized commodity contracts offers the potential of a much more liquid market.

At first glance, the commodity futures' "increased liquidity" story appears unconvincing as a full explanation of the success of financial futures markets. Historically, the cash markets for stocks and Treasury securities have been viewed as among the most liquid and least costly markets within which to transact. In particular, the New York Stock Exchange traditionally has been considered to be a low-cost, liquid centralized market. Likewise, the dealer markets in Treasury securities and currencies operated by commercial banks and investment banking houses have typically been mentioned as competing examples of well-functioning schemes for the organization of trade.

However, these traditional views of cash financial markets as "model" organizations of trade were formed in a world where financial futures markets did not exist. Recall that, prior to the October 1987 crash, S&P 500 stock index futures trading often generated twice the dollar volume of trading on the New York Stock Exchange. This somewhat surprising fact indicates that stock index futures in particular—and financial futures in general—offer traders significant liquidity and transactions cost advantages over the cash markets.

Lower Transactions Costs

For firms that do not engage in marketmaking activities, the total transactions costs for futures contracts can be substantially lower than those for the cash market. These transactions cost savings are especially significant for stock index futures. Table 1–2 presents a cost comparison for a "roundtrip" purchase and sale of $13.25 million worth of stocks versus the analogous roundtrip trade in 100 S&P 500 index futures contracts (an equivalent stock exposure at an index of 265.00). The total roundtrip transactions costs of buying and subsequently selling 100 S&P 500 index futures contracts is about $5,000, split evenly between the direct commission costs and the usual one-tick ($25 per contract) bid-ask spread. In contrast, assuming institutional commission costs of $0.07 per share, an average share price of $45, and a bid-ask spread of $0.125 per share, the total costs of buying and selling an equivalent amount of stocks ($13.25 million for an S&P 500 stock index equal to 265.00) in the cash market would be about $78,000. Thus, the stock index futures trade costs less than $1/15$ of the stock market trade.

Financial futures markets solve other problems faced by institutional traders. In particular, a stock market speculator can finance only 50% of a position with margin loans. With stock index futures, the effective leverage ratio can be significantly higher. A $6,500 initial margin payment controls one S&P 500 stock index futures contract that, when the underlying index equals 265.00, represents $132,500 in stock market value ($500 times the S&P 500 index).[3] Furthermore, all futures markets offer the opportunity to short the underlying asset conveniently. In some cash markets, shorting the cash asset directly by selling a borrowed asset is relatively costly.

These cost-reduction benefits accrue especially to nondealer institutions and the public. Cash market dealers already have access to low transactions costs. This extension of the low cash market transactions cost profiles of dealer firms to nondealer firms and the public via futures trading has been termed the "democratization of transactions costs."[4] Thus, futures contract purchases and sales provide investors with cost-efficient means of making desired portfolio adjustments and are properly viewed as institutional solutions to trading problems.

The Demand for Trading Services

Another reason for the remarkable growth of financial futures trading is reflected in the changing trading patterns of cash securities markets. Although precise data for trading volume growth in the dealer markets for fixed-income securities are unavailable, the data for stock exchange trading reveal dramatic increases in trading activity. For example, reported share volume on the New York Stock Exchange rose from 1.6 billion shares in 1965 to 4.7 billion shares by 1975 to 40.9 billion shares in 1988.

---

3. Initial margin levels change frequently in response to shifts in market volatility. The $6,500 figure was in force in May 1989.

4. See William Silber (1982).

Table 1–2. Comparing Roundtrip Transactions Costs on $13.25 Million of Stock Risk Exposure.

	Stock Market	Futures Market
Size	294,444 average shares (@ $45 average price)	100 S&P 500 contracts
Commissions	$20,611 on purchase (@ $0.07 per share)	$2,500 roundtrip (@ $25 per share)
	$20,611 on sale (@ $0.07 per share)	
Bid-ask market impact cost	$36,806 (@ $0.125 per share)	$2,500 (@ $25 [1 tick] per contract)
Total costs	$78,028	$5,000

A number of factors suggest themselves as contributing to this dramatic upward trend in trading activity. Certainly, the cast of characters playing in the securities markets has changed. Beginning in the early 1960s, the markets for stock and fixed-income securities have become dominated by institutional investors such as pension and mutual funds. It is likely that such institutional investors are more apt than private individuals to trade on a discretionary basis, swapping in and out of securities positions with the hope of achieving higher returns. Moreover, transactions costs in securities markets have fallen sharply in recent years. This is particularly true in the stock market, where, prior to May 1975, commissions were fixed by the exchanges and were immune to competitive pressures. It is not unreasonable to believe that some significant portion of the rise in discretionary trading is tied to lower transactions costs.

When viewed against the backdrop of the changes in cash securities market trading patterns, the successes of the new financial futures markets are quite understandable. First, financial futures markets cater to institutional investors. Second, the emergence of these super-low trading cost structure markets represents a continuance of a trend toward cost efficiency begun earlier within the cash securities markets.

Plan of This Book

The remainder of this book is organized as follows: Chapter 2 outlines the important institutional details of futures contracts themselves and the exchanges on which they are traded. Chapter 3 discusses futures contract pricing; the linkages between futures and cash market prices provided by arbitragers and basis traders are explained. Chapter 4 explains the special aspects of Treasury bond and note futures pricing and basis trading.

Chapter 5 begins a three-chapter section on hedging. Chapter 5 itself focuses on the simplest types of hedging problems; the concept of basis risk is explored, and the relationship between arbitrage sector performance and hedging effectiveness is discussed. Chapter 6 analyzes the regression model approach to more general "cross-hedging" problems, with special applications to stock index futures hedging. The problems accompanying uncritical applications of the statistical approach to hedging are discussed.

Chapter 7 presents analytical approaches to hedging Treasury bond and note positions. Here, the duration and price value of basis point concepts are applied to measuring futures versus cash security risk relationships. The use of futures-based strategies in portfolio management and the special problems associated with uncertainty over the identity of the cheapest deliverable Treasury issue are discussed.

Chapter 8 concludes the book with a discussion of recent market structure and regulatory issues. These include the effects of futures trading on the underlying cash market, the role of futures in the stock market crash, and the trading scandals of 1988–89.

All of the arbitrage and hedging strategies developed in this book are illustrated using actual market data. Reflecting the widespread interest in stock, Treasury note and bond, and money market portfolio risk management, the examples here stress applications to S&P 500 index, Treasury note and bond, and Eurodollar futures contracts.

CHAPTER 2

Futures Contracts and Their Markets

"Our life is frittered away by detail". . . . (Henry David Thoreau)

Definition and Terms

A futures contract is a standardized agreement to buy or sell a particular asset or commodity at some deferred date. The terms of the contract specify the amount and precise type of the asset to be delivered, the delivery date or dates, the place of delivery, and certain options that the contract seller may have with respect to the delivery process. Many contracts, especially the more recently designed ones, specify final settlement through a cash payment. Each contract's terms are established by a government-regulated futures exchange on whose floor and under whose auspices contracts are traded. The exchange also sets certain rules and regulations governing the conduct of trading in its contracts.

For example, the Chicago Board of Trade's March 1989 Treasury bond futures contract calls for delivery of $100,000 face value of U.S. Treasury bonds with at least 15 years to first call date (if the delivered issue is callable) or to maturity (if not callable). Delivery must take place by wire transfer through the Federal Reserve System on any business day during the month of March 1989. The seller has the option to deliver bonds bearing a coupon higher or lower than the 8% "par grade," but the invoice price is adjusted according to a predetermined system of premiums and discounts.

Long Versus Short

An investor who buys a March 1989 bond contract is said to have a long position, or simply to "be long". This investor must accept delivery of

$100,000 of bonds, or offset this obligation by selling a March 1989 futures contract prior to its last trading date (March 22, 1989). An investor who opens a position by selling a futures contract is said to "be short" and must either deliver the actual Treasury bonds at maturity, or cover the short position by buying a contract in the futures market prior to its last trading date.

Futures Prices

The price fluctuations in futures markets provide the potential for profits (and losses) from futures positions. Long positions will profit and short positions will lose as the futures contract's price rises. Short positions will profit and long positions will lose as the contract's price falls.

Price Convergence at Contract Maturity

The contract price is closely related to the cash market price of the security and, thus, to cash market supply and demand. Assuming a single delivery date and a single deliverable security, the futures price must converge to the security's cash market price so as to rule out the simplest of arbitrage strategies. If the futures price at maturity were *greater* than the cash market price of the deliverable security, an arbitrager could buy that security, sell the futures contract, and immediately deliver the security against the short futures position for a quick profit.

For example, suppose that the delivery date price of the security were $110, but that the delivery date futures contract price equalled $111. An arbitrager could buy the security in the cash market for $110, sell the futures contract and immediately deliver. Since the delivered security's acquisition price is $1 less than the delivery invoice price of $111, the arbitrager earned $1. Thus, the security is $1 underpriced relative to the futures. (Equivalently, the futures is $1 overpriced relative to the security.) Arbitrage trading would simultaneously generate security buy orders and futures sell orders. These orders would put the appropriate pressures on each market. The initial –$1 gap would narrow to $0.

This narrowing could take place by a rise in the security's price to $111, with the futures price remaining unchanged. Alternatively, the narrowing could take place by a fall in the futures price to $110, with the security's price remaining unchanged. The necessary narrowing also could occur by each market price showing some partial movement toward the other. For example, the futures price might decline by $0.45 and

Table 2–1. **Summary of Delivery Date Arbitrage Mispricing: Cash (110) Below Futures (111)**

Buy Cash Security	−110
Sell Futures, Immediately Deliver at Invoice Price	111
Total Profit on Delivery	1

the security's price might rise by $0.55 to achieve price convergence at $110.55. In any case, the exact price where convergence is achieved is irrelevant to the arbitrager. The important price signal was the negative *spread* between the security's price and the futures price on the delivery date.

If the futures price at maturity was *less* than the cash price, the arbitrager could buy the futures contract, take delivery of the cash asset, and immediately sell it in the cash market for a corresponding profit. For example, suppose that the delivery date price of the security were $110, but the future contract price equalled $109. An arbitrager could buy the futures contract, take delivery, and then sell the delivered security immediately in the cash market.

The arbitrager earns $1 without risk by acquiring the delivered security for the futures invoice price of $109 and selling the security for $110 in the cash market. Thus, the security is $1 overpriced relative to the futures. (Equivalently, the futures is $1 underpriced relative to the security.) Arbitrage trading would simultaneously generate security sell orders and futures buy orders. These orders would put the appropriate pressures on each market. The initial $1 gap would narrow to $0.

Again, the exact price where convergence is achieved is irrelevant to the arbitrager.

In sum, at least for simple single delivery date, single deliverable security futures contracts, price convergence at maturity is an arbitrage-

Table 2–2. **Summary of Delivery Date Arbitrage Mispricing: Cash (110) Above Futures (109)**

Buy Futures, Immediately Take Delivery at Invoice Price	−109
Sell Cash Security Upon Receipt	110
Total Profit Upon Cash Sale	1

enforced relation. For final cash settlement contracts, convergence is guaranteed by the contract terms themselves.

Basis

The "basis" is the cash price minus the futures price. For the simplest single delivery date, single deliverable security contracts, the delivery date's cash-futures basis must equal zero. By definition, cash settlement contracts guarantee a zero final expiration date basis.

A final basis of zero is the anchor for fairly valuing the futures contract on all days prior to maturity. The possibility of buying actual securities, selling futures, and holding either for delivery or offset at a zero final basis imposes a theoretical relation between the cash price, the futures price and the cost of carrying the securities until the delivery date. This fair pricing relationship will be analyzed in detail in Chapter 3.

Futures vs. Cash vs. Forward

A futures market differs considerably from a "cash" or "spot" market, such as the dealer market in Treasury securities or an exchange market for stocks like the New York Stock Exchange. In a cash market, securities are purchased and sold for prompt delivery. Funds and asset titles exchange hands in cash market transactions. In a futures contract market, the trading is in commitments to make a transaction at a later date. No money changes hands at the time a futures contract is initiated, since in reality nothing tangible is purchased or sold at the moment the contract is entered.

A futures market also differs in significant ways from "forward" markets,such as those in foreign currencies traded through the international banks. First, futures are traded on an exchange. Since all trade is unified in one marketplace, there is no need to search among a number of dealers to uncover the best price, and liquidity and depth of the market are maximized. In contrast, forward contracts are agreements privately entered between two parties.

Second, all aspects of a futures contract except the price are standardized. All investors who buy or sell March 1989 bond futures are trading identical contracts. This enhances continuous market liquidity. In contrast, forward contracts are usually tailored to meet the individual needs of the two specific parties.

Third, unlike forward contracts, futures do not usually result in delivery. Most futures positions are closed out before maturity by off-setting futures transactions.

Finally, futures are guaranteed against default by either party by the creditworthiness of the futures exchange. This eliminates the need to worry about the credit risk of other specific traders, though the investor must bear the risk of default by the exchange itself. Forward contracts are private agreements which bear trader-specific default risks.

Futures Trading

Trading in futures contracts takes place on the floor of organized futures exchanges. Each exchange provides the facilities through which its members can transact purchases and sales of the contracts listed by that exchange. An exchange membership is valuable since members have direct physical access to the trading floor, and they can react more quickly than outsiders to changes in the market. Exchange membership also reduces the direct costs of trading.

Memberships or "seats" on a futures exchange are limited in number. Seat prices fluctuate in value as determined by demand forces (given a predetermined supply). Seat prices can sometimes be more volatile than the prices of the futures contracts themselves. For example, the price of a seat on the CME's Index and Option Market—which trades the S&P 500 Index futures and futures options—fell from $175,000 during the week of October 12, 1987 to $95,000 during the week of October 26, 1987.

The Pit

Trading is done in an area of the exchange trading floor known as the pit, so called because of its shape. A trading pit is shaped like a miniature amphitheater, generally octagonal with several levels, descending toward the center, on which the traders stand facing each other.

Unlike the stock market, there is no specialist or designated marketmaker. Instead, the traders, who may be acting for their own account or as agents for off-the-floor customers, make competing bids and offers for the listed contracts in an open outcry auction. That is, at all times every trader in the pit is free to announce a bid to buy one or more contracts, an offer to sell, or be silent. The rules governing the pit are meant to ensure that transactions take place at either the highest bid or lowest offer quoted at the time of the trade.

The Floor Trader Population

The floor trader population is comprised of a diverse set of individuals. Some trade on their own account. Others are employed by trading firms. Specific subgroups segregated by their willingness to take risks can be identified. The most important of these subgroups are brokers, day traders, and scalpers ("locals").

Brokers. Brokers simply transmit the buy and sell orders of "off-the-floor" users of futures markets—hedgers and speculators. In some cases these orders are bids or offers for contracts that must compete with other bids and offers in the pit. Such orders provide liquidity to the pit. In other cases, the broker's customers place "market" orders. Market orders instruct the broker to buy contracts at the lowest offer price or to sell contracts at the highest bid price then prevailing in the pit. Market orders consume liquidity in the pit. In any event, brokers merely service the orders of their off-the-floor customers.

Day Traders. Day traders are short-term speculators who choose to place their own orders rather than work through brokers. Here "short-term" could mean a matter of minutes or hours, depending upon the individual trader's expectation of price movements. The "day trader" label implies that these speculators seldom hold open positions overnight.

Scalpers ("Locals"). Finally, scalpers (also referred to as "locals") are very short-term traders who perform a marketmaking function by servicing market orders placed by other floor traders. A scalper quotes a two-sided market and hopes to profit by turning over positions at the usual bid-ask spread. For example, a scalper's bid might be lifted by a broker placing a five-contract market sell order for a hedger customer. After acquiring this five-contract long position inventory, the scalper hopes that a five-contract market buy order will appear quickly to be filled at his initial asking price.

Under textbook circumstances, the off-the-floor order flow allows the scalper's five-contract inventory to be turned over in a matter of seconds at the anticipated bid-ask spread. However, it is possible that the anticipated market buy orders do not appear immediately and are only attracted by a lower price. Such a fall in price will cause the scalper to lose money on the trade if his ultimate sale price is lower than his initial purchase price. (To get out of a position, the scalper might even decide to liquidate by selling to another scalper at the prevailing bid price.) Conversely, the scalper would make more than the original bid-ask spread if there were a rise in the price structure during the time he held a long contract inventory.

Table 2-3 provides a revealing diary of one New York Futures Exchange NYSE index contract scalper's trading over a 22-minute interval in January 1983. Note especially this scalper's tendency to eliminate his existing inventory as quickly as possible.

With many traders simultaneously shouting bids and offers, and using hand signals to attract the attention of others and to announce their desired trades, a trading pit under normal circumstances gives an outsider the impression of near-bedlam. Yet, this highly competitive system of marketmaking has proved successful over the years. Active futures markets remain very liquid in the fact of large transactions volume and volatile prices. The bid-ask spread in most major futures contracts is equal to the smallest allowed price change (one tick).[1]

Nevertheless, problems with the organization of open-outcry trading have emerged. Because of inadequate time-sequence auditing capabilities, exchanges are unable to perfectly police adherence to the strict price priority rules for market orders. Furthermore, the practice of "dual trading"—allowing brokers to both service public orders as well as trade for their own account—raises obvious conflict of interest issues. Movements to reform open-outcry trading, or supplement or replace it with electronic exchanges, are gaining momentum and will be further discussed in Chapter 8.

The Clearinghouse

In order to execute trades on the trading floor, an exchange member must also be a member of the clearinghouse or affiliated with a clearing member. The clearinghouse is the guarantor of performance on all con-

---

[1]However, during the stock market crash of October 1987, stock index futures trading became very illiquid as many clearing firms pulled their sponsored traders off the floor. Instead of the usual 1-tick bid-ask spread, a 20-tick spread (one index point) was not unusual in the S&P 500 pit on October 19, 1987.

Table 2–3. Diary of a NYFE Scalper

Transaction	Time	Contracts Bought (+) Sold (−)	Q	Price
1	10:05:29	2	1	85.70
2	10:06:47	−2	1	85.75
3	10:08:10	5	1	85.80
4	10:09:15	−1	1	85.85
5	10:09:49	−2	0	85.85
6	10:10:25	−1	0	85.85
7	10:11:20	−1	0	85.80
8	10:12:56	6	0	85.90
9	10:13:29	−3	1	85.95
10	10:15:38	−1	1	85.95
11	10:16:58	−1	1	85.90
12	10:17:23	−1	1	85.90
13	10:22:25	−5	0	85.80
14	10:23:11	3	1	85.80
15	10:23:23	2	1	85.80
16	10:25:26	5	0	85.75
17	10:26:12	−1	1	85.75
18	10:26:18	−1	1	85.75
19	10:28:12	−3	1	85.70

$Q = 1$ indicates trade done on scalper's own market.
Source: Silber (1984).

tracts entered into on the floor of the exchange. After member A agrees on the exchange floor to sell member B a March 1989 Treasury bond contract at 90-28 (90 and 28/32s of 100% of the $100,000 par value) and the trade is verified by the clearinghouse, the clearinghouse interposes itself between the buyer and seller and becomes the legal opposite side to each party's trade. Thus, A is short one March 1989 Treasury bond contract and the clearinghouse is long the contract. Similarly, B is long one March 1989 contract, while the clearinghouse is short one to her.

The clearinghouse has no net position and bears no risk from price changes since it always takes on equal and opposite positions. However, since both A and B deal directly with the clearinghouse, and not with each other after the initial transaction, each party perceives default risk to be much lower. That is, even if B defaults on the agreed contract terms, A's position is unaffected. It also means that each of the original parties to a trade can liquidate her position—by entering a new offsetting contract position—without affecting the other's outstanding contract.

The contract performance guarantee granted by the clearinghouse is typically backed by a fund maintained by the exchange. Should any party to a contract default on the contract's provisions, the fund is available to fulfill the defaulted obligations. In addition, the exchange is authorized to assess its members to meet such obligations should the fund be depleted by a large default. The role of the clearinghouse as guarantor of contract performance is crucial in establishing a liquid contract market since it eliminates any need by market participants to investigate the creditworthiness of other individual traders in the pit.

Margin Requirements

Futures exchange clearinghouses require that investors opening positions in futures meet initial margin requirements. Essentially, initial margin amounts are "good-faith" deposits that investors must forward to their brokers (and brokers to their clearing members, and clearing members to the clearinghouse) to bind their performance on the contracts they undertake. Both long and short positions must make margin deposits.

Profits (and losses) are realized on a cash basis at the end of each day when the contracts are "marked to market." The investor will be required to post additional margin to bring the deposit back up to the initial margin level. These cash flows are known as variation margin. If the investor fails to meet the margin call, the position may be liquidated immediately by the clearinghouse at the going market price. Initial margin can be posted either in cash, U.S. government securities, or in letters of credit. Thus, an investor who posts Treasury bills as initial margin does not lose interest earnings on this good-faith deposit. However, all variation margin payments must be made in cash.

The initial margin deposits and subsequent variation margin payments are designed to guarantee that the investor will perform according to the terms of the contract. The variation margin payments provide the necessary pool of funds to finance the daily cash settlements.

The level of the initial margin requirement depends on the specific contract considered and on whether the position to be margined is a hedged or a speculative one. Margin requirements are set by the exchange and are usually directly related to the face value of the underlying contract and to the volatility of the contract's price. The objective of futures margins is simply to guarantee performance on the contracts.

Initial margin requirements are usually small relative to the contract's face value. As of May 1989, the initial margin for a speculative position in Treasury bill futures was $1,500 per contract, 1.5% of the $1 million par value of the bills controlled by the contract. At the same time, the initial margin for a S&P 500 index futures speculator was $6,500 per contract, representing 4.2% of the contract value as of May 7, 1988.

The exchanges move quickly to alter margin levels to reflect changes (either increases or decreases) in price volatility. In particular, the margin policy shifts in response to the October 19, 1987 stock market crash were swift and dramatic. Table 2-4 lists the margin requirements in effect just before and just after the stock market crash for a number of important contract markets.

Margin and Leverage

Because margin is so low in a futures position, leverage is very high. Leverage is defined as the ratio of the dollar value of resources controlled to the dollar value of funds invested. This means that a small change in the futures price can create a cash flow which is large relative to the margin posted by the investor. For example, a 10 basis point rise in a Treasury bill futures quote will generate an immediate $250 cash inflow (or outflow) to the long (or short) side of the contract. This

Table 2–4. Initial Per Contract Margin Requirements Before and After October 19, 1987

Contract	Net Speculative		Hedging	
	Before	After	Before	After
Treasury Bond (CBT)	2,500	5,000	2,000	4,000
Treasury Note (CBT)	2,000	4,000	1,500	3,000
GNMA (CBT)	2,500	5,000	2,000	4,000
Treasury Bill (CME)	750	1,500	500	1,000
Eurodollar (CME)	750	1,500	500	1,000
S&P 500 Index (CME)	10,000	20,000	7,500	15,000
NYSE Composite Index (NYFE)	3,500	7,000	1,750	5,000
Value Line Index (KCBT)	4,500	20,000	3,000	20,000

"small" futures price change, which would cause a 16.7% change in the value of an investor's position (given that $1,500 was deposited as initial margin), could easily happen in a single day.

While the leverage that low futures contract margin requirements create is important for individual speculators, this leverage issue per se is not of major importance for hedgers with offsetting cash market position risks. From the hedger's point of view, low initial margins on futures positions translate into lower effective costs of hedging, as only small amounts of capital need to be tied up in margin-acceptable assets such as Treasury bills.

Mark-to-Market Daily Settlement

The clearinghouse also manages the daily settlement procedure of futures markets. At the end of each trading day, all contracts "mark-to-market." The gain (or loss) from the price change on the contract during the day is immediately credited (or debited) to the winning (or losing) accounts. It is as if each outstanding contract position were settled at the close of trading and then reopened with a trade price equal to the day's settlement price. Thus, unless prices remain constant from day to day, all futures accounts will have some cash flow.

This daily settlement procedure is an important difference between futures markets and other markets. It prevents unsettled losses from building up which could lead to a default at maturity. Marking-to-market increases the safety of futures contracts, but it means that positions must be monitored constantly to service daily settlement.

To illustrate more clearly the cash flow consequences of the daily settlement aspect of futures, Table 2-5 shows the March 1989 Treasury bond contract as it traded over the week of February 3, 1989 to February 10, 1989. Column 1 of Table 2-5 presents the settlement price for this contract on each day. The settlement price is determined by an exchange committee to be representative of the transactions prices during the last 60 seconds of trading each day. Column 2 gives the change in the settlement price over each day. Finally, column 3 gives the daily cash flow consequences of the mark-to-market settlement procedure. These cash flows are computed by multiplying each 32nd of a point change in the quoted contract settlement price by $31.25. The $31.25 change per 32nd of a point is the correct cash flow for this contract since each 32nd (the price quotation unit or "tick") equals 0.03125 of 1% of face value and the contract's face value is $100,000.

Table 2–5. Cash Flow Consequences of Daily Settlement. Markings-to-Market of the March 1989 Treasury Bond Contract Over the Trading Week From February 3, 1989 to February 10, 1989

	Settlement Price	Change (Ticks)	Cash Flow ($) if Long	if Short
Friday, Feb. 3, 1989	90–28	—	—	—
Monday, Feb. 6	90–30	+2	+62.50	−62.50
Tuesday, Feb. 7	91–11	+13	+406.25	−406.25
Wednesday, Feb. 8	91–05	−6	−187.50	+187.50
Thursday, Feb. 9	89–20	−49	−1,531.25	+1,531.25
Friday, Feb. 10	88–28	−24	−750.00	+750.00
Net change over Feb. 3 close of 90–28		−64	−2,000.00	+2,000.00

All prices are end-of-day settlement prices (quoted in points and 32nds of 100%). Daily cash markings to market are worth $31.25 per tick per contract.

In light of the two-tick rise in the March 1989 contract's price between Friday, February 3 and Monday, February 6, the long would have received $62.50 from the clearinghouse and the short would have had to pay $62.50 to the clearinghouse in variation margin. On Tuesday, the 13-tick price rise has the long receiving $406.25, while the short pays the same amount. On Wednesday, fortunes begin to reverse with a six-tick or $187.50 loss (gain) for the long (short). On Thursday, the price drops by 49 ticks. On Friday, the price falls another 24 ticks. These drops generate payments of $1,531.25 and $750.00, respectively, from the long to the short.

For the week, the long would have had to make net payments to the clearinghouse of $2,000 since Treasury bond futures prices fell 64 ticks on net. Conversely, the short position would have pocketed $2,000.

The clearinghouse's role in the daily settlement process is one of a bookkeeper/treasurer. Funds collected from accounts with losses are transferred to those with gains. These cash flows occur down the entire account chain, from customer-to-broker-to-clearing member-to-clearinghouse, as appropriate. However, since the clearinghouse has no net position, it shows no net cash flow for the day.

Finally, the clearinghouse oversees the final settlement of positions by delivery. This process includes the acceptance of filings of intent to deliver by contract sellers, assignment of delivery notices to outstanding long positions, and communication with the banks of the seller and the buyer.

Price Limits

Usually, there are some exchange-imposed limits on how much a contract's price may change during a given day. For example, the Treasury bond contract is not permitted to trade at a price more than three points ($3000 per contract) above or below the previous trading day's closing price.

When the price which would clear the market is above the limit, active trading essentially ceases. One observes many bids for that contract at the limit price, but few transactions take place since most sellers are content to wait until after the contract's "pent-up" price advance has run its course. A corresponding plethora of sellers and few buyers emerge on a day when the market is limit down.

This effective halt in trading gives traders more time to digest the market's movement and to re-evaluate the soundness of the market's momentum. Daily price limits may offer investors some protection from abrupt short-run swings in market prices. They bound the day's losses for investors on the wrong side of the price move (and the day's gains for those on the right side).

However, they cannot limit these losses indefinitely. There is no long-term escape from fundamentally sound market movements since, as discussed above, losing positions are essentially frozen during limit move days. The effect of the daily limits in these cases is to distribute the total losses and gain over more than one day.

Price limits do not hold on the last day of trading in the delivery month. In some markets, price limits are lifted for the entire delivery month or when a contract closes "limit up" or "limit down" for a specified number of consecutive trading days. Table 2-6 presents a sampling of price limits currently in force, as of May 1989, on various futures contracts.

Position Limits

Futures exchanges reduce the probability that a single trader or group of traders may exert too much influence over prices through position limits. Position limits restrict the quantity of contracts that an investor may own or control through others. In addition to reducing the risk

Table 2–6. **Normal Daily Price Change Limits***

Contract	Size	Daily Price Change Limits	
Treasury Bond	$100,000	3 pts.	$3000
10-Year Treasury Note	$100,000	3 pts.	$3000
5-Year Treasury Note	$100,000	3 pts.	$3000
Treasury Bill	$1,000,000	None	
Eurodollars	$1,000,000	None	
S&P 500 Index	$500 × Index	30 pts.	$15,000

*Quoted figures are normal daily limits. For many contracts, daily limits may be expanded after a series of limit move days and/or removed during the delivery month.

of active price manipulation, the position limits bound the size of any losses the exchange itself might have to incur upon a default by one of its clearing members. Position limits vary according to whether the position holder is classified as a speculator or a bona fide hedger.

Settlement of Open Futures Positions by Offset

Most futures positions are closed out prior to the stated delivery date(s). An open futures position can be closed out at any time during its trading life by taking an offsetting futures position. An investor with a long March 1989 Treasury bond futures position could close that position any trading day prior to delivery by selling a March 1989 Treasury bond contract. Similarly, an investor with a short March 1989 Treasury bond futures position could close the position by buying a March 1989 Treasury bond futures contract. Therefore, an investor in a futures contract need not be fearful of having to make or take unwanted deliveries of the underlying asset as long as care is taken to offset the open position prior to the delivery period.

A typical strategy designed to avoid deliveries, but maintain the desired futures exposure, involves "rolling" the contract position forward. This would be done for an open long March 1989 bond futures contract by selling a March 1989 contract and buying a June 1989 contract. The roll replaces the long March 1989 position with a long June 1989 position. Likewise, the short could roll a position by buying March 1989 and selling June 1989. These rolls could take place in February 1989, prior to the start of the March 1989 contract's delivery period. Rolls are naturally executed as a "spread" trades (see Chapter 3).

Final Settlement by Delivery of the Physical Asset

Futures positions that have not been closed out prior to the end of trading in a contract must be settled through the delivery of the physical asset. For example, the holder of an open short position in a Treasury bond or note futures contract may file notice of intent to deliver to the exchange's clearinghouse any time during the contract's delivery notification period. This notification period begins two business days prior to the first business day of the delivery month (February 27, 1989 for the March 1989 Treasury bond and note futures). This notice period ends two days prior to the last business day of the delivery month (March 29, 1989 for March 1989 Treasury contracts). The day the short files a delivery notice is termed the "position day," and is the first day of a three-day delivery sequence. The day after the filing of the short's delivery notice is received, the clearinghouse assigns it to a holder of an open long position. Each incoming notice to deliver is assigned to the oldest (i.e., longest outstanding) long position which has not already been "matched up" with a delivering short. The short then invoices the accepting long. This invoicing day is termed the "notice of intention day."

Delivery of the specific Treasury issue actually is accomplished in concert with the banks of the seller and buyer on the day after the notice of intention day. The seller's bank wires the securities to the buyer's bank through the computerized system of the Federal Reserve. A cash payment is wired from the buyer's bank to the seller's bank in return. The respective banks then credit and debit the securities and cash accounts of the seller and buyer appropriately. The three-day delivery process ends.

The invoice price paid by the buyer to the seller at delivery is based on the contract's settlement price as of the "position" day. It is not necessarily the price at which either the seller or buyer initially opened his or her position. The differences between the delivery invoice price and the prices initially agreed to by the seller and buyer have previously been adjusted for through daily cash payments and receipts according to the mark-to-market daily settlement feature of futures contracts.

Sellers' Delivery Options

Sellers of futures contracts are granted certain options regarding delivery of the underlying security if final settlement by delivery is desired. The options relate to the quantity, quality grade, place, and date of delivery of the underlying security. Some of them, if elected, do not affect the cash value that the seller receives upon making delivery. Others add a premium to or deduct discount from the contract's invoice value.

The Treasury Bond Futures Contract

An important example of the invoice price adjustment procedure due to a contract's quality option occurs in connection with the Treasury bond futures contracts.[2] While the Chicago Board of Trade's Treasury bond futures contract is nominally written on $100,000 in face value of an 8% coupon rate bond, final settlement can be made through delivery of *any* issue with at least 15 years to its first call date (if callable) or maturity (if not callable). A system of premiums and discounts is applied to the invoice amount for delivered issues with coupon rates greater or less than the 8% standard. This system is summarized by a set of *conversion factors*. The invoice price (quoted ex-accrued) associated with the delivery of a specific issue is found by multiplying that issue's conversion factor by the position day's futures settlement price. Thus, if the futures settlement price equals 90-00, the invoice price of an issue with a conversion factor of 1.2000 would be 108-00, while that of an issue with a conversion factor of 0.9500 would be 85-16. The delivered issue's accrued interest as of the delivery date is added to the invoice price to obtain the total invoice amount.

Conversion Factors

The conversion factors for all deliverable bonds are published by the CBOT. The formulas determining the conversion factor for each bond essentially view the delivered bond as of the first day of the delivery month and discount its remaining cash flows (per $1 of face) using an 8% yield. Actually, the CBOT system only approximates the actual cash flows of each bond, since some shortcuts are taken in determining the size and timing of the cash flows of each deliverable bond.

In particular, before applying its present value formula, the CBOT rounds the maturity of each bond down to the number of whole quarterly periods until the bond's actual maturity or first call date (if callable). This rounding imposes some obvious distortions. It not only arbitrarily

---

[2]The CBOT Treasury note contracts have correspondingly similar terms.

shortens the bond's maturity, but also assumes that all bonds will be called on their first call date (even if the market assigns a low probability to such a call). Furthermore, the rounding will impose an inaccurate computation of interest accrual for fractional coupon periods.[3] Finally, the CBOT computes all factors as of the first day of the delivery month regardless of the day the bond actually is delivered.

The specific formulas to calculate CF^i, the conversion factor for bond i with a rounded CBOT maturity of n years and x months and an annual coupon rate of CR, are

$$CF^i = \frac{1}{(1.04)^{x/6}} \left\{ \frac{CR}{2} + [(\frac{CR}{0.08})(1 - \frac{1}{(1.04)^{2n}}) + \frac{1}{(1.04)^{2n}}] \right\}$$
$$-[\frac{CR}{2} \frac{6-x}{6}]$$

if $x = 0, 3,$ or 6; but

$$CF^i = \frac{1}{(1.04)^{3/6}} \left\{ \frac{CR}{2} + [(\frac{CR}{0.08})(1 - \frac{1}{(1.04)^{2n+1}}) + \frac{1}{(1.04)^{2n+1}}] \right\}$$
$$-[\frac{CR}{2} \frac{6-3}{6}]$$

if $x = 9$.

These formulas represent simple solutions to the general yield-to-price translation of the form:

$$CF_i = \sum_{t=1}^{q'} \frac{CR/2}{(1.04)^{t-w}} + \frac{1}{(1.04^{q'-w})} - w[CR/2],$$

where q is the number of *full* semiannual periods within the rounded CBOT maturity; w (equal to 0 or 0.5) is the fractional period remainder; and $q' = q + 2w$ is the number of coupons remaining.

An Illustration. Consider the 10.375% of November 2007-12 as a delivery candidate for the March 1989 futures contract. Rounded down from 18 years and 8.5 months to the nearest full quarter, this bond has a

---

[3]Of course, the accrued interest received by the delivering short is accurately determined for invoicing purposes.

maturity for invoice purposes of 18 years and six months, as calculated from the first day of the delivery month (March 1, 1989) to the first call date (November 15, 2007). From the formula above, this issue's conversion factor is calculated using the relevant inputs: CR = .10375; n = 18; and x = 6:

$$CF = \frac{1}{(1.04)^1}\left\{\frac{.10375}{2} + \left[(\frac{.10375}{0.08})(1 - \frac{1}{(1.04)^{36}}) + \frac{1}{(1.04)^{36}}\right]\right\}$$
$$- \left[\frac{.10375}{2}\frac{0}{6}\right]$$
$$= .9615[.051875 + 1.22454] - [0]$$
$$= 1.2273$$

The conversion factor for this 10.375% coupon, 18-year, six-month rounded CBOT maturity bond is 1.2273 (rounded to four decimal places as stipulated by the contract's terms). On February 27, 1989 (the first notice day), the March 1989 bond futures settlement price was 87-28. Thus, the short could give notice as of this date and subsequently deliver $100,000 in par value of these 10.375% bonds on March 1, 1989. The accepting long would be invoiced $107,848.99 in principal value (1.2273 × 87.875% × $100,000). The March 1, 1989 accrued interest on the 10.375% of November 2007-12 would be added to compute the full invoice amount.

In contrast, suppose that 7.25% of May 2016 were delivered against the March 1989 futures contract. The conversion factor of the 7.25% of May 2016 is determined by this issue's rounded CBOT maturity (from March 1, 1989) of 27 years and 0 months. The inputs to the conversion factor formula are CR = .0725; n = 27; and x = 0.

$$CF = \frac{1}{(1.04)^0}\left\{\frac{.0725}{2} + \left[(\frac{.0725}{0.08})(1 - \frac{1}{(1.04)^{54}}) + \frac{1}{(1.04)^{54}}\right]\right\}$$
$$- \left[\frac{.0725}{2}\frac{6}{6}\right]$$
$$= 1.0[0.03625 + 0.91753] - [0.03625]$$
$$= 0.9175$$

The resulting conversion factor is 0.9175. Thus, the invoiced principal amount would be 0.9175 × 87.875% × $100,000 or $80,625.31.

As a final illustration, consider delivery of the 11.25% of February 2015. From March 1, 1989, there are 25 years and 11.5 months until this issue's February 15, 2015 maturity date. Thus, the rounded down CBOT maturity is set at 25 years and nine months. In terms of the formula inputs, CR $= .1125$; $n = 25$; and $x = 9$. Because $x = 9$, the second form of the equation is used.

$$CF = \frac{1}{(1.04)^{.5}} \left\{ \frac{.1125}{2} + \left[(\frac{.1125}{0.08})(1 - \frac{1}{(1.04)^{51}}) + \frac{1}{(1.04)^{51}} \right] \right\}$$
$$- \left[\frac{.1125}{2} \frac{3}{6} \right]$$
$$= 0.9806[0.05625 + 1.35128] - [0.028125]$$
$$= 1.3521$$

The 11.25% of February 2015's conversion factor for a March 1989 delivery is 1.3521. Its invoice price is 1.3521 $\times$ 87.875% $\times$ $100,000.

In each case, accrued interest on the delivered bond as of the delivery date would be added to determine the total invoice amount. Table 2-7 presents the conversion factors associated with each issue eligible for delivery into the March 1989 bond futures contract.

Benefits of Delivery Options

The chief benefit of incorporating delivery options for short positions is reduction of the risk of an unintended tight supply of deliverable securities, or deliberate price manipulation. If no delivery options existed, the contract could be determined by the vagaries of supply and demand for the single issue. It might even be possible for a powerful investor (or consortium of investors) to accumulate a large long position in a particular contract and simultaneously gain control of a major proportion of the underlying cash market securities eligible for delivery. By broadening the contract to allow delivery of one of a number of securities, the exchange increases the deliverable supply of securities. Thus, the chances that the deliverable supply would become technically tight or that anyone could obtain control over a major proportion of this expanded list of securities are diminished.

Due to the delivery specifications of "market basket" contracts (those allowing delivery of one of a number of different specific securities for final settlement) one security is often cheapest to deliver. Such situations

Table 2–7. Conversion Factors for March 1989 Bond Futures Deliverable Supply

Deliverable Issue	Factor
12.375% May 2004	1.3783
13.75% Aug 2004	1.5011
11.625% Nov 2004	1.3188
12.00% May 2005	1.3575
10.75% Aug 2005	1.2474
9.375% Feb 2006	1.1255
9.125% May 2004–09	1.0973
10.375% Nov 2004–09	1.2089
11.75% Feb 2005–10	1.3322
10.00% May 2005–10	1.1787
12.75% Nov 2005–10	1.4310
13.875% May 2006–11	1.5408
14.00% Nov 2006–11	1.5599
10.375% Nov 2007–12	1.2273
12.00% Aug 2008–13	1.3893
13.25% May 2009–14	1.5196
12.50% Aug 2009–14	1.4473
11.75% Nov 2009–14	1.3749
11.25% Feb 2015	1.3521
10.625% Aug 2015	1.2860
9.875% Nov 2015	1.2051
9.25% Feb 2016	1.1369
7.25% May 2016	0.9175
7.50% Nov 2016	0.9447
8.75% May 2017	1.0833
8.875% Aug 2017	1.0972
9.125% May 2018	1.1262
9.00% Nov 2018	1.1126
8.875% Feb 2019	1.0986

occur because the structure of premiums and discounts tied to the delivery invoice prices of the alternative deliverable securities need not always reflect their true relative cash market values. Chapter 4 analyzes this issue from the perspective of Treasury bond and note futures pricing.

Final Settlement by Cash Payment

While most commodity and financial futures contracts specify final settlement by delivery, many contracts are settled through a final cash payment. For financials, these include stock index, Eurodollar and municipal bond futures.

Under cash settlement, the final settlement price of the futures contract is set equal to the value of a specific settlement index. All open positions go through a final marking-to-market at this settlement price and the resulting gains and losses are transferred among the accounts of the futures contract holders, under the usual daily procedure. By definition, the final cash settlement procedure provides "perfect" convergence of the final futures price to the settlement index (the "cash price").

Example: Eurodollar Cash Settlement.   Consider the cash settlement process for the highly successful Eurodollar futures contract traded on the CME's International Monetary Market (IMM). The contract is written on a $1,000,000 notional face amount of three-month Eurodollar time deposits. It is quoted on the IMM through an index equal to 100 minus the implied interest rate. Cash settlement is affected by marking all outstanding contracts to a final settlement index at the contract's expiration moment. This final settlement index equals 100 minus the three-month London Interbank Offered Rate (LIBOR) as determined by an authoritative poll of London banks on the contract's final trading day. The Eurodollar contract expires at 3:30 p.m. London time on the second London business day prior to the third Wednesday of the contract month. For the March 1989 contract expiration, this expiration date was March 13, 1989. The settlement LIBOR was 10.29%. Thus, the March 1989 Eurodollar contract was settled at an index of 89.71 ($= 100 - 10.29$). Each basis point in the index is valued at $25. All open positions were marked to this price and were settled in cash. The final marking-to-market on an open long position held since the close of trading on the previous trading day (when the March 1989 contract closed at 89.72) was $-$25 ($= $25 \times [-1$ basis point]). Conversely, an open short March 1989 Eurodollar position had a cash settlement marking-to-market over the final day of $25.

Pros and Cons of Cash Settlement

The cash settlement feature has become an important force in new contract design. Given an appropriate settlement index choice, cash settlement facilitates hedging by guaranteeing price convergence at maturity. Garbade and Silber [1982] argue that the gains from specifying a cash settlement scheme in lieu of delivery depend on three factors: (1) the need to promote convergence of cash and futures prices because delivery costs are large; (2) the ability to reduce the incidence of squeezes and corners; and (3) the accuracy of the settlement index.

Cash settlement has proven to be especially useful for financial contracts such as stock indexes. Here, delivery costs for physical delivery of stock index baskets would be large and otherwise inconvenient. Furthermore, broad indexes of stock prices (e.g., the S&P 500, the NYSE Composite index) can be computed accurately and would be difficult to manipulate.

Summary

In this chapter, some of the most important features of futures contracts and the markets in which they are traded have been reviewed. It is crucial that users of futures markets understand their specific contractual obligations. The specific terms of the contract will determine how it is priced by arbitragers. Chapters 3 and 4 discuss the arbitrage process in detail.

CHAPTER 3

Basis Trading: Linking Cash and Futures Markets

"Buy cheap, sell dear.". . . . (Anonymous [but rich])

Since a futures contract is a close substitute for the underlying cash asset, the futures price should be closely related to the cash price. Certainly, the tie between the futures price and the cash price is tight at the contract's maturity date when, either through a simple arbitrage or final cash settlement design, the two are equal. However, prior to the maturity date, the potential user of the futures should "comparison shop" to see whether the contract is overpriced or underpriced relative to the cash market.

For example, is it cheaper to buy a three-months-to-maturity S&P 500 stock index futures contract at 273 or the underlying portfolio of stocks if the cash S&P 500 index stands at 270? The futures position entails no initial investment, but receives no dividends. While both futures and cash indexes must converge in three months, there is usually a net cost to carrying the stock portfolio (i.e., financing costs are greater than dividend earnings). Thus, the futures should usually sell for more than the cash index. However, is 273 too high or too low?

As it happens, answering the question of fair relative pricing between futures and cash markets also explains how arbitragers make money by trading the basis. While comparison shopping by hedgers and speculators puts some limits on potentially abnormal deviations of futures prices from their fair values, most of the trading pressure aimed at maintaining fair pricing between the futures and cash markets is placed by members of the securities community who have come to specialize in basis trading.

Arbitrage traders attempt to extract profits from any discrepancy that arises between the futures contract's price and its fair value. They sell futures contracts and simultaneously buy the underlying cash asset when the futures price is too high. Conversely, they buy futures contracts and simultaneously sell the cash asset when the futures price is too low. With these trades, arbitragers create synthetic riskless positions at rates of interest more advantageous than those available in the money market.

Basis

As previously defined, the "basis" equals the cash price minus the futures price. On the contract's delivery or expiration date, the cash-futures basis must equal zero (at least for simple contracts). Guaranteed maturity date convergence of cash and futures prices is the anchor for fairly valuing the futures contract on all days prior to maturity. Given maturity date convergence, a trader who buys the cash asset and sells the futures has a riskless capital gain (if the initial basis is negative) or a riskless capital loss (if the initial basis is positive).

For example, suppose that the cash security sells for $100, while a futures contract for a given maturity date sells for $104. The basis equals −$4. A trader who buys the security and sells the future is "buying the basis." If this trader holds the position until the contract's maturity date, he will make a riskless capital gain of $4. This $4 gain is certain to occur since the long basis trader buys the basis at −$4 and, because of convergence, can sell it for $0 on the maturity date.

The maturity date basis "sale" at a $0 price is assured through either of two mechanisms. For a delivery-based contract, closing out the long basis trade at a $0 basis is accomplished simply by delivering the cash security in final settlement of the futures. In this example, the trader pockets a $4 gain since the effective futures delivery invoice price is $4 greater than the cost of acquiring the delivered cash security. For cash settlement contracts, the $4 profit is captured by selling the cash security position and settling the short futures position in cash at an identical final futures price. Here, a final basis of $0 is guaranteed by the contract's cash settlement provision.

Carry

The change in the basis is not the only return to the long basis trader. The long basis position also involves a profit (or loss) equal to its "carry." The long basis trade's carry equals the dollar earnings from the cash security's yield (if any) minus the cash security's financing cost, where both are calculated out to the contract's maturity date. If the cash position's yield provides dollar earnings higher than its corresponding financing cost, the position has *positive* carry. If the cash position's yield provides dollar earnings lower than its corresponding financing cost, the position has *negative* carry.

For example, suppose that the futures contract above matures in one year; that the cash security has a riskless current yield of 5% per year; and that the financing rate is 9% per year. Given an initial price of $100, the cash position has current yield earnings of $5 and financing costs of $9. The position's carry equals current dollar yield minus financing costs, or –$4 for the holding period until contract maturity.

Carry Determines The Fair Basis

For either a single grade/single delivery date or a final cash settlement contract, the underlying cash security's carry determines the fair cash-futures basis. In the example above, the market prices the current basis at –$4 such that the long basis trader has a known capital gain of $4. This pricing makes sense in equilibrium only if the position entails a carry of –$4.[1]

An arbitrager looking at the basis would not find any special opportunities. If a trader buys the basis with borrowed capital, and holds the trade until maturity, the position earns $4 in capital gains and $5 in current yield for a total income of $9. However, this $9 income is precisely what the trader needs to cover the position's $9 financing cost. For a simple delivery or cash settlement futures contract, the basis is fairly priced when basis equals carry.

Basis After Carry

A simple measure of the richness or cheapness of the basis is "basis after carry." Basis after carry equals basis minus the cash position's carry. In the example above, basis after carry equals $0 (= –$4 – [–$4]). A

---

[1]Actually, this "basis equals carry" condition holds for forward contracts. Because futures contracts entail financing/reinvestment risks on mark-to-market daily settlements, an additional risk adjustment related to the co-movement of interest rates and the asset price should enter. See Richard and Sundaresan (1980).

Table 3–1. Summary of a Long Basis Trade.	
Fair Pricing: Basis (−4) = Carry (−4)	
Buy Basis Now	−4
Sell Basis at Expiration	0
Gain on Long Basis Position	4
Cash Asset Yield	5
Cash Position Financing	−9
Loss on Negative Carry	−4
Total Profit	0

basis after carry of $0 expresses a fair cash-futures pricing relationship for a contract which does not grant special delivery options.

A *negative* basis after carry indicates basis cheapness and is a signal for the trader to buy the basis (i.e., buy the cash asset and sell the futures) and carry the position until contract maturity. In the example above, suppose that the futures were priced at $105 (not $104), but that all other data were unchanged. The basis would equal -$5 (= $100 − $105), carry would remain –$4, and the new basis after carry would equal –$1 (= –$5 − [–$4]). Thus, the long basis trade earns $5 in capital gains from convergence, but loses only $4 in negative carry. The long basis trade's net profit equals $1, the negative of the basis after carry at which the position is entered.

Conversely, a *positive* basis after carry indicates basis richness and is a signal for the arbitrager to sell the basis. The basis is sold by selling the cash asset short and buying the futures. Selling the cash asset short involves temporarily borrowing the asset and selling it in the market. The funds generated by the short sale are invested until the contract's delivery month at the interest rate. At that time, the short basis trader takes delivery of the cash asset (effectively, at the present futures price) in final settlement of the long futures position. He then uses the delivered security to cover his short position and reimburses the lender of the borrowed security for the loss of any yield over the borrowing period.

In the context of the original example, assume that the futures were priced at $103 (not $104), but that all other data were unchanged. The basis would equal –$3 (= $100 − $103), carry would remain –$4, and the new basis after carry would equal 1 (= –$3 − [–$4]). This short basis trade loses $3 in capital gains from convergence, but gains $4 in carry. (The short cash position earns interest on the funds raised through

Table 3–2. Summary of a Long Basis Trade.

Mispricing: Basis (−5) < Carry (−4)
Basis After Carry = −1

Buy Basis Now	−5
Sell Basis at Expiration	0
Gain on Long Basis Position	5
Cash Asset Yield	5
Cash Position Financing	−9
Loss on Negative Carry	−4
Total Profit	1

Table 3–3. Summary of a Short Basis Trade.

Mispricing: Basis (−3) > Carry (−4)
Basis After Carry = 1

Sell Basis Now	−3
Buy Basis at Expiration	0
Loss on Short Basis Position	−3
Yield Owed on Short Position	−5
Interest on Short Sale Proceeds	9
Gain on Carry	4
Total Profit	1

the short sale [here, $9], but must pay the borrowed security's current yield to the security's lender [here, $5].) This short basis trade's net profit is $1, the basis after carry at which the position is entered.

Basis Fluctuations: Yield, Financing and Time

Table 3–4 presents some simple calculations on the effects of yield, financing rates and time-to-delivery on carry and, therefore, the fair basis. This table calculates the fair basis (i.e., the carry) associated with a cash security priced at $100 for a range of times-to-delivery (one year, six months and three months); a range of current yields (0% to 15%); and a range of term financing rates (1% to 15%).

At a 3% yield and a 7% term financing rate, the one-year contract basis is fairly priced at –$4. A basis of –$5 would represent a buying opportunity (basis after carry of –$1). Conversely, a basis of –$3 would

Table 3–4. Carry as Function of Asset Yield, the Financing Rate and Time to Delivery for a Cash Price of $100.

Time to delivery: one year

Financing	Yield								
	0%	1%	3%	5%	7%	9%	11%	13%	15%
1%	−1	0	2	4	6	8	10	12	14
3%	−3	−2	0	2	4	6	8	10	12
5%	−5	−4	−2	0	2	4	6	8	10
7%	−7	−6	−4	−2	0	2	4	6	8
9%	−9	−8	−6	−4	−2	0	2	4	6
11%	−11	−10	−8	−6	−4	−2	0	2	4
13%	−13	−12	−10	−8	−6	−4	−2	0	2
15%	−15	−14	−12	−10	−8	−6	−4	−2	0

Time to delivery: six months

Financing	Yield								
	0%	1%	3%	5%	7%	9%	11%	13%	15%
1%	−0.5	0	1	2	3	4	5	6	7
3%	−1.5	−1	0	1	2	3	4	5	6
5%	−2.5	−2	−1	0	1	2	3	4	5
7%	−3.5	−3	−2	−1	0	1	2	3	4
9%	−4.5	−4	−3	−2	−1	0	1	2	3
11%	−5.5	−5	−4	−3	−2	−1	0	1	2
13%	−6.5	−6	−5	−4	−3	−2	−1	0	1
15%	−7.5	−7	−6	−5	−4	−3	−2	−1	0

Time to delivery: three months

Financing	Yield								
	0%	1%	3%	5%	7%	9%	11%	13%	15%
1%	−0.25	0.0	0.5	1.0	1.5	2.0	2.5	3.0	3.5
3%	−0.75	−0.5	0.0	0.5	1.0	1.5	2.0	2.5	3.0
5%	−1.25	−1.0	−0.5	0.0	0.5	1.0	1.5	2.0	2.5
7%	−1.75	−1.5	−1.0	−0.5	0.0	0.5	1.0	1.5	2.0
9%	−2.25	−2.0	−1.5	−1.0	−0.5	0.0	0.5	1.0	1.5
11%	−2.75	−2.5	−2.0	−1.5	−1.0	−0.5	0.0	0.5	1.0
13%	−3.25	−3.0	−2.5	−2.0	−1.5	−1.0	−0.5	0.0	0.5
15%	−3.75	−3.5	−3.0	−2.5	−2.0	−1.5	−1.0	−0.5	0.0

represent a selling opportunity (basis after carry of $1). At an 11% current yield and a 9% term financing rate, the one-year contract basis is fairly priced at $2. A basis of $1 would represent a buying opportunity (basis after carry of –$1). Conversely, a basis of $3 would represent a selling opportunity (basis after carry of $1).

For fixed yields and financing rates, the fair basis (i.e., carry) converges toward $0 as time-to-expiration decreases. Compare the 3% yield/7% financing rate cells of the three alternative times-to-expiration. The one-year basis is priced at –$4; the six-month basis is priced at –$2; and the three-month basis is priced at –$1. Carry becomes less negative as time-to-maturity decreases. Alternatively, compare the 11% yield/9% financing rate cells of the three alternative times-to-expiration. The one-year basis is priced at $2; the six-month basis is priced at $1; and the three-month basis is priced at $0.5. Here, carry becomes less positive as time-to-maturity decreases. For the simple contracts under consideration, full convergence is guaranteed by rational arbitrage pricing on the single delivery date.

Finally, carry also depends on the market value of the cash position. Table 3–5 presents a comparison of the fair basis for a range of market levels, times-to-maturity and financing rates. Short-run fluctuations in the fair basis (via carry) depend on cash market value shifts. Nevertheless, full convergence (a final basis of 0) at maturity still occurs.

The Fair Futures Price

The fair cash-futures pricing relationship can be expressed as

Cash Price − Futures Price = Current Earnings − Financing Cost

or

$$\text{Basis} = \text{Carry};$$

or

$$\text{Basis After Carry} = \text{Basis} - \text{Carry} = 0$$

Unfortunately, these relations can also be expressed algebraically. Let $F_{0,T}$ be the date 0 price of the futures that matures at date T; P_0 be the date 0 cash price; r be the known financing rate; y be the known percentage yield on the cash asset; and let n_0 measure the fraction of a year until the expiration of the futures contract (i.e., fraction of a year between date 0 and date T). Then, in equilibrium,

Table 3–5. Carry and Market Levels. Asset Yield = 3%.

Time to delivery: one year

Cash Price	Financing Rate						
	1%	3%	5%	7%	9%	11%	13%
80	1.6	0.0	−1.6	−3.2	−4.8	−6.4	−8.0
85	1.7	0.0	−1.7	−3.4	−5.1	−6.8	−8.5
90	1.8	0.0	−1.8	−3.6	−5.4	−7.2	−9.0
95	1.9	0.0	−1.9	−3.8	−5.7	−7.6	−9.5
100	2.0	0.0	−2.0	−4.0	−6.0	−8.0	−10.0
105	2.1	0.0	−2.1	−4.2	−6.3	−8.4	−10.5
110	2.2	0.0	−2.2	−4.4	−6.6	−8.8	−11.0
115	2.3	0.0	−2.3	−4.6	−6.9	−9.2	−11.5
120	2.4	0.0	−2.4	−4.8	−7.2	−9.6	−12.0

Time to delivery: six months

Cash Price	Financing Rate						
	1%	3%	5%	7%	9%	11%	13%
80	0.8	0.0	−0.8	−1.6	−2.4	−3.2	−4.0
85	0.9	0.0	−0.9	−1.7	−2.6	−3.4	−4.3
90	0.9	0.0	−0.9	−1.8	−2.7	−3.6	−4.5
95	1.0	0.0	−1.0	−1.9	−2.9	−3.8	−4.8
100	1.0	0.0	−1.0	−2.0	−3.0	−4.0	−5.0
105	1.1	0.0	−1.1	−2.1	−3.2	−4.2	−5.3
110	1.1	0.0	−1.1	−2.2	−3.3	−4.4	−5.5
115	1.2	0.0	−1.2	−2.3	−3.5	−4.6	−5.8
120	1.2	0.0	−1.2	−2.4	−3.6	−4.8	−6.0

Time to delivery: three months

Cash Price	Financing Rate						
	1%	3%	5%	7%	9%	11%	13%
80	0.4	0.0	−0.4	−0.8	−1.2	−1.6	−2.0
85	0.4	0.0	−0.4	−0.9	−1.3	−1.7	−2.1
90	0.5	0.0	−0.5	−0.9	−1.4	−1.8	−2.3
95	0.5	0.0	−0.5	−1.0	−1.4	−1.9	−2.4
100	0.5	0.0	−0.5	−1.0	−1.5	−2.0	−2.5
105	0.5	0.0	−0.5	−1.1	−1.6	−2.1	−2.6
110	0.6	0.0	−0.6	−1.1	−1.7	−2.2	−2.8
115	0.6	0.0	−0.6	−1.2	−1.7	−2.3	−2.9
120	0.6	0.0	−0.6	−1.2	−1.8	−2.4	−3.0

$$P_0 - F_{0,T} = (y - r)n_0 P_0$$

For some assets, the y component is positive. For example, stock portfolios yield dividends. Bonds yield coupon interest income. In contrast, gold will have a negative y since the metal itself yields no cash flows, but requires certain storage and insurance expenses.

The basis market equilibrium condition above can be rearranged to solve for the fair futures price:

$$F_0 = P_0 + (r - y)n_0 P_0$$

Thus, the fair futures price is determined by the current cash price plus the net financing cost (financing cost minus current yield earnings) until the contract reaches maturity. Ignoring transactions costs, the fair futures price equates the holding period value changes of the futures position and a 100%-financed cash asset position. At the fair futures price, the riskless long basis position earns the current riskless rate of interest.

Convergence

Fair basis pricing implies strong restrictions on futures pricing as the delivery date approaches. Table 3–6 illustrates how the convergence process might occur, given constant yields and financing rates, for a range of cash prices (from 80 to 120) and a range of times-to-delivery (0 to 24 months). For each cash price, a time path of futures prices consistent with fair basis pricing is determined.

In the first example, the yield is 3% and the financing rate is 7%. In this negative carry environment, the futures price is higher (so that the basis is more negative) as the time-to-delivery increases. Thus, at a fixed cash price of 100, a one-year futures is initially priced at 104 (basis of –$4). In six months, this six-months-to-expiration contract would be priced at 102 (basis of –$2). In 9 months, this three-month-to-expiration contract would be priced at 101 (basis of –$1). In 11 months, this one-month-to-expiration contract would be priced at 100.3 (basis of –$.3). Finally, on the delivery date the futures would equal the cash price of 100 (basis of $0).

In the second example, the yield is 11% and the financing rate is 9%. In this positive carry environment, the futures price is lower (so that the basis is more positive) as the time-to-delivery increases. Thus,

Table 3–6. Futures Prices and Convergence.

Asset Yield: 3%; Financing Rate: 7%

Cash Price	Months-to-delivery							
	0	1	3	6	9	12	18	24
80	80.0	80.3	80.8	81.6	82.4	83.2	84.8	86.4
85	85.0	85.3	85.9	86.7	87.6	88.4	90.1	91.8
90	90.0	90.3	90.9	91.8	92.7	93.6	95.4	97.2
95	95.0	95.3	96.0	96.9	97.9	98.8	100.7	102.6
100	100.0	100.3	101.0	102.0	103.0	104.0	106.0	108.0
105	105.0	105.4	106.1	107.1	108.2	109.2	111.3	113.4
110	110.0	110.4	111.1	112.2	113.3	114.4	116.6	118.8
115	115.0	115.4	116.2	117.3	118.5	119.6	121.9	124.2
120	120.0	120.4	121.2	122.4	123.6	124.8	127.2	129.6

Asset Yield: 11%; Financing Rate: 9%

Cash Price	Months-to-delivery							
	0	1	3	6	9	12	18	24
80	80.0	79.9	79.6	79.2	78.8	78.4	77.6	76.8
85	85.0	84.9	84.6	84.2	83.7	83.3	82.5	81.6
90	90.0	89.9	89.6	89.1	88.7	88.2	87.3	86.4
95	95.0	94.8	94.5	94.1	93.6	93.1	92.2	91.2
100	100.0	99.8	99.5	99.0	98.5	98.0	97.0	96.0
105	105.0	104.8	104.5	104.0	103.4	102.9	101.9	100.8
110	110.0	109.8	109.5	108.9	108.4	107.8	106.7	105.6
115	115.0	114.8	114.4	113.9	113.3	112.7	111.6	110.4
120	120.0	119.8	119.4	118.8	118.2	117.6	116.4	115.2

at a fixed cash price of 100, a one-year futures is initially priced at 98 (basis of $2). In six months, this six-months-to-expiration contract would be priced at 99 (basis of $1). In nine months, this three-month-to-expiration contract would be priced at 99.5 (basis of $0.5). In 11 months, this one-month-to-expiration contract would be priced at 99.8 (basis of $0.2). Finally, on the delivery date the futures would equal the cash price of 100 (basis of $0). Of course, during the span of a year's trading, cash prices, financing rates and yields will change. Thus, the typical convergence process will not follow the simple linear progression. Nevertheless, full convergence by the contract delivery date is inevitable.

The Implied Repo Rate

The fair cash-futures pricing relation is supported in single grade/single delivery date contracts by a simple arbitrage argument. If the basis is less than carry, there is an incentive to sell the futures contract and buy the cash asset with funds borrowed at the current financing rate. The position is planned to be carried until the delivery month and would be closed out through the delivery of the cash asset as final settlement of the short futures position.

The annualized internal rate of return on this riskless long basis trade, termed the "implied repo rate," equals

$$\text{irr}_{0,T} = (1/n_0)[F_{0,T} - P_0)/P_0] + y$$

In equilibrium, the implied repo rate cannot be greater than the actual financing rate (r). Otherwise, a simple long basis arbitrage trade would be possible.[2]

Conversely, suppose that the basis is higher than carry. There is an incentive for the arbitrager to buy the futures contract, sell the cash asset short and invest the short sale proceeds at rate r. The short basis trade is similar to borrowing P_0 dollars for a period of n_0 years. Again, the implied repo rate is the important return variable. However, for this short basis trade, it is interpreted as a cost of using funds. In equilibrium, the implied repo rate cannot be less than the actual riskless interest rate (r).

From the imposition of these two-sided restrictions, the equilibrium-implied repo rate must equal the interest rate:

$$(1/n_0)[F_{0,T} - P_0)/P_0] + y = r$$

This condition is equivalent to the futures pricing formula:

$$F_{0,T} = P_0[1 + (r - y)n_0]$$

This equation is also applicable to cash settlement contracts like stock index futures. For a cash settlement contract, the annualized return on a long basis trade unwound on the expiration date equals

$$\text{irr}_{0,T} = (1/n_0)[(P_T - P_0) - (F_{T,T} - F_{0,T})]/P_0 + y$$
$$= (1/n_0)[(P_T - F_{T,T}) - (P_0 - F_{0,T})]/P_0 + y$$

---

[2]For Treasury futures arbitrage (see below), basis trade financing can be arranged through the repurchase agreement ("repo") market. Thus, hedged returns from basis trades are naturally termed "implied repo rates." This jargon has been appropriated by arbitragers in other markets, who would not have access to repo rate financing.

However, for cash settlement contracts, $F_{T,T} = P_T$ by definition, so that the date T basis equals 0. Thus, the long basis trade's rate of return simplifies to

$$\text{irr}_{0,T} = (1/n_0)[(F_{0,T} - P_0)/P_0] + y$$

or

$$\text{irr}_{0,T} = -(1/n_0)[\text{Basis}_{0,T}/P_0] + y$$

This derivation neatly shows how the long basis trade's implied repo rate decomposes into two parts: the convergence return and the cash asset's yield. Finally, one can present a similar argument in the case of a short basis trade supporting the usefulness of the implied repo rate as a cost of synthetic riskless money market funding for cash settlement contracts.

Table 3–7 presents two sets of calculated implied repo rates. The upper panel generates implied repo rates for different combinations of initial basis and time-to-delivery, assuming a cash price of 100 and an asset yield of 3% per year. The lower panel generates corresponding implied repo rates for different combinations of initial basis and time-to-delivery, assuming a cash price of 100 and an asset yield of 11% per year.

Consider first the results for the 3% yield value given in the upper panel. For a six-month-to-delivery contract, a basis of –2 gives an implied repo rate of 7%. If the term financing rate equals 7%, the basis is fairly priced at –2. In this case, a basis of –3 would be cheap since the implied repo rate of 9% would be greater than the 7% financing rate. The 2% spread between the implied repo rate over the financing rate indicates that the long basis trade is attractive.

On the other hand, if the basis were –1.5, the implied repo rate would be 6%. In this case, the implied repo rate is 1% less than actual market interest rate. Thus, the basis market offers cheap financing and a short basis trade is indicated. The trade would earn the 1% spread between the assumed 7% market interest rate and the 6% rate at which funds could be raised through shorting the basis.

Now consider the results for the 11% yield value given in the lower panel. For the same six-month-to-delivery contract, an implied repo rate of 7% is obtained only if the basis equals +2. Thus, if the term financing rate equals 7%, the basis is fairly priced at 2. If the term financing rate equals 9%, the basis would be fairly priced—that is, have an implied

Table 3–7. Implied Repo Rates.

Asset Yield: 3%; Cash Price: 100

Basis	Months-to-delivery						
	1	3	6	9	12	18	24
−4.00	51.00	19.00	11.00	8.33	7.00	5.67	5.00
−3.50	45.00	17.00	10.00	7.67	6.50	5.33	4.75
−3.00	39.00	15.00	9.00	7.00	6.00	5.00	4.50
−2.50	33.00	13.00	8.00	6.33	5.50	4.67	4.25
−2.00	27.00	11.00	7.00	5.67	5.00	4.33	4.00
−1.50	21.00	9.00	6.00	5.00	4.50	4.00	3.75
−1.00	15.00	7.00	5.00	4.33	4.00	3.67	3.50
−0.50	9.00	5.00	4.00	3.67	3.50	3.33	3.25
0.00	3.00	3.00	3.00	3.00	3.00	3.00	3.00
0.50	−3.00	1.00	2.00	2.33	2.50	2.67	2.75
1.00	−9.00	−1.00	1.00	1.67	2.00	2.33	2.50
1.50	−15.00	−3.00	0.00	1.00	1.50	2.00	2.25
2.00	−21.00	−5.00	−1.00	0.33	1.00	1.67	2.00
2.50	−27.00	−7.00	−2.00	−0.33	0.50	1.33	1.75
3.00	−33.00	−9.00	−3.00	−1.00	0.00	1.00	1.50
3.50	−39.00	−11.00	−4.00	−1.67	−0.50	0.67	1.25
4.00	−45.00	−13.00	−5.00	−2.33	−1.00	0.33	1.00

Asset Yield: 11%; Cash Price: 100

Basis	Months-to-delivery						
	1	3	6	9	12	18	24
4.00	−37.00	−5.00	3.00	5.67	7.00	8.33	9.00
3.50	−31.00	−3.00	4.00	6.33	7.50	8.67	9.25
3.00	−25.00	−1.00	5.00	7.00	8.00	9.00	9.50
2.50	−19.00	1.00	6.00	7.67	8.50	9.33	9.75
2.00	−13.00	3.00	7.00	8.33	9.00	9.67	10.00
1.50	−7.00	5.00	8.00	9.00	9.50	10.00	10.25
1.00	−1.00	7.00	9.00	9.67	10.00	10.33	10.50
0.50	5.00	9.00	10.00	10.33	10.50	10.67	10.75
0.00	11.00	11.00	11.00	11.00	11.00	11.00	11.00
−0.50	17.00	13.00	12.00	11.67	11.50	11.33	11.25
−1.00	23.00	15.00	13.00	12.33	12.00	11.67	11.50
−1.50	29.00	17.00	14.00	13.00	12.50	12.00	11.75
−2.00	35.00	19.00	15.00	13.67	13.00	12.33	12.00
−2.50	41.00	21.00	16.00	14.33	13.50	12.67	12.25
−3.00	47.00	23.00	17.00	15.00	14.00	13.00	12.50
−3.50	53.00	25.00	18.00	15.67	14.50	13.33	12.75
−4.00	59.00	27.00	19.00	16.33	15.00	13.67	13.00

repo rate equal to its term financing rate—at 1. The same rich/cheap analysis used above would be applied here as well.

Note that the table contains negative values. These negative values indicate that there is no (positive) interest rate that could justify the associated basis value. Under the single grade/single delivery date contract assumptions, the basis is unambiguously rich.

Pricing Stock Index Futures: An Example

Consider pricing a three-month S&P 500 stock index futures contract assuming a current S&P 500 stock index of 270.00. Suppose that the current annualized dividend yield on the underlying cash market S&P 500 stock portfolio is 3.5% (9.45 index points per year, 2.3625 points per quarter); that the annualized interest rate is 7.5% (20.25 index points per year, 5.0625 points per quarter); and that transactions costs can be ignored.

In this example, the stock portfolio has negative carry: it gains 2.3625 in dividends, but loses 5.0625 in financing costs. Specifically, for the three-month holding period until contract maturity, carry equals –2.7 index points (= 2.3625 – 5.0625).

In order to preclude simple arbitrage, the basis must equal the stock position's carry (basis after carry must equal zero). Thus, the basis must also equal –2.7. Given the initial stock index value of 270, the basis will equal –2.7 only if the futures is priced at 272.70.

Alternatively expressed, the annualized net cost of financing this stock position equals 4%—the 7.5% financing rate less a 3.5% dividend yield. Since the futures position entails no net financing, a three-month-to-expiration S&P 500 index futures contract is still competitively priced at 2.7 index points above the current cash index. These 2.7 index points equal the net financing rate, 1% (= [3/12] × 4%), times the current cash index value of 270. Finally, the fair S&P 500 stock index futures price level for the three-month-to-expiration contract analyzed above can be written as

$$F_{0,T} = 270(1 + [.075 - .035][3/12])$$
$$= 270(1.01)$$
$$F_{0,T} = 272.70$$

To see why this pricing structure makes sense, consider what happens when a "program trader" (a stock index futures basis arbitrager) purchases the stocks and sells the futures. He is assured of making the current futures-cash index spread (272.70–270 = 2.7 index points) via convergence, regardless of whether the final stock index is higher than, equal to, or lower than its current level. Recall that cash settlement contracts like those for stock index futures legislate the expiration day futures price to equal the underlying cash asset price. Thus, if the expiration day index value is 290, the cash position gains 20 points (290–270) and the short futures position loses 17.3 (272.7–290) for a net gain of 2.7. If, instead, the index closes out at 260, the cash position loses 10 points (260–270) while the futures position gains 12.7 (272.7–260). This position also will earn 2.3625 points in dividends. Thus, total gross earnings for this riskless investment will be 5.0625 index points. This gross profit is exactly what the initial capital of 270 would return if invested at the current interest rate of 7.5% ([3/12][0.075] [270] = 5.0625).

If the futures were selling at 273, this riskless buy program would gross 5.3625 points (3 through convergence and 2.3625 in dividends). The program's annualized implied repo rate would equal

$$100 \times [360/90] \times [5.3625/270] = 7.94\%$$

Of this 7.94% return, 4.44% is traceable to convergence return and 3.5% is due to dividend yield.

Such a program would dominate the simple 7.5% riskless investment. Arbitragers, seeking to swap the riskless cash/futures program for a plain vanilla money market investment whenever discrepancies arise in the rates of return, would bid the futures price down (and/or the cash price up) if the futures rose above 272.70.

Likewise, if the futures price fell below 272.70, arbitragers would profit from the reverse trade of selling the stock basket and buying the underpriced futures. For example, suppose that this three-month index futures were priced at 272.40. The arbitrager would buy the futures, short the basket of stocks, and invest the proceeds of the short sale at 7.5%. He would lose 2.40 points since the basis converges to 0 at expiration and would also owe 2.3625 points in dividends on the stocks borrowed to make the short sale. These cash flows translate into an implicit borrowing rate of 7.056% (= 100 × [360/90] × [4.7625/270]).

However, the short basis arbitrager can invest the short sale proceeds at a rate of 7.5%. Thus, this yield spread is attractive. Again, the result would be pressure on both cash and futures prices to return to their fair relative values.

Transactions Costs

These calculations ignore transactions costs. Typically, the largest play-
ers in index futures program trading are the major stock brokerage
houses. These firms already have invested in developing economical
systems for trading stocks. These transactions costs include the bid-ask
spread on the basket of stocks, direct stock commissions (or implied
overhead if done by a brokerage firm for its own account), futures commissions, and one market impact (bid or ask) cost on the futures for a
trade held until expiration day cash settlement.

For an S&P 500 index futures program trade by a major institutional
arbitrager, total transactions costs might be reasonably approximated as
0.5% of the S&P 500 cash index (or, 1.35 index points in the example
above).[3] Thus, the futures price could wander anywhere from 271.35 to
274.05 without violating fair pricing boundaries.

One critique of the seemingly wide transactions cost boundaries outlined above focuses on the maintained assumption that each particular
trade is held until the expiration date. However, the hold-to-expiration
trade is just one possible way in which the arbitrager can take profits.
In fact, it usually will be rational for the arbitrager either to unwind or
rollover his position sometime before the initial contract's maturity date.

Early unwindings or rollovers of futures-cash arbitrage trades usually
make sense as alternatives to the hold-to-expiration trade because of
interim changes in contract mispricings between the date the position
is entered (date 0) and contract maturity (date T). If the return to fair
pricing happens earlier, the arbitrager will earn his anticipated profit
and perhaps more if the position can be unwound at a basis which is
mispriced in the opposite direction.

In practice, arbitragers constantly look either to unwind their positions early at a reversed mispricing or to roll their hedges into the next
contract at a more favorable price spread. These active arbitragers effectively place additional arbitrage trades without incurring the full set of
additional transactions costs.[4] Thus, the effective average cost per trade
might be closer to 0.80 or 1.00 index points, depending upon the fre-
quency of opportunities to unwind early or rollover. Using the 1-point
average cost per trade, the transactions cost bounds for the particular

---

[3]See Hans Stoll and Robert Whaley (1986).
[4]See Merrick (1989).

example shrink to 271.70 to 273.70. Buy programs (long basis trades) are attractive at futures prices greater than 273.70. Sell programs (short basis trades) are attractive at futures prices less than 271.70.

Pricing Treasury Bill Futures: An Example

The CME's three-month Treasury bill futures contract can be priced through a relatively simple carry and deliver trade. To price the contract relative to currently traded Treasury bills, the specifics of the contract's delivery and invoicing terms must be clearly understood.

The Treasury bill contract trades on a quarterly cycle: March, June, September and December. Contracts that are not offset by the end of trading on the last trading date are settled through delivery. The contract's first delivery date is the first day of the spot contract month on which the Treasury issues a new 13-week bill *and* a previously issued one-year bill has 13 weeks to maturity. Deliveries may be made on this day or either of the next two business days.[5] The final trading date is the first business day before the first delivery date.

For the June 1989 Treasury bill futures contract, the first delivery date was June 1, 1989 and the last trading date was May 31, 1989. For the September 1989 contract, the first delivery date was September 21, 1989 and the last trading date was September 20, 1989.

The invoice price for all deliveries is based on the last trading date's final settlement index. This index determines the implied discount rate. The invoice price is determined by this discount rate, assuming first delivery date settlement. Thus, if the final settlement index were 91.50, the implied discount rate would equal 8.50% ($= 100 - 91.50$), and the invoice price for a delivered bill would equal

$$\text{Invoice Price} = \$100 \times \{1 - [0.0850 \times (91/360)\}$$
$$= \$97.851389 \text{ per } \$100 \text{ of face value}$$

This price would imply a total invoice amount of $978,513.89 per contract ($1,000,000 face value).[6]

Before delivery, the Treasury bill contract is priced through the basis equals carry arbitrage condition. The basis equals the price of a currently

---

[5]It is always rational to deliver on the first delivery day. See below.

[6]This invoice price applies regardless of whether delivery occurs on the first, second or third possible delivery date. Thus, deliveries later than the first delivery date are treated as "fails."

traded deliverable bill (issued previously as a six-month or one-year bill, but having 13 weeks to maturity as of the contract's first delivery date) minus the current invoice price (as implied by the current settlement index). Carry on any Treasury bill is always negative since it is a discount instrument. Carry is determined by the term repo rate quoted in the repurchase agreement market for the specific deliverable bill. The implied repo rate can be computed from market prices and then compared to the market repo rate to judge profit opportunities.

Consider pricing the June 1989 Treasury bill futures contract on April 25, 1989. The deliverable bill for this contract is the current 128-day bill maturing on August 31, 1989 (i.e., 13 weeks after the first delivery date). On April 25, 1989 this bill traded at an asked discount rate of 8.58%, an asked cash price of $96.973167 per $100 of face value for next day settlement:

$$\text{Price of 8/31 Bill} = \$100 \times \{1 - [0.0858 \times (127/360)]\}$$
$$= \$96.973167$$

The June futures closed at an IMM index of 91.48 (futures discount rate of 8.52%). The current invoice price using the implied discount rate equals

$$\text{Invoice Price} = \$100 \times \{1 - [0.0852 \times (91/360)]\}$$
$$= \$97.8463 \text{ per } \$100 \text{ of face value}$$

The deliverable bill's basis equals -0.873133 ($= 96.973167 - 97.8463$) per $100 of face. In equilibrium, the deliverable bill's basis should equal the bill position's carry over the 36-day period from April 26, 1989 to June 1, 1989.

Recall the definition of the implied repo rate:

$$\text{irr}_{0,T} = -(1/n_0)[\text{Basis}_{0,T}/P_0] + y$$

Since the current income on a Treasury bill is 0 by construction, $y = 0$ and the implied repo rate simplifies to

$$\text{irr}_{0,T} = -(1/n_0)[\text{Basis}_{0,T}/P_0]$$

Thus, the implied repo rate for the deliverable June 1989 contract bill equalled

$$\text{irr}_{0,T} = -(360/36)(-0.873133/96.973167)$$
$$= 0.0900 \text{ or } 9.00\%$$

If the term repo rate to June 1, 1989 on the August 31, 1989 bill were less than 9.00%, the long bill basis position would be profitable.

If the term repo rate were more than 9.00%, the long basis trade would not be profitable. However, the short basis trade might be attractive. A short Treasury bill basis trade involves shorting the deliverable bill and buying the bill futures. The trader invests the proceeds of the short sale to the delivery date, accepts delivery, and uses the delivered bill to cover the short bill position. The implied *reverse* repo rate is computed from the bid price of the bill.

On April 25, 1989, the bid discount rate on the deliverable August 31, 1989 maturity bill was 8.62%, with a bid price of $96.959056. The bid price basis was –0.911189. Thus, the implied reverse repo rate equalled

$$irr_{0,T} = -(360/36)(-0.887244/96.959056)$$
$$= 0.0915 \text{ or } 9.15\%$$

If the term reverse repo rate to June 1, 1989 on the August 31, 1989 bill were more than 9.15%, the short bill basis position would be profitable.

Pricing Eurodollar Futures: An Example

The fundamental basis versus carry argument applies in principle to pricing Eurodollar futures off of the cash Eurodollar deposit market. However, some reinterpretation is necessary due to the fact that the underlying instrument, a three-month Eurodollar time deposit, is non-negotiable.

Assume the following market data for August 19, 1988: one-month LIBOR of 8.375%, four-month LIBOR of 8.792%, and a September 1988 Eurodollar futures index of 91.25.[7] Given the IMM quotation index, this 91.25 Eurodollar futures price implies an 8.75% rate. Using four-month LIBOR to value a 122-day Eurodollar deposit due December 19, 1988, the known end-of-period deposit proceeds equals $1.029795 (= 1 + [.08792(122/360)]) per $1 of deposit principal.[8]

Consider now a synthetic 122-day time deposit created by investing in an 8.375% 31-day deposit maturing on September 19, 1988 (the futures' expiration date), buying 1.0184 (= {1 + [.08375(31/360)]}[91/90])

---

[7]This four-month rate was interpolated from available quotes for three-month and six-month LIBOR.

[8]The term "known" is used somewhat loosely here, since the issuing bank could default on the deposit. Eurodollar deposits are uninsured.

September Eurodollar futures contracts per million dollars of deposits, and then on September 19 rolling over the total position's value into new 91-day deposits due December 19, 1988.[9]

Rolling this deposit over implies reinvesting in 31 days at an unknown future 91-day rate. September futures were priced on August 19 at an implied three-month LIBOR rate of 8.75%. On September 19, 1988, this contract will be settled in cash at an index value reflecting this date's actual three-month LIBOR.

The total value on December 19, 1988 of this synthetic 122-day deposit strategy per \$1 million of initial principal value will be

$$
\begin{aligned}
(1 + R^s_{122}[122/360]) &= (1 + 0.08375[31/360])(1 + R^f_0[91/360]) \\
&= (1 + 0.08375[31/360])(1 + 0.0875[91/360]) \\
&= 1.02949
\end{aligned}
$$

where R^f_0 represents the implied futures rate at date 0 and R^s_{122} is interpreted as the synthetic 122-day deposit rate.[10] Thus, the synthetic 122-day deposit rate equals

$$
R^s_{122} = (360/122)\{(1 + 0.08375[31/360])(1 + 0.0875[91/360]) - 1\}
$$
$$
R^s_{122} = 0.08702
$$

The Implied Forward Rate.   Ignoring the impact of bid-ask spreads in the futures and deposit markets, both issuers and investors will be indifferent between actual and synthetic 122-day deposits only if both rates are identical. A comparison of the synthetic 122-day deposit rate with actual four-month LIBOR reveals the synthetic rate to be nine basis points too low (8.702% versus 8.792%). Given the initial August 19 one-month LIBOR and four-month LIBOR, the synthetic 122-day deposit rate would equal 8.972% only if the implied futures rate on the September Eurodollar contract were 8.87%. Thus, ignoring bid-asked spreads, the fair September futures index is 91.13. Only at this price

---

[9]The [91/90] term is a scale adjustment to the number of contracts necessitated by the fact that the Eurodollar contract pays off at a 90-day equivalent. Moreover, this futures position must be further scaled to offset the interest-compounding effects on daily variation margin payments. The appropriate adjustments will be discussed in Chapter 5.

[10]The strategy used to generate this synthetic 122-day return involves buying the 31-day deposit and a certain amount of September Eurodollar futures contracts. A discussion of the exact number of contracts to buy is deferred until the Eurodollar strip section of Chapter 5. Again, as with all futures positions, a full appreciation of the strategy requires understanding of "tailing" a position to offset the effects of variation margin flows. For now, less is more.

would issuers and investors be indifferent between using an actual four-month deposit versus a synthetic four-month deposit created by Eurodollar futures hedging of a rollover of a current one-month deposit into a new three-month deposit in one month.

The fair implied futures equals the current forward rate for the 122-day period beginning in one month.[11] This forward rate is directly solved from the definition

$$(1 + R_{1,4}^{fwd}[91/360]) = (1 + 0.08792[122/360])/(1 + 0.08375[31/360])$$

The one-month forward rate on a three-month deposit, $R_{1,4}^{fwd}$, equals

$$R_{1,4}^{fwd} = .0887$$

Basis Versus Carry. Eurodollar deposits are non-negotiable instruments. Thus, to consider the cash and carry trade of buying a 122-day deposit and selling a September 1988 Eurodollar futures contract on August 19, 1988, and unwinding the position on September 19, 1988, is a somewhat misleading exercise. Nevertheless, such a strategy completes the correspondence between the equilibrium condition above and the general basis versus carry valuation approach.

To make the translation into basis versus carry terms, think of the December 19, 1988 maturity deposit viewed on August 19 as a $(31 + 91)$-day deposit that, on September 19, will become $(0 + 91)$-day maturity paper returning principal plus a coupon. The coupon rate is set to equal $R_{0,122}$, the four-month LIBOR as of August 19, 1988. The value of such a deposit on September 19, 1988 depends on that day's three-month LIBOR. By selling September Eurodollar futures on August 19, the September 19 portfolio value is locked-in to equal that determined by the initial August 19 implied Eurodollar rate. The fictitious forward price implied by the current futures rate for the December 19, 1988 maturity deposit as of the September 19 settlement date is

$$\text{Forward Price} = [1 + R_{0,122}(122/360)]/[1 + R_{0,T}^{f}(91/360)]$$

Finally, the cash-futures basis on August 19 can be thought of as

$$\text{Basis}_{0,T} = 1 - \{[1 + R_{0,122}(122/360)]/[1 + R_{0,T}^{f}(91/360)]\}$$

per $1 of the initial 122-day deposit.

---

[11] Actually, this is only an approximation because of mark-to-market risks.

Under the contract's cash settlement terms, the final September 19 implied futures rate equals three-month cash LIBOR. For the 31-day holding period until September 19, there is no cash inflow from the long-dated deposit, but the earnings from a 31-day deposit maturing on September 19 are forgone. Thus,

$$\text{Carry}_{0,T} = -R_{0,31}[31/360]$$

per $1 of the initial 122-day deposit.

Equilibrium is reached when prices or rates adjust such that basis equals carry:

$$\text{Basis}_{0,T} = \text{Carry}_{0,T}$$

or

$$1 - \{[1 + R_{0,122}(122/360)]/[1 + R_{0,T}^f(91/360)]\} = -R_{0,31}[31/369]$$

Clearly, basis after carry equals zero as long as

$$R_{0,T}^f = (360/91)\{[1 + R_{0,122}(122/360)]/[1 + R_{0,31}(31/360)] - 1\}$$

This zero basis after carry condition is identical to the implied futures rate/forward rate equivalence equilibrium condition developed above.

The Maturity Structure of Futures Prices

Futures contract markets offer trading in a number of delivery or expiration months (hereafter, "maturity" months). For single grade, single date delivery-based contracts and for all cash settlement contracts, the fair value of each traded maturity month is determined by applying the basis equals carry pricing relationship. A fair maturity month structure of futures prices also emerges from such analyses. This maturity structure is determined by differences in each contract's carry to maturity. Carry differences arise because of differences in term to maturity; term financing rates; and the effective term yield on the cash asset.

Consider pricing three-month, six-month, nine-month and 12-month maturity contracts on the same underlying security. Assume a three-month financing rate of 8%; a six-month rate is 8.5%; a nine-month rate of 8.75%; and a 12-month financing rate of 9%. Furthermore, assume that the cash security yields a flat annualized rate of 5% regardless of maturity. Given an initial cash security price of 100, the fair futures prices for this set of contract maturities are easily computed.

Table 3–8 presents these fair futures prices along with their associated basis versus carry justifications. The tenth column from Table 3–8

Table 3–8. The Maturity Structure of Futures Prices.

Time to Maturity	n_0	Cash Price	Financing Rate (r)	Yield (y)	$(r - y)n_0$	Fair Futures Price	Cash Basis	Carry	Forward Carry	Fair Maturit Basis
3 Months	.25	100	.0800	.05	.0075	100.75	−0.75	−0.75	—	—
6 Months	.50	100	.0850	.05	.0175	101.75	−1.75	−1.75	−1.00	−1.00
9 Months	.75	100	.0875	.05	.0281	102.81	−2.81	−2.81	−1.06	−1.06
1 Year	1.00	100	.0900	.05	.0400	104.00	−4.00	−4.00	−1.19	−1.19

presents the carry differential between successive contract maturities (i.e., the carry on the six-month contract minus the carry on the three-month contract). It is this carry differential—the current forward carry for the three-month period between successive contract maturity dates—that determines the fair maturity basis ("calendar spread"). The maturity basis is the price of one contract minus the price of the contract with the next deferred maturity. The fair maturity basis reflects the forward carry between the contract maturity dates.

In the special case of a flat term structure of interest rates and cash yields, the fair deferred versus near contract price spread reduces to a simple linear function of the differential time to expiration. Such carry structures were presented earlier in Tables 3–4, 3–5 and 3–6.

In the example above, suppose a flat term structure of financing rates (at $r = 0.09$) and current yields (at $y = 0.05$) prevailed. The three-month contract would be priced at 101.00; the six-month contract would be priced at 102.00; the nine-month contract would be priced at 103.00; and the one-year contract would be priced at 104.00. Note that these futures prices are identical to those in Table 3.6 for the 7% financing rate/3% yield case. Both situations imply a –4% carry (or 4% net financing rate).

A Stock Index Example

Table 3–9 reports the maturity structure of prices from the S&P 500 futures market on April 8, 1989. Since the dividend rate is less than the interest rate, the cash S&P 500 stock portfolio has negative carry. Thus, deferred contracts are priced higher than near ones.

Speculating on Carry

Hold-to-delivery basis versus carry trades are the primary sources of discipline to basis market pricing. However, this discipline also invites other types of traders who use basis relationships to speculate on changes in carry.

Return to the analysis of Table 3–4. This table reveals the basis market to be an excellent short-term vehicle through which to speculate on carry (even if the cash price is expected to remain flat). For example, assume a current yield of 3% and financing rates of 7%. Suppose that the trader expects cash prices to remain flat, but sees a 200 basis point rise in financing rates over a six-month horizon. With this outlook, a short basis position in a one-year maturity contract using term financing (at 7%, assuming a flat term structure) for six months makes sense. The

Table 3–9. The Maturity Structure of S&P 500 Index Futures Prices.

Date: April 7, 1989   Cash S&P 500 Index: 297.15

	Futures Price	Cash Basis	Maturity Basis
June	300.90	−3.75	—
September	305.30	−8.15	−4.40
December	309.70	−12.55	−4.40

initial basis would be –$4. If the trader is correct, the basis in six months will equal –$3 (check the Table 3.4 entry for a six-month-to-delivery contract at 9% financing rates and a 3% yield).

This short basis position will lose $1 on the basis change (sell short at –$4, buy back at –$3), but gain $2 in carry. This $2 gain in carry on the short position is generated through $3.50 of investment earnings on the short cash position (six months of interest on $100 at the initial 7% six month term rate) minus $1.50 owed on the short position (six months of yield due to the owner of the borrowed cash position).

Thus, this speculative short basis position would net $1 if the trader's views were actually realized. If rates did not rise, the $2 in carry on the short basis position for six months would be offset by a full $2 capital loss (since the position would be covered at a basis of –$2). If rates *fell* 200 basis points to 5%, the position would lose $1, since the position would be covered at a basis of –$1. The capital loss of $3 would be $1 more than the $2 gain through the short position's carry.

Of course, since carry depends upon price levels, the short-term profits and losses of a basis trade also depends upon movements in market levels. The market level risks of the basis trade P&L could be gauged through analysis of the results of Table 3–5.

Calendar Spreads

A spread position consists of a long position in one contract and a short position in another contract. Spreads using contracts of different maturity dates within the same market are called "calendar spreads." Calendar spreads are trades designed to profit from anticipated changes in the price spread of futures contracts with different maturities. Thus, calendar spread positions provide another means of speculating on forward carry.

Return to the example of Table 3–8. However, suppose that the three-month contract is priced at 100.70, while the six-month contract is priced at 101.85. At these prices, the three-month contract is underpriced relative to the cash market by 0.05 and the six-month contract is overpriced relative to the cash market by 0.10. Alternatively, the three-month minus six-month contract calendar spread of −1.15 (= 100.70 − 101.85) is underpriced by 0.15 relative to forward carry. Anticipating a return to their proper fair carry price spread relationship, spreaders would buy the underpriced calendar spread by buying the cheap three-month maturity contract and selling the expensive six-month maturity contract.

Conversely, suppose that the three-month contract is priced at 100.80, while the six-month contract is priced at 101.70. The three-month minus six-month contract price spread of −0.90 is overpriced by 0.10. Here, spreaders would sell the calendar spread by selling the expensive three-month contract and buying the cheap six-month contract.

In both cases, the spreader will profit from the return of the initially mispriced spread to its current fair value. This return to fair relative contract prices may occur quickly or only after some delay—or not at all.

It is important to understand that calendar spread trades are not arbitrages. Like short-term basis trades, they actually are bets on forward carry. Positions reacting to a mispriced futures maturity basis are most attractive when the trader is poised to bet the same way on a shift in forward carry. That is, if the trader believes that financing rates will rise, the short calendar spread is an especially attractive position if it is already overpriced relative to current rates. Conversely, if the trader believes that financing rates will fall, the long calendar spread is an especially attractive position if it is already underpriced relative to current rates.

Generally, forward carry will shrink if (1) the forward interest rate for the three-month period between contract maturities rises, (2) forward cash asset earnings over this same period fall, and/or (3) the level of cash asset prices rises. Forward carry will rise if (1) the forward interest rate for the three-month period between contract maturities falls, (2) forward cash asset earnings over this same period rise, and (3) the level of cash asset prices falls.

Intermarket Spreading

So far, the trading examples have emphasized cash-futures basis transactions and intramarket futures maturity spread positions. Such trades are easiest to analyze because they are driven by carry. In contrast, *inter*market futures contract spreads are speculative trades designed to profit from price shift differentials in two distinct, but related, futures markets. Two important examples of such intermarket spread trades are the "Treasury bill over Eurodollar" ("TED") spread and the Treasury "Note Over Bond" ("NOB") spread.[12]

The TED Spread

For a given maturity month, the TED spread is defined as the IMM index price of the Treasury bill contract minus the index price of the Eurodollar contract. For example, on March 10, 1989, the June 1989 Treasury bill contract closed at 90.80 (implied futures discount rate of 9.20%), while the June 1989 Eurodollar contract closed at 89.27 (implied LIBOR rate of 10.73%). Thus, the TED spread equalled 153 basis points (= 9080 − 8927).

The TED spread reflects the default premium attached to the riskiness of uninsured three-month Eurodollar deposit returns over the riskless three-month U.S. Treasury bill return. Given default risk and investor risk aversion, the three-month LIBOR rate must exceed the three-month Treasury bill rate. Thus, the TED spread is always positive. However, the TED spread fluctuates because of shifts in the riskiness of bank creditworthiness and because of shifts in investors' attitudes toward risk.

Figure 3–1 plots the near contract TED spread for daily closing prices between December 16, 1981 and March 7, 1989. For most of this period, the TED spread trades within a band of 80 and 170 basis points. However, the TED spread also is vulnerable to extreme movements (e.g., the 350 levels of 1982). Such extreme movements — investor "flight to quality" episodes — show up in Figure 3.1 relating to economic recession (1982), the international debt crisis (1984, May 1987), and the stock market crash (October 1987).

Buying the June 1989 TED spread involves buying one June Treasury bill contract and selling one June Eurodollar contract. This long TED spread trade will show profits of $25 for each basis point that the TED spread rises and will show losses of $25 for each basis point that the TED spread falls. Thus, this long TED spread is a bet that the June LIBOR-Treasury bill rate differential will strengthen from its currently priced level.

---

[12]The TED and NOB are just two of the more important intermarket spreads. Here, the BED spread (Bond over Euros) is left uncovered and no connections are made to the MOB spread (Municipals over Bonds).

Figure 3–1. The TED Spread.

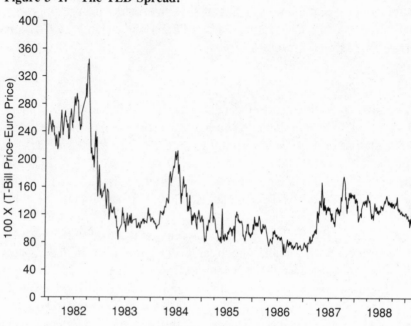

Selling the June 1989 TED spread involves selling one June Treasury bill contract and buying one June Eurodollar contract. This short TED spread trade profits from a fall in the TED spread. Thus, the short TED spread is a bet that the June LIBOR-Treasury bill rate differential will weaken from its currently priced level.

On May 2, 1989, the June 1989 Treasury bill contract closed at 91.55, while the June 1989 Eurodollar contract closed at 90.04. Thus, the June 1989 TED spread closed at 151 basis points. The trader who bought the June TED on March 10 at 153 had lost two basis points ($50 per contract). Conversely, the trader who sold the June TED on March 10 at 153 had gained two basis points ($50 per contract).

The NOB Spread

For a given maturity month, the NOB spread is defined as the price of the CBOT 10-year Treasury note futures contract minus the price of the CBOT Treasury bond futures contract. For example, on March 10, 1989, the June 1989 10-year Treasury note contract closed at 91-22, while the June 1989 Treasury bond contract closed at 87-29. Thus, the NOB spread equalled 3-25 (= 91-22 − 87-29), or 121 ticks.

Buying the June 1989 NOB spread involves buying one June Treasury note contract and selling one June bond contract. This long NOB spread trade will show profits of $31.25 for each tick that the NOB spread rises and will show losses of $31.25 for each tick that the NOB spread falls. Thus, this long NOB spread is a bet that the June note minus June bond price differential will strengthen from its currently priced level.

Selling the June 1989 NOB spread involves selling one June Treasury note contract and buying one June bond contract. This short NOB spread trade profits from a fall in the NOB spread. Thus, the short NOB spread is a bet that the June note minus June bond price differential will weaken from its current level.

Figure 3–2 plots the NOB spread over the period between August 1982 and March 7, 1989.

The NOB spread is both a yield spread and market directional play. The yield spread play is obvious. Holding bond yields fixed, a decrease (or increase) in 10-year note yields will cause the NOB spread to rise or fall). Thus, the NOB spread benefits from a steepening of the yield curve between the 10-year and 30-year sectors.

Figure 3–2.   The NOB Spread.

Furthermore, since the price response of long-term bonds to a basis point change in yield is much larger than that of 10-year notes, the NOB spread is extremely market-directional. In particular, the NOB spread is a bearish trade. Figure 3–3 shows the NOB spread to have a distinctive negatively sloped profile versus the bond futures price level. Since there are simpler ways to construct bearish trades (e.g., by shorting the bond contract), the NOB spread is especially attractive only to traders who are both bearish *and* anticipate a curve steepening between 10-year and 30-year sectors.

On May 2, 1989, the June 1989 Treasury note contract closed at 93-10, while the June bond contract closed at 89-26. Thus, the June 1989 NOB spread closed at 3-16 (112 ticks). Thus, the trader who bought the June NOB at 121 ticks on March 10 lost nine ticks ($281.25 per contract) since the 52-tick rise in the note contract held long is more than offset by the 61-tick rise in the bond contract held short. Conversely, the trader who sold the June NOB on March 10 gained nine ticks ($281.25 per contract).

Figure 3–3.   The NOB Spread versus Bond Levels.

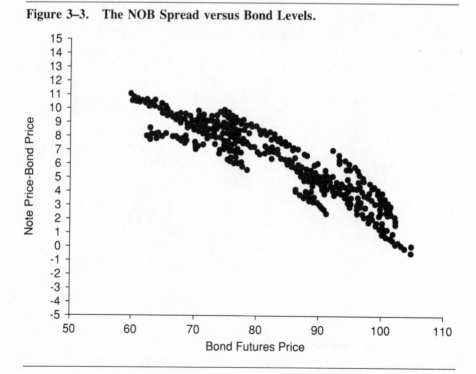

Weighted NOB Spreads

Traders who anticipate a curve steepening, but who are either bullish or neutral, must trade the NOB in a price value of a basis point-weighted fashion (see Chapter 7). On March 10, 1989, the price value of a basis point yield change for the note contract was about two-thirds of that of the bond contract. Thus, the NOB spread had yield risk equivalent to being short one-half of a 10-year note contract.

A *weighted* long NOB trade would involve buying three CBOT 10-year note contracts for every two CBOT bond contracts sold.[13] This position would profit (or lose) with a steepening (or flattening) of the 10-year to 30-year portion of the yield curve, but remain approximately neutral to small shifts in the absolute level of yields.

Consider the P&L on such a weighted June 1989 NOB spread between March 10 and May 2. The trader who was long the weighted June NOB (long 3 notes/short 2 bonds) has a net gain of 34 ticks ($1,062.50 per position or $531.25 per bond). This 34-tick gain occurs since the 156-tick profit from the three long note contracts (3 × 52 ticks) is more than enough to offset the 122-tick loss from the two short bond contracts. The profit from the long weighted NOB position occurs since the yield curve between 10-year and 30-year maturities steepened over the period by six basis points.

Note that, while the NOB fell over this specific period, the weighted NOB rose. Again, the weighted NOB rose since the yield curve between 10-year and 30-year maturities steepened over the period by six basis points. While such a steepening also helps the unweighted NOB, the fall in the unweighted NOB occurred because the market simultaneously rallied and the unweighted NOB is a bearish position. Here, the latter effect was enough to offset the favorable curve steepening.

Summary

This chapter has focused on basis relationships and certain futures spread positions. For simple single grade/single delivery date contracts, the futures is priced off of the deliverable cash market security through a

---

[13]Think of the position as two NOB spreads plus one outright long 10-year contract. The position is hedged since the two NOBs have a risk equivalent to one short 10-year contract (the extra 10-year contract in the weighted spread position offsets this exposure).

carry and deliver trade. In equilibrium, futures must be priced such that basis equals carry.

Two exceptions to the basis equals carry equilibrium rule apply to financial futures. First, in some markets, the concept of the carry trade becomes ill-defined. For example, it may be difficult to short sell the underlying asset (especially commodities) or arrange term financing for holding periods of more than one year. Indeed, for Treasury bills, the deliverable bill for contract delivery months more than nine months in the future will not yet have been auctioned.

Second, the basis equals carry rule breaks down when the futures contract grants delivery options relating to quality grade, delivery date, etc. Chapter 4 discusses basis pricing in Treasury bond and note futures markets. These Treasury contracts grant the short a number of potentially valuable delivery options. Pricing the basis for such complicated contracts involves both carry and option value considerations.

CHAPTER 4
Treasury Basis Trading

"It is quality rather than quantity that matters." . . . . (Lucius Annaeus Seneca)

As with stock index, Treasury bill, and Eurodollar futures, analysis of Treasury bond and note futures pricing begins by comparing basis with carry. However, because of the conversion factor system applied to invoice price determination for each deliverable issue, the terms basis and basis after carry must be carefully reviewed. Furthermore, because of the delivery options granted by these contracts, basis trading is much more complex. In fact, the main equilibrium condition, that basis after carry must equal zero, will not hold. Long Treasury basis trades can be attractive even at a positive basis after carry. This occurs because basis and carry no longer exhaust the cash flows to a basis trade. One more source of value emerges: the short's delivery options.

Treasury bond and note futures contracts grant the short position a number of important quality and timing options concerning final settlement through delivery. These delivery options are crucial to the pricing of the Treasury basis. The most important of these delivery options is the "quality option," giving the short the right to deliver a particular issue selected from a menu of specified issues.[1] The quality option is important because the conversion factor system of premiums and discounts which determines the delivery invoice prices of the alternative deliverable issues contains important yield-related biases.

---

1. See Garbade and Silber (1983), Gay and Manaster (1984, 1986, 1989), Cheng (1985), Kane and Marcus (1986), Hegde (1987), Hemler (1988), and Boyle (1989).

The Cheapest Deliverable Treasury Issue

Determining the cheapest deliverable Treasury issue under the premium and discount structure of a Treasury futures contract involves comparison of the net difference between each deliverable issue's market price and its invoice price (conversion factor times futures price). It is convenient to express the delivering short's P&L statement in terms of the "loss on delivery." At the time of delivery, the short acquires the deliverable issue at its current market price (plus accrued interest) and tenders it at its invoice price (plus accrued interest). Thus, the loss on delivery equals the delivered issue's flat price minus its invoice price. The difference between the cash market bond price and its futures invoice price is called the issue's "raw basis." In fact, large differences among the raw bases of eligible issues will typically occur.

The cheapest deliverable issue (CDI), as its name implies, is the one which minimizes the loss on delivery. For any particular day throughout the delivery month, the CDI is the issue with the lowest raw basis. For example, compare the short's alternatives after filing a delivery notice on March 16 to settle a March 1989 Treasury bond contract short position. On March 20 (two business days later), the short must deliver $100,000 in face value of any of the 29 deliverable bonds (see Chapter 2). On March 16, the short computes the basis of each deliverable issue (flat price minus invoice price). The bond with the minimum raw basis is the issue which minimizes the cost of delivery.

Table 4–1 presents the relevant invoice price and basis computations. Clearly, the 7.25% of May 2016 is the issue with the minimum raw basis. Its basis equals zero ticks. Thus, on March 16, there is no implied loss upon delivering the 7.25% of May 2016 in final settlement of the March contract. The 7.50% of November 2016—with a raw basis of one tick—is a very close second choice as the deliverable issue. In contrast, the on-the-run bond, the 8.875% of February 2019, would not be an appropriate delivery choice since its 17-tick raw basis implies a delivery loss of equal size. The worst choice through which to settle the contract would be the 13.75% of August 2004. Delivery of this bond would imply a 109-tick loss on delivery.

The delivering short would file a delivery notice with the CBOT clearinghouse. The short would then buy $100,000 of face value of the 7.25% of May 2016 at a flat price of 81-01. Excluding accrued interest, this implies a cost of $81,031.25 per $100,000 of face value. The long

Table 4–1. **March 1989 Bond Futures Delivery Alternatives for March 16, 1989 Delivery Notice Filing (March Futures Price: 88–10).**

Deliverable Issue	Price	Factor	Invoice Price	Raw Basis (Ticks)
12.375% May 2004	124–22	1.3783	121–23	95
13.75% Aug 2004	135–31	1.5011	132–18	109
11.625% Nov 2004	118–31	1.3188	116–15	80
12.00% May 2005	122–12	1.3575	119–28	80
10.75% Aug 2005	112–06	1.2474	110–05	65
9.375% Feb 2006	101–08	1.1255	99–13	59
9.125% May 2004–09	98–15	1.0973	96–29	50
10.375% Nov 2004–09	108–07	1.2089	106–24	47
11.75% Feb 2005–10	119–17	1.3322	117–21	60
10.00% May 2005–10	105–08	1.1787	104–03	37
12.75% Nov 2005–10	128–09	1.4310	126–12	61
13.875% May 2006–11	138–07	1.5408	136–02	69
14.00% Nov 2006–11	139–25	1.5599	137–24	65
10.375% Nov 2007–12	109–00	1.2273	108–12	20
12.00% Aug 2008–13	123–13	1.3893	122–22	23
13.25% May 2009–14	135–02	1.5196	134–06	28
12.50% Aug 2009–14	128–14	1.4473	127–26	20
11.75% Nov 2009–14	122–06	1.3749	121–13	25
11.25% Feb 2015	120–09	1.3521	119–13	28
10.625% Aug 2015	114–09	1.2860	113–18	23
9.875% Nov 2015	106–26	1.2051	106–14	12
9.25% Feb 2016	100–24	1.1369	100–13	11
7.25% May 2016	81–01	0.9175	81–01	0(CDI)
7.50% Nov 2016	83–15	0.9447	83–14	1
8.75% May 2017	95–21	1.0833	95–21	10
8.875% Aug 2017	97–08	1.0972	96–29	11
9.125% May 2018	99–29	1.1262	99–15	14
9.00% Nov 2018	98–24	1.1126	98–08	16
8.875% Feb 2019	97–18	1.0986	97–01	17

accepting this delivered bond would be invoiced at $81,026.72 (the flat invoice price) plus the March 20, 1989 accrued interest of $2,503.45.[2]

---

2. If the 7.25% of May 2016 is bought for next day (March 17, 1988) settlement, it must be carried for the weekend. The carry on this bond was slightly negative at this time, so that the short would have incurred an additional loss of about $7.

One useful way to describe the delivering short's choice set for a March 16 notice is as a set of options. In particular, the short's option to deliver the 7.25% of May 2016 instead of the 13.75% of August 2004 is 109 ticks in-the-money. The short's option to deliver the 7.25% of May 2016 instead of the 8.875% of February 2019 is 17 ticks in-the-money. The option to deliver the 7.25% of May 2016 instead of the 7.50% of November 2016 is just one tick in-the-money. However, the option to deliver any bond as a substitute for the 7.25% of May 2016 has finished out-of-the-money.

Determinants of Deliverability

For a March 16, 1989 delivery notice filing, shorts are not indifferent to the choice of the delivered issue. Preference for delivery of the 7.25% of May 2016 implies that the conversion factor system does not produce fair Treasury issue values. Why is the 7.25% of May 2016 the cheapest issue to deliver? Why are the higher coupon, shorter maturity issues much more expensive? The answers can be found by examining the CBOT's conversion factor system. These conversion factors determine the premiums and discounts for delivering non-standard issues.

Yield-Related Biases of CBOT Factors

The CBOT's conversion factor system equalizes the delivery costs among all deliverable issues only in the unlikely event that each issue actually yields 8% in the market at the time of delivery. The fixed conversion factor system works in this 8% yield case because each issue's *converted price*—flat price divided by conversion factor—would be approximately identical.[3] However, for every other yield pattern, the conversion factors contain clear and important biases. The CBOT factor biases occur because the relative prices of any set of bonds change as a function of both absolute and relative yield shifts, whereas their conversion factors remain fixed. Thus, away from the 8% standard, the relative prices of a set of bonds quoted by their CBOT factors will not equal their true relative values. Relative bond prices change on parallel yield shifts due to differences in the yield-to-price sensitivities among bonds. Relative bond prices also change because of shifts in yield spreads.

---

3. Each issue's converted price is only approximately identical because of the system's shortcuts (rounding of maturity, etc.). Exact delivery cost equivalence among all deliverable bonds still would not be obtained in this scenario.

Since the CBOT factors are biased, one bond typically is cheapest to deliver. Delivering shorts choose, from among the set of eligible issues, the particular issue which minimizes the cost of delivery. Longs should expect that deliveries will be made using this cheapest deliverable issue. In other words, shorts should be expected to rationally exercise the contract's quality option.

Yield Level Impacts: A Simple Example

Table 4–2 presents a numerical example of the yield level CBOT conversion factor bias under a full convergence final futures price assumption. Full convergence implies that the final futures price equals the converted price of the cheapest deliverable issue. For simplicity, the analysis assumes a single delivery date. Table 4–2 compares the delivery date's converted price of a hypothetical 7%, 30-year Treasury with that of a hypothetical 12%, 15-year Treasury.[4]

On the delivery date, the cheapest deliverable issue is the bond with the lowest converted price. At the critical 8% yield level, the bonds have identical converted prices (100). Thus, the two bonds are equally cheap to deliver. At yields below 8%, the 12%, 15-year bond is the cheaper issue. At yields above 8%, the 7%, 30-year bond is the cheaper issue.

Table 4–2. Yield Level Related CBOT Conversion Factor Bias.

| Yield | 7%, 30-year Bond (Factor = .8869) | | 12%, 15-year Bond (Factor = 1.3458) | | Futures Price | Final Raw Basis | |
	Market Price	Converted Price	Market Price	Converted Price		7%, 30-yr.	12%, 15-yr.
6.0	113–27	128–12	158–26	118–00	118–00	9–06	0
6.5	106–18	120–05	152–06	113–03	113–03	6–08	0
7.0	100–00	112–24	145–31	108–15	108–15	3–26	0
7.5	94–02	106–02	140–04	104–04	104–04	1–23	0
8.0	88–22	100–00	134–19	100–00	100–00	0	0
8.5	83–26	94–16	129–12	96–04	94–04	0	2–06
9.0	79–12	89–15	124–14	92–15	89–15	0	4–01
9.5	75–10	84–29	119–25	89–00	84–29	0	5–20
10.0	71–20	80–24	115–12	85–23	80–24	0	6–22

---

4. Assume the delivery date is also the ex-coupon date for both bonds.

The CBOT factor biases stem from the fact that the ratio of any two issues' factors implicitly quotes their relative price for delivery. At a 7% (< 8%) yield level, the market values the 7%, 30-year bond at par (100-00), while the 12%, 15-year issue sells for 145-31. The market value ratio of the former to the latter is 0.685. Thus, while the market judges the 7%, 30-year issue to be worth about 0.685 of the value of the 12%, 15-year issue, the fixed CBOT factor system constrains its value in delivery to be only 0.6590 (= .8869/1.3458) of the value of the 12%, 15-year bond. Because of this discrepancy between market and CBOT factor relative values, the 12%, 15-year bond is cheap to deliver and the 7%, 30-year bond, expensive.

Conversely, at a yield of 8.5% (> 8%), the market judges the 7%, 30-year bond to be worth only 0.6478 of the value of the 12%, 15-year issue. Since the CBOT system still constrains the relative value of this issue to be 0.6590 of the 12%, 15-year bond, the 7%, 30-year bond is cheap to deliver and the 12%, 15-year bond, expensive.

Furthermore, under the single delivery date assumption, the final futures price will equal the converted price of the cheapest deliverable issue. Thus, the futures price will equal the converted price of the 12%, 15-year bond for yields lower than 8%, and equal the converted price of the 7%, 30-year bond for yields higher than 8%. These futures prices are reported in Table 4-2.

Figure 4-1 plots the converted price of each issue versus the common schedule of bond yields. The final futures price is assumed to converge to the lower of the two converted prices. The futures price would lie on the 12%, 15-year bond's converted price curve for yields below 8% and on the 7%, 30- year bond's converted price curve for yields above 8%. Thus, the futures price curve is "kinked" at the critical 8% yield level.

Table 4-2 also presents the final raw basis of each issue. Under the full convergence assumption, the futures is priced to make the final raw basis of the CDI equal zero. While both bonds have a raw basis of zero at the 8% yield, the two raw bases diverge away from this critical level. If the market rallies to yield levels below 8%, the 12%, 15-year bond becomes the CDI. Its final raw basis remains at zero, but that of the 7%, 30-year bond becomes positive. Conversely, if the market falls and yields increase above 8%, the 7%, 30-year issue becomes the CDI. Here, its final raw basis finishes at zero, but that of the 12%, 15-year bond turns positive.

Figure 4–1. CBOT Conversion Factor Bias.

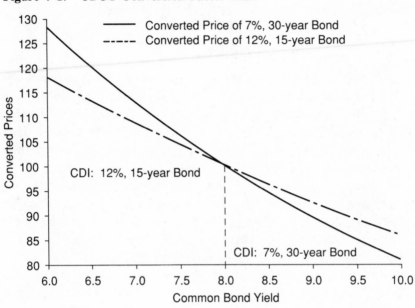

Relative Yield Impacts

Shifts in relative bond yields also play an important role in determining relative cheapness for bond futures delivery. It is straightforward to solve for the yield increase of any bond that, given fixed yields for the remaining deliverable issues, would make it the new CDI.

For example, suppose that yields on both bonds equal 8.5%. The 7%, 15-year issue is cheaper to deliver by 1-20 (= 96-04 − 94-16) of converted price (see Table 4–2). Holding the yield of the 7%, 30-year bond fixed at 8.5%, what increase in the yield of the 12%, 15-year bond would make it equally cheap to deliver? In order to sell at a converted price of 94-16, the 12%, 15-year bond would have to yield 8.72%. In other words, if the 12%, 15-year bond cheapened by more than 22 basis points in yield relative to the 7%, 30-year issue, it would become the CDI. This 22 basis point change is commonly referred to as the 12%, 15-year bond's "yield cheapening to delivery."

The cheapest deliverable issue concept is crucial during the settlement month delivery process. Not too surprisingly, traders find that predicting the cheapest deliverable Treasury issue is the key to establishing the cash and carry trade that underlies Treasury bond futures pricing.

Delivery Experience: Issue Choice

The biases of the conversion factor system usually make it rational to deliver issues that are relatively homogeneous in their interest rate characteristics. For example, Tables 4–3 and 4–4 present data summarizing deliveries against the March 1989 and June 1989 Treasury bond futures contracts, respectively. For the March 1989 contract, the low coupon, long maturity, 7.25% of May 2016 accounted for all of the 16,190 contract deliveries. In contrast, for the June 1989 contract, the high coupon, callable issues (the 12% of August 2008-13, the 10.375% of November 2007-12 and the 12.5% of August 2009-14) accounted for 21,301 of the 21,320 total contract deliveries (99.9%). The remaining 19 contracts were settled through delivery of the 7.50% of November 2016 (18) and the 7.25% of May 2016 (1).

As detailed in Table 4–1, deliveries of a low coupon, long maturity issue such as the 7.25% of May 2016 were rational for the March 1989

Table 4–3. Treasury Bond Futures Contract Delivery Experience: March 1989

Delivery Date	Issue Delivered		Amount Delivered
March 31	7.25%	May 2016	2
March 30	7.25%	May 2016	154
March 29	7.25%	May 2016	322
March 28	7.25%	May 2016	1,700
March 27	7.25%	May 2016	300
March 23	7.25%	May 2016	8,812
March 22	7.25%	May 2016	62
March 21	7.25%	May 2016	797
March 20	7.25%	May 2016	206
March 17	7.25%	May 2016	896
March 16	7.25%	May 2016	2,935
March 3	7.25%	May 2016	1
March 1	7.25%	May 2016	3
Total			16,190

Table 4–4. **Treasury Bond Futures Contract Delivery Experience: June 1989**

Delivery Date	Issue Delivered		Amount Delivered
June 30	10.375%	November 2007–12	4,551
June 29	10.375%	November 2007–12	151
June 27	10.375%	November 2007–12	10
	12%	August 2008–13	24
June 26	10.375%	November 2007–12	1,185
June 23	10.375%	November 2007–12	12
	12%	August 2008–13	20
	12.5%	August 2009–14	50
June 22	10.375%	November 2007–12	473
	12%	August 2008–13	4
June 21	10.375%	November 2007–12	7,722
	12%	August 2008–13	3,810
	12.5%	August 2009–14	397
June 20	12%	August 2008–13	25
June 19	12%	August 2008–13	1,760
June 16	10.375%	November 2007–12	67
June 15	10.375%	November 2007–12	1,040
June 14	7.25%	May 2016	1
June 5	7.50%	November 2016	8
June 2	7.50%	November 2016	1
June 1	7.50%	November 2016	9
Total			21,320

yield environment. The bases of such issues were substantially lower than those of other issues.

In contrast, given the subsequent May-June 1989 market rally, the delivery mathematics implied that deliveries of high coupon, callable issues were rational for the June 1989 contract. Yield levels and spreads were such that these issues were cheaper to deliver than the low coupon, long maturity issues. The shorts who closed out the 19-contract positions by delivering the low coupon, long maturity issues suffered losses on delivery which were unnecessarily large. On May 30, 1989, the basis on the 7.50% of November 2016 for a June 1 delivery was 4 ticks higher than that of the 12% of August 2013. Thus, delivery of the 7.50% of November 2016 entailed an excess delivery cost of $125 per contract.

Isolated irrationalities aside, note that more than one issue of the high coupon, callable issues were delivered against the June 1987 contract. The 10.375% of November 2007-12 accounted for 71.5% of all deliveries, the 12% of August 2008-13 accounted for 26.5%, and the 12.5% of August 2009-14 accounted for 2.0% of the total.

Multiple issue deliveries may be somewhat disconcerting to those wedded to the delivery mathematics concept of a single "cheapest deliverable issue." Nevertheless, some diversity among delivered issues should be expected. To a naked short position, one specific issue—say, the 10.375% of November 2007-12—would usually appear to be the single most economical delivery choice. However, because of bid-ask spreads in the cash market, current holders of a specific deliverable issue may find it cheaper to deliver the issue in hand—say, the 12.5% of August 2009-14—rather than swap into the 10.375% of November 2007-12 prior to delivery. Thus, the 4-tick loss on a June 1, 1989 delivery of the 7.5% of November 2016 against the June bond futures contract would not seem unduly large in this perspective.

Treasury Basis Trading and the Quality Option

The quality option has important effects on the nature of Treasury basis trading. However, before examining the trade's quality option component, it is helpful to review the concepts of basis, carry, forward price, and basis after carry as they relate to Treasury trading.

The Raw Basis

The raw basis of each deliverable issue is defined as the difference between the bond's flat price and its futures invoice price. A bond's invoice price equals the futures settlement price multiplied by the bond's conversion factor. On January 20, 1989, the 7.25% of May 2016 was priced at 83-04, while the March 1989 bond futures was priced at 90-10. Since the 7.25% of May 2016 has a conversion factor of 0.9175 for invoicing purposes versus the March 1989 contract, its invoice price is 82-28. The 7.25% of May 2016's March basis equalled 8 ticks (= 83-04 − 82-28).

Figure 4–2 plots the closing marks for the March 1989 bond futures and the March raw basis for each of three issues— the 7.25% of May 2016, the 10.375% of November 2007-12, and the 12% of August 2008-13—between January 3, 1989 and March 20, 1989.

Figure 4–2.   March 89 Bond Basis Pricing.

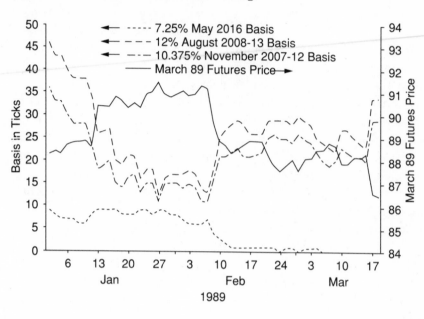

Carry

A bond's *carry* is defined as the difference between interest earnings (including reinvested coupons) and financing charges from the current date until the planned delivery date. Here, assume that March 31 delivery will be optimal. For the 7.25% of May 2016 issue purchased on January 20, 1989 (January 21 settlement), the coupon interest earned until March 31, 1989 equals 44 ticks. At an 8.75% term repo rate, the financing cost of the position to March 31 equals 45 ticks. Thus, the bond's carry to March 31 equals −1 tick (= 44 − 45). Since interest earnings are less than financing costs, the bond exhibits negative carry.

Forward Price

A bond's forward price for a specific forward settlement date equals its current flat price minus its carry until that settlement date. For CDI applications, the relevant forward settlement date is the expected futures delivery date. Thus, the forward price for the 7.25% of May 2016 for March 31, 1989 settlement equals 83-05 (= 83-04 − [−1]).

Basis After Carry

Basis after carry is defined as the bond's raw basis minus its carry.[6] Thus, the 7.25% of May 2016 priced on January 20, 1989 for March 31, 1989 delivery has a basis after carry of nine ticks (= 8 − [−1]). These nine ticks represent the loss incurred by the trader who buys the bond, sells a conversion factor-weighted number of futures contracts, and carries and delivers this particular bond.[7] The first eight ticks of this nine-tick loss can be traced to the long basis trader's delivery of the bonds for an invoice price (82-28) which is eight ticks lower than the bond acquisition price (83-04). The remaining one-tick loss comes from the position's negative carry.

The naive analyst might conclude from the observed positive nine-tick basis after carry for the 7.25% of May 2016 (on January 20, 1989, the anticipated CDI for March 1989 deliveries) that this March Treasury bond futures was underpriced in the sense that a riskless arbitrage was available through a short basis trade. However, unlike the stock index and Eurodollar markets previously studied, a positive basis after carry for each deliverable Treasury bond (or note) does not necessarily imply that futures are underpriced.

This apparent contradiction occurs because basis after carry calculations do not adequately represent the true payoff structure of a Treasury basis trade. In particular, the basis after carry calculation ignores the possibility that the identity of the cheapest deliverable issue will change between the January 20 start of the trade and the March delivery period.

For bonds, the long basis trade consists of buying a deliverable bond and selling a conversion factor-weighted number of Treasury bond futures contracts. The 7.25% of May 2016 long March basis trader would actually deliver the 7.25% of May 2016 issue to close out the short futures position only if this issue turns out to be the CDI in March. Otherwise, this trader would sell the 7.25% of May 2016, buy the then current CDI, and deliver that specific issue.

---

6. Equivalently, the basis after carry can be viewed as the bond's forward price minus its invoice price. Some analysts refer to basis after carry as the "value basis" (see Leibowitz [1981]).

7. Note that the actual trade involves selling a conversion factor-weighted (CF) number of futures contracts per $100,000 of bonds and then, on the delivery date, buying (CF − 1) additional bonds to have CF × $100,000 in par value of the bond to deliver into the CF futures contracts.

The long basis trader would benefit from this "CDI switch" outcome relative to the initial basis versus carry P&L. The difference between the initial basis after carry and the final P&L of a particular basis trade is determined by the value of the issue's final raw basis. Assuming a single delivery date and full convergence, the final raw basis for any issue must either be zero (if the bond held turns out to be the CDI) or positive (if some other issue is the CDI). Thus, the P&L of a long basis trade in a particular issue equals that issue's final raw basis minus its initial basis after carry.

Because of this possible extra payoff, the long basis trade is attractive at an initial basis equal to carry. The long basis trader would be willing to pay a premium (sell the futures at a lower price) to enter the trade.

The short basis trade consists of shorting a deliverable bond and buying a conversion factor-weighted number of futures contracts. The 7.25% of May 2016 short March basis trader would actually be delivered the 7.25% of May 2016 only if it is the CDI in March. Otherwise, delivering shorts will choose the then current CDI. Since the short basis trader needs to obtain the 7.25% of May 2016, the trader is at risk that some relatively less valuable issue actually will be delivered. The short basis trader would lose under this outcome relative to the initial basis versus carry P&L.

The P&L of a short basis trade in a particular issue equals that issue's initial basis after carry minus its final raw basis. Because of this possible loss, the short basis trade is unattractive if the initial basis just equals carry. The short basis trader needs to receive a premium (buy the futures at a lower price) to be induced into the trade.

CDI Identity Switches and Basis Trading: A Simple Two-Bond Example

Insights into the impact of CDI identity switches on basis trade returns can be gained by sketching out a simple example based on the Treasury contract conversion factor bias discussion above. For simplicity, assume that only two bonds within the menu of deliverable issues can possibly become the March 1989 CDI: the 7.25% of May 2016 (with a conversion factor of 0.9175) and the 12% of August 2008-13 (with a conversion factor of 1.3893). Furthermore, assume that the last trading date, March 22, 1989, is the contract's only possible delivery date.

What will be the profit and loss statement on each issue's long basis trade? The 7.25% of May 2016 long basis trade consists of buying the

7.25% of May 2016 and selling 0.9175 March bond futures (i.e., 918 contracts per $100,000,000 of par value in bonds). If, on the contract's delivery date, the 7.25% of May 2016 is the cheapest deliverable issue, the long basis trader will close out the position by delivering these bonds.[8] The P&L from this set of transactions corresponds exactly to that which underlies the basis after carry calculation. Thus, if the 7.25% of May 2016 turns out to be the delivered issue, this long basis trade will lose its initial basis after carry.

However, suppose that the 12% of August 2008-13 turns out to be cheaper to deliver than the 7.25% of May 2016.[9] Here, the long 7.25% of May 2016 basis trade has a higher payoff than under the "no switch" case. Why? Because the initial "no switch" basis after carry calculations assumed that the long basis trader delivers bonds worth the converted price of the 7.25% of May 2016 per contract. However, the trader ultimately delivers bonds worth only the converted price of the 12% of August 2013-08 per contract. Since, by assumption, the converted price of the latter bond is worth less than that of the former, the long 7.25% of May 2016 basis trader earns an extra

$$0.9175 \times [\text{Converted price of } 7.25\% - \text{Converted price of } 12\%]$$

or

$$\text{Price of } 7.25\% - [\text{Factor of } 7.25\% \times (\text{Price of } 12\%/\text{Factor of } 12\%)]$$

This latter form of the payoff is interpreted as the final 7.25% of May 2016 raw basis (here, the final futures price would equal the converted price of the 12% of August 2008-13). A positive final raw basis *offsets* the loss from the initial positive basis after carry. If the final raw basis is sufficiently large, the long basis trade becomes profitable.

Market Level Effects

Table 4–5 presents an analysis of how the identity of the CDI for March 1989 and the corresponding final March 1989 raw bases of the 7.25% of

---

8. Actually, the mechanics of the trade involve delivering $100,000 in bond par value for each contract. If the trader had $100,000,000 in par value of the 7.25% of May 2016 and sold 918 bond futures, he must deliver only $91,800,000 in par value to settle his futures position. He sells the remaining $8,200,000 at the current market price. (However, see the discussion of the wild card option below.)

9. On the delivery date, the short will deliver the bond with the minimum raw basis. Under our assumption of full convergence, this bond also has the lowest converted price (flat price divided by the bond's conversion factor).

Table 4–5. March 1989 Treasury Bond Futures Deliverability and Basis Pricing (Settlement Date: 03/22/89; Yield Spread: 20 bpts).

Final Futures*	Bond 7.250% 05/15/16 Factor: 0.9175			Bond 12.000% 08/15/08–13 Factor: 1.3893			CDI
	Yield	Price	Basis	Yield	Price	Basis	
95-06	8.360	88-05	25.5	8.560	132-08	0.0	12.000%
94-30	8.390	87-27	23.6	8.590	131-29	0.0	12.000%
94-22	8.420	87-18	21.8	8.620	131-18	0.0	12.000%
94-14	8.450	87-09	20.0	8.650	131-07	0.0	12.000%
94-06	8.480	87-00	18.3	8.680	130-28	0.0	12.000%
93-31	8.510	86-23	16.5	8.710	130-17	0.0	12.000%
93-23	8.540	86-14	14.8	8.740	130-06	0.0	12.000%
93-15	8.570	86-05	13.1	8.770	129-27	0.0	12.000%
93-07	8.600	85-28	11.4	8.800	129-16	0.0	12.000%
92-31	8.630	85-19	9.7	8.830	129-05	0.0	12.000%
92-23	8.660	85-11	8.1	8.860	128-27	0.0	12.000%
92-16	8.690	85-02	6.4	8.890	128-16	0.0	12.000%
92-08	8.720	84-25	4.8	8.920	128-05	0.0	12.000%
92-00	8.750	84-17	3.2	8.950	127-26	0.0	12.000%
91-25	8.780	84-08	1.6	8.980	127-16	0.0	12.000%
91-17	8.811	83-31	0.0	9.011	127-05	0.0	Switch pt.
91-08	8.840	83-23	0.0	9.040	126-27	2.2	7.250%
90-31	8.870	83-14	0.0	9.070	126-16	4.6	7.250%
90-21	8.900	83-06	0.0	9.100	126-06	6.9	7.250%
90-12	8.930	82-30	0.0	9.130	125-27	9.1	7.250%
90-03	8.960	82-21	0.0	9.160	125-17	11.4	7.250%
89-26	8.990	82-13	0.0	9.190	125-07	13.6	7.250%
89-17	9.020	82-05	0.0	9.220	124-28	15.8	7.250%
89-08	9.050	81-29	0.0	9.250	124-18	18.0	7.250%
88-31	9.080	81-20	0.0	9.280	124-08	20.1	7.250%
88-22	9.110	81-12	0.0	9.310	123-30	22.3	7.250%
88-14	9.140	81-04	0.0	9.340	123-20	24.4	7.250%
88-05	9.170	80-28	0.0	9.370	123-10	26.5	7.250%
87-28	9.200	80-20	0.0	9.400	122-32	28.5	7.250%
87-20	9.230	80-12	0.0	9.430	122-22	30.6	7.250%
87-11	9.260	80-04	0.0	9.460	122-12	32.6	7.250%
87-02	9.290	79-28	0.0	9.490	122-02	34.6	7.250%
86-26	9.320	79-21	0.0	9.520	121-24	36.5	7.250%
86-17	9.350	79-13	0.0	9.550	121-14	38.5	7.250%
86-09	9.380	79-05	0.0	9.580	121-04	40.4	7.250%
86-00	9.410	78-29	0.0	9.610	120-26	42.3	7.250%
85-24	9.440	78-22	0.0	9.640	120-17	44.2	7.250%
85-16	9.470	78-14	0.0	9.670	120-07	46.1	7.250%
85-08	9.500	78-07	0.0	9.700	119-29	47.9	7.250%
84-31	9.530	77-31	0.0	9.730	119-20	49.7	7.250%
84-23	9.560	77-23	0.0	9.760	119-10	51.5	7.250%
84-15	9.590	77-16	0.0	9.790	119-01	53.3	7.250%
84-07	9.620	77-09	0.0	9.820	118-23	55.1	7.250%
83-31	9.650	77-01	0.0	9.850	118-14	56.8	7.250%
83-23	9.680	76-26	0.0	9.880	118-04	58.5	7.250%

*Note: Assumes that the raw basis of the cheapest deliverable issue on the settlement date equals zero.

May 2016 and the 12% of August 2008-13 are affected by market levels. The example works out the same conversion factor bias effects explored in Table 4–2, except that now (1) two *actual* issues, not hypothetical ones, are examined and (2) the bonds are assumed to trade at a positive yield spread instead of even yields.

The numbers in Table 4–5 were generated as follows: A schedule of yields on the 7.25% of May 2016 for March 22, 1989 between 8.36 and 9.68 was set down in increments of three basis points. It was then assumed that the 12% of August 2008-13 traded at a constant 20 basis point spread above the yield of the 7.25% of May 2016. Given the implied yield schedules for these two bonds, corresponding schedules of March 22, 1989 prices for these issues are easily generated. A final futures price associated with each price pair in the schedules is defined as that which sets the final raw basis on the cheapest deliverable issue equal to zero. This final futures price assumes full convergence and is calculated as the minimum of the two converted bond prices. (For each element in the schedule, divide each bond's price by its conversion factor. The futures price equals the lower of the two price-to-conversion factor ratios.) Given the prices of the bonds and the futures, a final raw basis schedule for each issue is constructed.

Interpret the final basis for each issue as the extra payoff to the long basis trade beyond the loss of the initial basis after carry. From Table 4–5, at the assumed 20 basis point yield spread, as long as the yield on the 7.25% of May 2016 finishes above 8.811% (a full convergence futures price below 91-17), the 7.25% of May 2016 will finish as the CDI and the extra payoff to the long basis trade on this issue will be zero. Thus, the long 7.25% of May 2016's March basis trade's P&L will show a loss equal to the initial basis after carry.

However, for final full-convergence futures prices below 91-17, the final basis for the 12% of August 2008-13 will be positive. The amount of the extra payoff on the long 12% of August 2008-13 basis is a direct function of the final futures price. At a futures price of 90-03, the 12% of August 2008-13's final basis would be 11.4 ticks. At a final futures price of 87-02, this "in-the-money" final 12% of August 2008-13 basis would equal 34.6 ticks.

In contrast, if the delivery date yield on the 7.25% of May 2016 falls below the critical 8.811% level (a full-convergence futures price above 91-17), the basis payoff picture reverses since the 12% of August 2008-13 would finish as the CDI. The 12% of August 2008-13's final basis would converge to zero, while the 7.25% of May 2016 issue's final basis will be positive. For a final futures price of 92-16, the extra payoff to this bond's long basis trade would be 6.4 ticks. For a final futures price of 94-06, the extra payoff to the 7.25% of May 2016's long basis trade would rise to 18.3 ticks.

Because of the dramatic differences in the price/yield characteristics of these two highlighted issues, the consequences of the CDI identity switch for either issue's final basis are quite important. The 7.25% of May 2016's final basis is a bullish position resembling a special type of bond call option. In contrast, the 12% of August 2008-13's final basis is a bearish position resembling a special type of bond put option. Finally, under the maintained assumptions, both basis trades would finish "out-of-the-money" if the yields on the 7.25% of May 2016 and the 12% of August 2008-13 on the delivery date were 8.811% and 9.011%, respectively. At these yields, the bonds are equally deliverable.

Yield Spread Effects

Table 4–6 presents results similar to those in Table 4–4, except that the yield spread is assumed to narrow to 15 basis points. The effect of the narrower yield spread is to increase the critical futures price at which the 12% of August 2008-13 becomes the CDI from 91-17 to 93-23. Furthermore, at every yield level at which the 7.25% basis finishes "in-the-money," this issue's final basis is about 12 ticks lower than for the 20 basis point yield spread case.

As a comparison of Tables 4–5 and 4–6 indicates, the long 7.25% of May 2016 basis trade benefits from a widening of the yield spread and is hurt by a narrowing of this spread. Conversely, the long 12% of August 2008-13 basis trade is hurt by a widening, and benefits by a narrowing of the yield spread.

Basis Trade P&Ls: An Options Interpretation

The difference between the initial basis after carry and the final P&L of a particular basis trade is determined by the value of the issue's final raw basis. Under the simplifying assumptions, the final raw basis must either be zero (if the bond held turns out to be the CDI) or positive (if some other bond is the CDI). Thus, the P&L of a long basis trade in a particular issue equals that issue's final raw basis minus its initial basis

Table 4–6. March 1989 Treasury Bond Futures Deliverability and Basis Pricing (Settlement Date: 03/22/89; Yield Spread: 15 bpts).

Final Futures*	Bond 7.250% 05/15/16 Factor: 0.9175			Bond 12.000% 08/15/08–13 Factor: 1.3893			CDI
	Yield	Price	Basis	Yield	Price	Basis	
95-20	8.360	88-05	13.1	8.510	132-27	0.0	12.000%
95-12	8.390	87-27	11.3	8.540	132-16	0.0	12.000%
95-04	8.420	87-18	9.5	8.570	132-05	0.0	12.000%
94-28	8.450	87-09	7.8	8.600	131-26	0.0	12.000%
94-20	8.480	87-00	6.1	8.630	131-14	0.0	12.000%
94-12	8.510	86-23	4.4	8.660	131-03	0.0	12.000%
94-04	8.540	86-14	2.7	8.690	130-24	0.0	12.000%
93-23	8.589	85-31	0.0	8.739	130-06	0.0	Switch pt.
93-19	8.600	85-28	0.0	8.750	130-02	0.9	7.250%
93-10	8.630	85-19	0.0	8.780	129-23	3.3	7.250%
93-00	8.660	85-11	0.0	8.810	129-13	5.8	7.250%
92-23	8.690	85-02	0.0	8.840	129-02	8.2	7.250%
92-13	8.720	84-25	0.0	8.870	128-23	10.6	7.250%
92-04	8.750	84-17	0.0	8.900	128-12	12.9	7.250%
91-26	8.780	84-08	0.0	8.930	128-02	15.2	7.250%
91-17	8.810	83-31	0.0	8.960	127-23	17.5	7.250%
91-08	8.840	83-23	0.0	8.990	127-12	19.8	7.250%
90-31	8.870	83-14	0.0	9.020	127-02	22.1	7.250%
90-21	8.900	83-06	0.0	9.050	126-23	24.3	7.250%
90-12	8.930	82-30	0.0	9.080	126-13	26.5	7.250%
90-03	8.960	82-21	0.0	9.110	126-02	28.7	7.250%
89-26	8.990	82-13	0.0	9.140	125-24	30.8	7.250%
89-17	9.020	82-05	0.0	9.170	125-14	33.0	7.250%
89-08	9.050	81-29	0.0	9.200	125-03	35.1	7.250%
88-31	9.080	81-20	0.0	9.230	124-25	37.2	7.250%
88-22	9.110	81-12	0.0	9.260	124-15	39.2	7.250%
88-14	9.140	81-04	0.0	9.290	124-05	41.3	7.250%
88-05	9.170	80-28	0.0	9.320	123-26	43.3	7.250%
87-28	9.200	80-20	0.0	9.350	123-16	45.3	7.250%
87-20	9.230	80-12	0.0	9.380	123-06	47.2	7.250%
87-11	9.260	80-04	0.0	9.410	122-28	49.2	7.250%
87-02	9.290	79-28	0.0	9.440	122-18	51.1	7.250%
86-26	9.320	79-21	0.0	9.470	122-08	53.0	7.250%
86-17	9.350	79-13	0.0	9.500	121-30	54.9	7.250%
86-09	9.380	79-05	0.0	9.530	121-20	56.8	7.250%
86-00	9.410	78-29	0.0	9.560	121-11	58.6	7.250%
85-24	9.440	78-22	0.0	9.590	121-01	60.4	7.250%
85-16	9.470	78-14	0.0	9.620	120-23	62.2	7.250%
85-08	9.500	78-07	0.0	9.650	120-13	64.0	7.250%
84-31	9.530	77-31	0.0	9.680	120-04	65.8	7.250%
84-23	9.560	77-23	0.0	9.710	119-26	67.5	7.250%
84-15	9.590	77-16	0.0	9.740	119-16	69.2	7.250%
84-07	9.620	77-09	0.0	9.770	119-07	70.9	7.250%
83-31	9.650	77-01	0.0	9.800	118-29	72.6	7.250%
83-23	9.680	76-26	0.0	9.830	118-20	74.3	7.250%

*Note: Assumes that the raw basis of the cheapest deliverable issue on the settlement date equals zero.

after carry. Conversely, the P&L of a short basis trade in a particular issue equals that issue's initial basis after carry minus its final raw basis.

With this quality option in mind, an easy description of basis after carry in P&L terms is (1) the maximum loss that a long basis trade can incur and (2) the maximum gain that a short basis trade can earn. As such, basis after carry represents the market delivery options "premium" associated with a particular basis.

Because of the quality option, Treasury basis trades have payoff profiles that can be interpreted within an options framework. However, the option is not a conventional call or put, but a particular type of exchange option. Nevertheless, the specific biases of the contract's conversion factors give rise to bond call and put option interpretations for specific basis positions.

Review of March 1989 Basis Pricing

Tables 4–5 and 4–6 show final basis values which, since carry is no longer a consideration, reflect the quality option's final payoff (final intrinsic value) for each basis trade. Prior to delivery, each basis should reflect its carry as well as the value of the implicit quality option.

The period between January and March 1989 was especially interesting for bond basis pricing because market levels remained near the critical deliverability switching region for an extended length of time. Thus, the fluctuations of alternative March 1989 bond bases during this period provides a good example of how the contract's quality option affects basis pricing.

As discussed above, the final settlement date payoff of the 12% of August 2008-13 March basis resembles a special type of bond put option over the relevant trading range.[10] The put's "strike price" is determined by the yield spread between the 12%'s final yield spread to the 7.25%. Since basis equals carry plus option value, the 12% of August 2008-13 basis could be priced on any trading day through its carry and put values.

---

10. Actually, an issue like the 10.375% of November 2004-09, or the 12.75% of November 2005-10 would have become deliverable for prices above 97 and the 12% of August 2008-13's basis would have turned positive once again. Thus, this basis had a deep-out-of-the-money call attached to its put value.

In contrast, the final settlement date payoff of the 7.25% of May 2016 March basis resembles a bond call option. Since basis equals carry plus option value, the 7.25% of May 2016 March basis could be priced on any trading day through its carry and call values.

Review the plots of the 7.25% of May 2016 basis, the 12% of August 2008-13 basis, the 10.375% of November 2007-12 basis and the March futures price for the January 3 to March 20, 1989 period presented in Figure 4–2. Two factors were notable for basis pricing within this period. First, financing rates rose, decreasing carry on all three issues, which depressed all three bases.

Second, the implicit option values of all three bases were greatly affected by the swings in market levels. The implied put values of both the 12% of August 2008-13 basis and that of the 10.375% of November 2007-12 bases (a similar issue) also fell as the market rallied to 90 and 91 levels. Thus, the carry and option components of these bases worked in the same (negative) direction. However, the put value of these bases subsequently recovered with the market's sharp drops on February 9 and 10.

In contrast, while the rise in financing rates also decreased the carry value of the 7.25% of May 2016 March basis, its implicit call option value rose with the rally in the market. The rise in call value offsets the fall in carry, keeping the 7.25% of May 2016 basis relatively constant. However, with the market's sharp fall, this basis dropped quickly.[11] The 7.25% of May 2016 was indeed the cheapest deliverable issue for the March 1989 contract. Its final basis converged to zero ticks.

Two-Directional Switching

For the relevant trading range, the two-bond switching example for March 1989 deliveries captured the essence of the then current basis pricing environment. However, given the market's subsequent May-June rally, deliverability switched from the 7.25% of May 2016 to issues like the 12% of August 2008-13 and the 10.375% of November 2007-12. Furthermore, the rally focused the market's attention on a further switch between the 12% of August 2008-13/10.375% of November

---

11. This basis never turned negative, since its remaining option value was always at least enough to offset the slightly negative carry that the 7.25% of May 2016 exhibited during the latter half of the period.

2007-12 family of issues and the 12.75% of November 2005-10/14% of November 2006-11 family of issues. Due to conversion factor bias, this further switch would occur (for June 1989 deliveries) at just about 100-17 if all of these issues traded at identical yields.

Figure 4–3 depicts the deliverability profile for the June 1989 bond futures contract assuming a 20 basis point yield spread of both the 12% of August 2008-13 and the 12.75% of November 2005-10 to the 7.25% of May 2016. Note that three distinct deliverability regions are determined here for parallel yield shifts. As a consequence, the 12% of August 2008-13's basis has both put and call option components. The put option component is implicit in the bear market deliverability switch to the 7.25% of May 2016. The call option component is implicit in the bull market deliverability switch to the 12.75% of November 2005-10.

Finally, it should be emphasized that the specific parallel yield shift delivery profiles analyzed here are accidents of history. Basis market opportunities are determined by the risk characteristics of the specific menu of deliverable issues. The market swings of the 1980s produced

---

Figure 4–3. Multiple Issue Switching (Converted Prices of 7.25s of '16, 12s of '13 and 12.75s of '10 Assuming 20 Bpt. Yield Spread of High Coupons to 7.25s of '16).

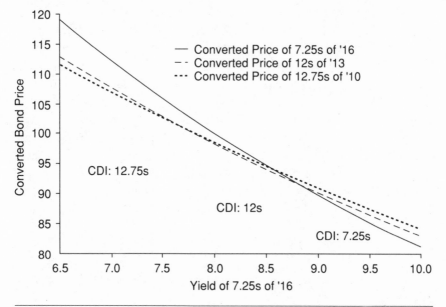

a particular menu of bonds that highlights parallel yield shift delivery plays. However, the specific menu of deliverable issues changes over time. Bonds become ineligible for delivery once their time to maturity or first call is less than 15 years. Furthermore, new bonds are auctioned through the Treasury's quarterly refunding cycle. Thus, delivery plays and basis market profit profiles are subject to an evolutionary process, though the basic conversion factor biases remain.

The Role of Simulation Analysis

How can a Treasury basis trade's quality option component be valued? A number of approaches are possible. As a starting point, Margrabe's (1978) exchange option model can be applied to the problem for a two-issue setting.[12] This model, which is detailed in the discussion of Treasury futures hedging in Chapter 7, provides some basic insights into quality option valuation.

Simulation analysis is an alternative method of evaluating basis trade payoffs under a variety of yield shift scenarios. This analysis can be used to project the entire distribution of possible basis trade payoffs as they might be more reasonably thought to actually occur. A joint probability distribution for yield shifts of the *entire menu* of deliverable issues is postulated; this distribution generates a large sample of yield curve draws. For each draw, the set of bond yields is used to derive the associated set of bond prices and converted bond prices and determine the identity of the CDI and each basis (zero or positive). Inferences about (1) the probability that each particular issue will actually become the final CDI and (2) the expected payoff of each basis trade can then be developed.

Simulated payoff structures permit a more complete analysis of the correspondences between the payoffs of basis trades and bond option positions. The accuracy of such inferences depends on the appropriateness of the presumed yield curve model. Kane and Marcus (1984) were the first to show how such a simulation study could be applied to

---

12. Garbade and Silber [1983] and Gay and Manaster [1984] apply the Margrabe model to two-asset quality delivery options for commodity futures. Cheng (1987) extended the model to a three-asset setting and applied the approach to Treasury bond futures. Subsequently, Hemler (1988) generalized the approach model to the n-issue case for Treasury bonds.

Treasury futures delivery options. Gay and Manaster (1989) suggest a short-cut method which permits simulations encompassing Treasury delivery options to be conducted in a cost-effective manner.

Timing Options

Under the terms of the Treasury bond and note futures contracts, shorts have the option of delivering on any business day within the delivery month. Treasury contract timing options can be described in terms of the accrued interest option, the wild card option and the end-of-month option.

A key determinant of delivery timing is the deliverable bond or note's carry. For any specific holding period, a Treasury issue's carry equals the difference between the accruing interest earnings and the position's financing cost. In *positive* carry markets (where the coupon interest accruing to the issue's holder is higher than the cost of financing the issue), the short will tend to deliver near the last business day of the month (the last possible delivery date). By deferring delivery, the short captures the positive carry as well as the full value of the contract's delivery options.

In contrast, in *negative* carry markets (where the coupon interest accruing to the issue's holder is lower than the cost of financing the issue), the short must compare the cost of the negative carry with the contract's remaining delivery option value. Early deliveries, possibly on the first business day of the month (the first eligible delivery date), may occur if the loss from negative carry is large and the remaining delivery options are not very valuable.

The available evidence on the timing of bond and note deliveries lends some support the effects of the accrued interest option.[14] During the period between December 1977 and June 1987, approximately 75% of all bond deliveries were made during the last five days of a delivery month. In contrast, only 7% of all bond deliveries occurred during the first five days of a delivery month. However, during periods of high short-term financing rates, a greater percentage of total deliveries take place early in the month. For example, during the high financing rate

---

14. For more details, see the Shearson Lehman Hutton, Inc. publication "Delivery Strategies and the Royal Flush Option in the Treasury Bond and Note Futures Markets," Derivative Products Research Group, April 1988.

environment of June 1979, 1,770 out of a total of 2,341 deliveries (76%) were made during the month's first three delivery days.

Of course, even in a negative carry market, the time dimensions implicit in, say, the Treasury contract quality option, may convince the short to bear the cost of negative carry in the hope that a cheaper deliverable issue or a profitable wild card delivery opportunity might emerge. In fact, in the 7.25% of May 2016 March 1989 basis position priced on January 20, 1989, the negative carry environment would not have signalled an early delivery. The long basis trader's delivery options would be too valuable to kill through early delivery to recoup a fraction of one tick of negative carry. The delivery timing evidence presented above in Table 4–3 supports this assertion. Furthermore, in a positive carry market, the possibility of delivering on relatively advantageous terms during the contract's wild card period may induce deliveries early in the month.

The Wild Card Option

Treasury bond and note contracts extend the short position another special timing-related delivery option: the "wild card" option.[15] During the delivery month, the short may notify the clearinghouse of its intent to deliver until as late as 8:00 P.M. (Chicago time). If delivery is chosen, the invoice price is based upon that day's *earlier* 2:00 P.M. closing price. The six-hour delivery window is referred to as the day's "wild card" period.

This delivery window grants the short a potentially valuable option. To understand the option, consider a simple example where the identity of the cheapest deliverable issue is known with certainty. This implies that, while the market remains open, the futures is priced off of this issue through a simple conversion factor weighting.[16]

Recall that a basis trader is short a conversion factor-weighted number of futures contracts against the face value of the bonds held long.

---

15. See Gay and Manaster (1986) and Arak and Goodman (1987).

16. The futures price change will equal (1/CF) times the CDI's cash price change. If the CDI's conversion factor is more than 1.0, the contract moves by a smaller than one-for-one proportion to CDI price changes. If the CDI's conversion factor is less than 1.0, the contract moves by a greater than one-for-one proportion.

For example, assuming a conversion factor of 1.3893 for a particular high coupon issue, a $100 million long basis position is long $100 million in par value of these bonds and short 1,389 futures contracts. However, $138.9 million of face value must be delivered against 1,389 contracts. Thus, the basis trader is somewhat short relative to delivery requirements. To deliver the high coupon issue, the basis trader must buy an additional $38.9 million in par value (referred to as the position's "tail") of these bonds.

For bonds with conversion factors greater than 1.0, the special value of the wild card play stems from the fact that a fall in bond prices between 2:00 P.M. and 8:00 P.M. (Chicago time) will imply an artificially low value of the tail's basis. (Remember that the futures price is fixed as of 2:00 P.M.) For some critical price drop, the profit on the delivery of the tail exceeds the loss of the initial raw basis incurred through delivery of the original $100 million bond position. Thus, the wild card play for an issue with a conversion factor greater than 1.0 resembles a special type of *put* option on the bond.

Suppose instead that the issue under consideration has a conversion factor that is less than 1.0. If the factor were 0.9175, the long basis position is long $100 million in bonds and short 918 futures contracts. However, only $91.8 million in par value of bonds are necessary to deliver against 918 contracts. Thus, the basis trader is slightly long relative to delivery requirements. The trader must sell off the additional $9.2 million in par value at the time the delivery decision is made. This $9.2 million of residual par value is this position's "tail."

For issues with conversion factors less than 1.0, the special value of the wild card stems from a rise in bond prices between 2:00 P.M. and 8:00 P.M. Delivery is announced at the 2:00 P.M. invoice price and the tail position of bonds can be sold off in the cash market at the favorable price. For some critical price rise, the profit on the cash market sale of the tail exceeds the loss of the initial raw basis incurred on the delivery of the $91.8 million in bonds. Thus, the wild card play for an issue with a conversion factor less than 1.0 resembles a special type of *call* option on the bond.

For both basis positions, the six-hour fixed futures price delivery period extends special value relative to the alternative of simply carrying the position. The "action" in the wild card play depends upon the size of the tail (i.e., the absolute difference between the bond's conversion factor and 1.0).

Finally, the best issue to deliver in a wild card play need not be the issue that the trader is holding. After the market moves, the best issue to deliver is that with the minimum raw basis, regardless of which issue was initially cheapest to deliver.

Mechanics of the Wild Card Payoff

Insight into the value of the wild card option can be obtained through a simple static breakeven analysis. Consider a trader who opens a long basis position at the market's close in anticipation of a profitable wild card delivery. The static breakeven point for a wild card delivery is defined to be where the delivery loss on the base position is just offset by the gain on the tail. Two cases must be examined, since the factor is either greater than or less than 1.0.

Factor > 1.0. The value in the trade occurs if the bond price falls after the futures market closes. The wild card trade is profitable if

$$CF(CF \times F_0) - [(CF - 1)B_1 + B_0] > 0$$

or

$$[(CF \times F_0) - B_0] + (CF - 1)[(CF \times F_0) - B_1] > 0$$

where the subscript 0 refers to the 2:00 PM. closing time and the subscript 1 refers to the 8:00 PM. deadline.

Thus, the critical static breakeven bond price *fall* equals

$$B_0 - B_1 = [CF/(CF - 1)] \times \text{Closing Basis}$$

On March 5, 1987, the March 1987 contract closed at 102-09 and the 13.875% of May 2006-11 was priced at 160-29. Thus, given its conversion factor of 1.5689, this issue's closing March 1987 basis equalled 14 ticks. Assume the trader buys $100 million of this basis at 14 ticks (i.e., buys $100 million of bonds and sells 1,569 bond futures). The breakeven afternoon price fall equals 38.6 ticks (= [1.5689/.5689] 14 ticks).

Later that afternoon, assume that the bond side trades down 49 ticks to 159-12.[17] The trader gives the exchange notice of an intention to

---

17. Actually, some poetic license is invoked here. This 159-12 quote is the next day's closing mark. It is used here for illustrative purposes.

deliver and buys the extra $56.9 million of the 13.875% May 2011-16. As before, the P&L can be divided into two components: (1) the loss on delivery of the base position and (2) the gain on delivery of the tail. The loss on delivery of the 1,000 contract base position equals

Loss on Base Position: $1,000 \times 14$ ticks $\times \$31.25 = \$437,500$

The gain from the purchase and delivery of the $56.9 million tail bond position more than offsets this loss. The basis on the delivery of the tail ·portion is -35 ticks (49 ticks lower than the initial 14-tick afternoon quote). Thus, the gain on delivery of the 569 contract tail is

Gain on Tail: 569×35 ticks $\times \$31.25 = \$622,343.75$

The 49-tick afternoon price fall of the 13.875% of May 2011-16 is more than sufficient to provide a profitable exercise of the wild card option. The exercise of the wild card option provides a profit of $184,843.75 per $100 million of the initial basis position.

Factor < 1.0.   The extra value of the trade occurs if the bond price rises after the futures market closes. The static breakeven point for the wild card delivery occurs where the loss of the closing raw basis from delivery of the CF futures contracts equals the gain from selling the tail bond position at an appreciated price:

$$CF \times \text{Closing Basis} = (1 - CF) \times (B_1 - B_0)$$

Thus, the critical price *rise* equals

$$B_1 - B_0 = [CF/(1 - CF)] \times \text{Closing Basis}$$

On March 14, 1989, at the 2:00 P.M. (Chicago) futures market close, the March 1989 contract was priced at 88-05 and the 7.25% of May 2016 was priced at 80-28. On a broker's screen, the March 1989 basis was quoted at 0.0 ticks bid/0.2 ticks asked. Assume that the trader buys $100 million of the 7.25% basis for 0.2 ticks (i.e., buys $100 million of bonds and sells 918 bond futures contracts). The breakeven price rise equals 2.2 ticks ($= [0.9175/0.0825] \times 0.2$ ticks).

By the end of the day's cash market trading, the 7.25% of May 2016 issue rises four ticks to 81-00. The trader files a delivery notice on the 918 contracts and sells the extra $8.2 million in bonds. As above, the P&L can be divided into base and tail components. The loss on delivery of the 918 contracts equals

Loss on Base Position: 918×0.2 ticks $\times$ $31.25 = $5,737.50$

The gain on the sale of the $8.2 million tail bond position equals

Gain on Tail Sale: $8.2 million $\times$ 4 ticks $\times$ $312.50 = $10,250$

Thus, the four-tick rise in the bond's price is sufficient to provide a profitable exercise of the wild card option. The P&L of the trade equals $4,512.50 per $100 million of the initial basis position.

Switching Issues. The best issue to deliver in a wild card play need not be the issue that the trader is holding. The traders above would have made even greater profits if, in the late afternoon trading, another issue had replaced their bonds as the minimum raw basis issue.

Dynamic Elements of Wild Card Valuation. The static breakeven analysis above gives some insight into wild card valuation, yet it ignores the dynamic element associated with the decision to deliver versus holding and carrying the basis position. By delivering, the trader closes out the short futures position and therefore gives up the right to exercise the contract's delivery options in the future. Furthermore, the basis position entails carry (either positive or negative). Thus, the value of the future opportunities lost by delivering versus holding the position open an extra day must be considered. Kane and Marcus (1986) and Gay and Manaster (1989) analyze dimensions of the dynamic nature of the wild card play.

The End-of-Month Option

The bond futures contract stops trading on the eighth last business day of the month (e.g., June 21, 1989 for the June 1989 contract). However, the contract allows the short the option to deliver on *any* business day within the month (e.g., through June 30, 1989). Deliveries during this end-of-month window are invoiced at the contract's final settlement price (from the last trading date).

As on any delivery date, the optimal bond for the short to deliver is the bond with the minimum raw basis. Because the invoice price of each deliverable issue is fixed as of the last trading day, each bond's basis changes during the end-of-month delivery window solely because of changes in the bond's price.

Consider two bonds that are equally deliverable (i.e., have identical raw bases) as of the last trading day, but have different price values of a basis point change in yield (PVBP).[18] For equal increases in yields, the bond with the higher PVBP will become unambiguously cheaper to deliver. Conversely, for equal decreases in yields, the bond with the lower PVBP will become unambiguously cheaper to deliver.

To capitalize on the end-of-month option, buy both issues and sell futures contracts of equal par value. If yields rise, sell the low PVBP issue, buy more of the high PVBP issue, and deliver the entire high PVBP issue position against the contract. The trade is profitable if the appreciation of the low PVBP issue relative to the high PVBP issue covers the loss of the sum of the two initial bond bases (less the combined carry to delivery).

Conversely, if yields fall, sell the high PVBP issue, buy more of the low PVBP issue, and deliver the entire low PVBP issue against the contract. The trade is profitable if the appreciation of the high PVBP issue relative to the low PVBP issue covers the loss of the combined initial basis (less the sum of the bonds' carries to delivery).

For example, at the expiration of trading in the June 1989 bond futures contract, on June 21, 1989, the 10.375% of November 2007-12 (PVBP = 0.1072) and the 12% of August 2008-13 (PVBP = 0.1203) each traded at a raw basis of two ticks. The trader who buys both bases (say, $50 million of each issue versus 1,000 contracts) is buying volatility. If yields on both bonds rise 20 basis points, the price of the 10.375% of November 2007-12 would fall 69 ticks, while that of the 12% of August 2008-13 would fall 77 ticks. In this case, the trader would sell the 10.375% issue (absorbing a capital loss of 69 ticks on $50 million) and buy $50 million more of the 12% of August 2008-13. The trader would then deliver $100 million of the 12% issue to settle the 1,000 contract position. The trader delivers the initial $50 million piece at a capital loss of two ticks. However, the second $50 million piece is delivered at a capital gain of 75 ticks (77-2). In this scenario, the trader gains two ticks, or $62,500 (i.e., 2 × 312.50 × 100), plus the carry on each bond position. The $62,500 capital gain is the net result of the $1,078,125 loss on the sale of the $50 million 10.375% of November 2007-12 position (−69 × $312.50 × 50); the $31,250 loss on the delivery of the first $50 million piece of the 12% of August 2008-13 (−2 × $312.50 × 50); and the $1,171,875 gain on the delivery of the second $50 million piece of the 12% of August 2008-13 (75 × $312.50 × 50).

---

18. The PVBP concept will be discussed more thoroughly in Chapter 7.

Alternatively, if yields on both issues should fall by equal amounts, the initial position in the 12% of August 2008-13 would be swapped for $50 million more of the 10.375% of November 2007-12, which would then be delivered.

Of course, changes in the yield spread between the two issues would also cause relative deliverability changes. Finally, it is also possible that some third issue's price would shift, giving it the minimum raw basis. In this case, both $50 million bond positions would be swapped for a new $100 million position in the third issue. This third bond would now be delivered.

Implied Repo Rates/Calendar Spreads

Delivery option value depresses the futures invoice price relative to its pure carry value. As in simple contracts, if the implied repo rate were greater than the market repo rate, a pure carry arbitrage would exist. However, for Treasury bond and note futures, such carry mispricing means that the long basis trader is being *paid* to acquire valuable delivery options. Thus, market forces almost always ensure that the implied repo rate from a Treasury bond or note contract will be less than the appropriate term repo rate (i.e., there will be a positive basis after carry).

Furthermore, since option value increases with time to expiration, the delivery option value of any deferred maturity contract is larger than that associated with a near contract. Thus, near minus deferred month calendar spreads will always appear somewhat high relative to pure carry differences.

Treasury Basis Pricing: Summary

Treasury bond and note contracts' delivery options lead to very different conclusions for pricing basis trades from those applicable to the much simpler stock index futures, Treasury bill, or Eurodollar futures contracts. In particular, the delivery option value extended to the short implies that futures will be priced below the forward price implied by the "basis equal carry" argument. In equilibrium, a Treasury bond or note futures will have a positive basis after carry even for the currently most likely CDI. This positive basis after carry value represents the premium that the long basis trader pays for obtaining the trade's delivery options. From the short basis trade's perspective, the positive basis after carry represents the premium that the short basis trader receives for granting these options. The hedging implications of Treasury contract deliverability and basis pricing issues are examined in Chapter 7.

CHAPTER 5

An Introduction to Hedging

"A bad hedge is one that loses money and a good hedge is one that makes money. Extending this, a perfect hedge is one that makes all the money." . . . . (Thomas Hieronymous, *The Economics of Futures Trading* (1971). [Author's Note: Not the classic definition.])

Why Hedge?

Asset values fluctuate. Holders of stocks, bonds, bills and other securities face risks. Futures hedges restructure the risk and return characteristics of the investor's initial unhedged position. Thus, futures hedges are entered because the investor is dissatisfied with at least one aspect of her initial portfolio.

In certain cases, the hedger may desire to eliminate all price level risk from the original cash market position. In other cases, the investor may prefer to hold an unbalanced futures-cash portfolio—and bear some hedgeable risks—with the expectation of returns higher than those expected on the fully hedged position. These decisions will depend on the value the investor places on the profit potential in not-fully-hedged positions relative to the risk reduction possible through more complete hedging. Thus, whether the investor hedges fully, hedges partially or does not hedge at all depends on the individual investor's personal risk preferences.

Regardless of the risk-return profile the investor chooses, futures contract positions are a quick and low-cost means to accomplish significant portfolio re-alignments. For example, in the case of large stock portfolios, "market risk" is under consideration. Achieving the desired change in risk exposure is easily accomplished through a single stock index

futures transaction. Only the costly liquidation of the entire stock portfolio would eliminate market risk. Thus, transactions costs and "convenience" may explain why traditional cash market participants turn to
futures contracts as a substitute for rearranging the cash portfolio.

Who Hedges?

A Treasury bond dealer might sell Treasury bond futures contracts to
hedge the price risk of her long cash bond inventory. A marketmaker like
this bond dealer carries inventories (net security positions) from which to
service customer buy and sell orders. Typically, a marketmaker desires
to hedge any abnormally large exposures. Treasury bond futures sales
are viewed as temporary substitutes for corresponding cash market sales.
Since the dealer *sells* bond futures, her position is termed a *short* hedge.

The dealer's original cash bond position is transformed into a particular
basis position. The price risk exposure is changed into basis risk—i.e.,
the risk of the *spread* between cash bond and Treasury bond futures
prices. Basis risk typically is much less than the original price level risk.
Through hedging, the dealer gives up the possibility of windfall gains
on the underlying position from favorable cash price level changes, in
order to gain protection against losses due to adverse cash price level
changes.

In other circumstances, suppose that the dealer, having sold Treasury
bonds to one customer which the dealer had originally borrowed from
another, has a net short cash bond position. The dealer might buy
Treasury bond futures to offset her short cash position's risk to upward
movements in bond prices. Because the dealer *buys* futures contracts in
this instance, the position would be termed a *long* hedge.

Typically, a dealer's net cash market position is constantly changing.
As she makes further cash bond purchases or sales, her futures position
would have to be adjusted to balance out the dollar risks of her futures
position with those of her changing cash bond position. Quick and cheap
temporary hedges of net bond positions allow the dealer to provide better
quotes to cash market customers. Thus, an important effect of futures
trading is to add liquidity to the underlying cash markets.

Other major cash market participants, such as pension funds, mutual
funds and insurance companies, typically desire to hold a net long
position in either the bond or stock markets, or both. However, from
time to time, in response to new information, institutional portfolio man-

agers decide to change their portfolio mix. Traditionally, such portfolio allocation changes have been accomplished solely through cash market transactions. For instance, a manager could lower the stock market exposure of his portfolio by selling stocks and buying short-term Treasury bills or bank certificates of deposit.

With the advent of financial futures trading, however, such portfolio risk reallocations also can be made through futures market transactions. The same decrease in the portfolio's stock market exposure could be accomplished through a sale of stock index futures contracts. In this scenario, the underlying cash portfolio is left untouched. Furthermore, the stock index futures price normally commands a premium over the stock market cash index. This premium, along with the dividends that continue to be received on the long stock position, should be sufficient to provide the same income that otherwise would have been earned from investing the proceeds of the cash stock sales. The transaction would be completed in a fraction of the time and cost of a cash market sale.

Factors Influencing Hedge Construction and Effectiveness

The futures-cash arbitrage trades studied in Chapter 3 were based upon the simplest type of textbook hedge. The arbitrager sought matched opposite positions in a futures contract and its underlying cash asset that eliminated all portfolio value risk and promised a return greater than the riskless interest rate. The riskless nature of this specific hedge portfolio is assured as long as the position is held to the futures contract's delivery or expiration date.

However, most hedgers are not in the arbitrage business. Thus, most hedgers hold a cash portfolio which differs from that underlying the traded futures contract and, in addition, plan to liquidate their hedge on a date different from the futures contract's expiration. In fact, the hedging horizon may be very short (e.g., one day) compared to the time left to the futures contract's expiration.

In most cases, the hedger can significantly alter the risk exposure of the cash asset position through futures trading. However, because of cash asset quality and hedge horizon differences, the price convergence property which anchors the returns in a true arbitrage hedge portfolio will not be in force. Thus, the typical hedger faces uncertain slippages between cash and futures position values on the actual hedge-lifting date. Like the basis traders of Chapters 3 and 4, hedgers have a particular basis position. However, unlike those basis trades, the hedger may enter a basis position out of fear of losses on an outright cash market exposure, in addition to strategic thoughts on futures basis movements.

Identifying When A Hedge Will Work

The key to a good hedging vehicle is a high correlation between changes in the price of the futures contract used and changes in the price of the cash asset. Put more simply, the relevant question is: *Do* cash and futures prices move together in a predictable way? If the answer is "yes," then risk reduction through futures trading will be possible. If the answer is "no," then futures trading will not reduce risk (and may increase it substantially). Suppose that significant correlations do exist between the changes in specific cash asset price and those of alternative futures contract prices. The prospective hedger must then choose the most suitable hedging vehicle from the available menu of traded futures contracts. This choice usually results in the contract which has the highest cash price change correlation among those that trade in liquid contract markets.

Balancing Risks

Finally, given a suitable hedging vehicle, the remaining choice concerns the number of contracts that must be entered. Assume that the goal of the hedge is to minimize portfolio risk. The futures position should be chosen to balance the dollar risk of the cash side of the portfolio. Thus, an appropriate *hedge ratio* must be chosen.

In order to find the proper balancing futures position, one further question must be answered: *How* do futures and cash prices move together? In particular, given a one-tick change in the futures contract price, by how much will the cash asset price change? On average, will the cash price change by the same one tick, by more than one tick, or by less than one tick?

If the corresponding cash price change equals one tick on average, then a futures position which matches the size of the cash position will be appropriate. If the corresponding cash price change is predictably *more* than one tick, the futures position must be scaled higher than merely matching the size of the cash position. This must occur because the cash side of the equally weighted portfolio is riskier than the futures side.

In contrast, if the corresponding cash price change is predictably *less* than one tick, the futures position should be scaled down versus the value of the total cash position. Scaling the futures position down makes sense in this case because the futures side of the equally weighted portfolio is riskier than the cash side.

Example 1: Perfect Quality and Timing Matches

Consider the case of a pension fund manager holding a large stock portfolio which reflects the composition of the S&P 500 stock index. Suppose that the initial date's cash S&P 500 index value is 275.00; that the cash portfolio will earn a fixed 1.00 index points in dividends a month (initially implying about a 4.36% annual dividend payout rate); that the two-month horizon money market interest rate is 8.0% per year; and that the S&P 500 stock index futures is selling at 276.66.[1]

Suddenly, this manager becomes bearish on the stock market for a short period. In particular, this manager decides to withdraw from the market for two months. As it happens, the near S&P 500 index futures contract expires at the end of this same two-month period. The manager implements the strategy by selling stock index futures contracts. These contracts will undergo a final cash settlement in two months on the contract's expiration date.

At the end of the two-month hedging period, the cash index may have fallen (as the fund manager feared) or it may have risen. As representative cases, assume that the cash index either falls to 265.00 or rises to 285.00 on the hedge-lifting date. These index values are chosen arbitrarily for expositional purposes. The arguments presented below hold regardless of what cash index expiration date value (e.g., 256.50, 297.10, etc.) occurs. Finally, recall that the futures also will be priced at either 265.00 or 285.00 on the hedge-lifting date due to the final cash settlement procedure used on contract expiration dates.

In the down market case, the hedge portfolio loses 10 points on the change in cash prices (265.00−275.00), but gains 11.66 on the short futures position (276.66−265.00). Thus, the basis change component of the hedge return is 1.66 index points (−10.00 + 11.66). The position

---

1. Here, the requirement that the S&P 500 index contract must trade in round five-tick increments (e.g., either 276.65 or 276.70), is ignored.

also receives 2.00 points in dividends and 0.0067 points as one-month's interest earnings on the first month's payment. The portfolio's total P&L in this case is 3.6667 index points. Expressed as an annual percentage yield on the initial value of the cash stock portfolio, the hedge earns 8.0% (i.e., compute [12/2][3.6667/275] = 0.0800).

Alternatively, in the up market case, the hedge portfolio gains 10 points on the rise in stock prices (285.00−275.00) and loses 8.34 points on the short futures position (276.00−285.00). Again, the basis change component of the hedge return equals 1.66 (= 10 − 8.34). The position earns the same 2.0067 points in dividends. The portfolio's total return in this up market case is exactly the same 3.6667 point or 8.0% yield achieved in the down market case.

Table 5–1 summarizes the payoffs of the hedge for both the up and down market cases.

Table 5–1. Perfect Quality and Maturity Match Hedge Results.

Final Cash Index	Cash Index Change	Div	Total Unhedged Return	Short Futures Change	Total Hedged Return	=	Basis Change	+	Div.
285.00	+10	+2.01	+12.01	−8.34	+3.67		+1.66		+2.01
265.00	−10	+2.01	−7.99	+11.66	+3.67		+1.66		+2.01

Interpretation of Ex. 1.   Why does this hedge work? Express the value change on this hedge position over the two-month period between date 0 and date T as

$$V_T - V_0 = -(F_T - F_0) + (P_T - P_0) + \text{Div}(0, T)$$

or

$$V_T - V_0 = (P_T - F_T) - (P_0 - F_0) + \text{Div}(0, T)$$

The hedge's value change equals the hedge-lifting date's cash-futures basis, $(P_T - F_T)$, minus the initial date's basis, $(P_0 - F_0)$, plus the value of dividends paid between dates 0 and T, $\text{Div}(0, T)$. Here, the dividends term, $\text{Div}(0, T)$, is interpreted as fixed in absolute index points, as opposed to being fixed as a percent of the index value.

In general, a hedge-lifting date's cash-futures basis is subject to some risk. However, because the hedge-lifting date in this specific example happens to coincide with the futures contract expiration date, the cash-futures basis at date T must equal 0 (either [285.00−285.00] or [265.00−265.00]) due to the final cash settlement terms of the index futures. Thus, for this very special example, the hedge portfolio value change entails no basis risk. The portfolio's P&L simplifies to

$$V_T - V_0 = -(P_0 - F_0) + \text{Div}(0, T)$$

Substituting the figures from the numerical example above, the riskless 3.67 point earnings of the hedge result from 1.66 points in convergence income (276.66−275.00) and 2.01 in dividends.

Qualifications

Clearly, the example above represents a very stylized hedging situation. First, stock index futures expiration dates occur only four days a year. The majority of hedges will naturally end on dates which do not coincide with expirations. For these hedges, the hedge-lifting date's cash-futures spread will be uncertain when the hedge is begun. Thus, even hedges of the underlying cash market portfolio will bear risk due to uncertainty about the actual cash-futures price relation on the hedge-lifting date.

The second reason why the example is highly stylized is not as obvious as the first. Note that this "riskless" hedge was priced to yield 8.0%, precisely the assumed yield on other riskless investments. While such a result seems reasonable, it depends crucially on the pricing performance of the futures market. Expressed somewhat differently, the hedger in this example entered the hedge at the "fair" date 0 futures price (276.66) as based upon the arbitrage model of Chapter 3. If the futures had been selling at 275.50 (i.e., 1.16 points underpriced at date 0), the total return would have been only 2.51 points (0.5 points of convergence income plus 2.01 dividend points) or a 5.48% annual yield. Instead, had the futures been sold at 277.90 (1.24 points overpriced at date 0), the hedge would have returned 4.91 index points (2.90 in convergence income plus 2.01 dividend points) for a 10.71% annualized yield.

The exact return that this simple textbook futures hedge risklessly delivers depends crucially on the initial date's futures price. This futures hedge is riskless in that it guarantees that the originally quoted futures-cash spread will be earned in addition to the stock position's dividends. It does not promise that the initially quoted basis is "fair." The fairness of the futures pricing that hedgers accept depends on the efficiency of the arbitrage sector's performance. In the chaos of the stock market crash of 1987, the S&P 500 index futures sometimes closed as much as 9%

below its "fair" relative cash market value. Hedges placed at such prices and unwound at expiration actually lost significant amounts of money ("risklessly") through unfavorable convergence.

Daily Mark-to-Market Settlement Effects

The hedging examples above ignored the impact of daily mark-to-market settlement on the futures side of the hedges. Variation margin payments due to losses on the futures side of the position over the life of a hedge will generate financing costs. Cash inflows from gains on the futures side over the life of a hedge will generate interest earnings. While the capital gains components of the daily variation margin payments "add up" in the appropriate way to ensure that the hedge still works, the financing/interest component is a new source of risk.

There are two implications of mark-to-market settlement for hedging over periods longer than one day. First, the hedger must manage the daily cash flows. Second, the hedger must underhedge somewhat in order to offset the hedge-lifting date value risk of the position caused by the financing/interest component. This underhedging adjustment is known as the hedge's "tail." Essentially, a hedge's tail is a present value factor.

As in the example above, assume that the hedge will be lifted on the futures contract's expiration date in two months (60 days). For a perfect quality and maturity matching hedge, the sale of one futures contract will not perfectly balance the value risks of the futures and cash sides of the position. Instead, at the hedge's inception, only 0.9871 contracts should be sold. Why? Because any gain or loss on the futures side over the first day of the hedging period results in an actual cash flow that will involve interest compounding for 59 days. The future value factor for 59 days at an interest rate of 8% is 1.0131 ($= 1 + [0.08 \times 59/360]$). In order to offset this future value "exaggeration factor" of 1.0131, the hedger should scale the futures position down by the corresponding present value factor of 0.9871 ($= 1/[1 + (0.08 \times 59/360)]$).

After the first day passes, only 59 days remain until the end of the hedge. Furthermore, the gain or loss on the futures over the second day of the hedging period will compound for only 58 days. Thus, at a constant 8% interest rate, the future value factor falls to 1.01289 ($= 1 + [0.08 \times 58/360]$) and the present value scaling factor for the hedge rises to 0.9873.

For an unchanged interest rate, the appropriate scaling factor gets a little bit closer to 1.0 with each successive day in the hedging period. Thus, more futures contracts are sold as the contract's time-to-expiration shortens. A week prior to the hedge-lifting/contract expiration date, the six remaining days of compounding imply a scaling factor of 0.9987. With one day left until expiration, no underhedging is needed since there is no differential compounding period between flows from the futures and cash positions. The "tail" disappears and the 1-to-1 hedge ratio is appropriate.

Basis Fluctuations and Maturity Cross-Hedging

A "maturity cross-hedge" refers to a hedge in which the natural hedge-lifting date is not identical to the futures contract's maturity date. For example, a hedge might be lifted while the contract still has one month to maturity. Such futures hedges of the underlying cash position are basis positions. However, in such hedges, the final basis is not anchored by assured convergence.

Recall the pension fund manager who has turned bearish on the stock market over the short-term. This manager still desires to withdraw from the market for only two months. However, suppose that the nearest stock index futures contract currently has three months to expiration. Thus, the pension fund manager will start the hedge by selling index futures when they are three months from their expiration date. He plans to lift the hedge in two months by buying back these same futures when they are only one month from their expiration date. Assume an initial stock index value of 275, an 8.50% three-month term financing rate, and reinvested dividend inflows to maturity of 3.02 index points. The initial fair three-month futures price equals 277.82 ($= 275 + 5.84 - 3.02$). Thus, the initial fair basis equals -2.82 ($= 3.02 - 5.84$).

Since the hedge is lifted with one month remaining to contract maturity, the cross-hedge's P&L can be understood by studying determinants of the fair cash-futures basis on a one-month maturity contract. The discussion of basis determination in Chapter 3 provides considerable insight into maturity cross- hedging. In particular, the hedge-lifting date basis should equal the stock index portfolio's carry (to the contract's expiration date). In turn, the one-month carry on the stock index portfolio will depend on the index level, the financing rate, and the remaining dividend income until contract expiration.

The upper panel of Table 5–2 projects the hedge-lifting date basis as a function of stock index levels and financing rate (assuming a constant 1.00 index points of remaining dividend income). The hedge-lifting date's basis will be high for low cash stock index levels and low financing rates. Conversely, the hedge-lifting date's basis will be low for high cash stock index levels and high financing rates.

Table 5–2.   The Hedge-Lifting Date Basis (= One-Month's Carry).

Months-to-maturity: 1
Dividends: 1.00 Index Points Per Month
Final Basis = Cash Price − (1.0 × Futures Price)

	Financing Rate (%)					
	4	6	8	9.375	10	12
Cash Price						
260	0.1	−0.3	−0.7	−1.0	−1.2	−1.6
265	0.1	−0.3	−0.8	−1.1	−1.2	−1.7
270	0.1	−0.4	−0.8	−1.1	−1.3	−1.7
275	0.1	−0.4	−0.8	−1.1	−1.3	−1.8
280	0.1	−0.4	−0.9	−1.2	−1.3	−1.8
285	0.1	−0.4	−0.9	−1.2	−1.4	−1.9
290	0.0	−0.5	−0.9	−1.3	−1.4	−1.9

The Maturity Cross-Hedge P&L.

Months-to-maturity: 1
Dividends (two month's): 2.01
Initial Hedge Basis: −2.82 = 275 − (1.0 × 277.82)
Hedge P&L = Final Hedge Basis − Initial Hedge Basis + Dividends.

	Financing Rate (%)					
	4	6	8	9.375	10	12
Cash Price						
260	5.0	4.5	4.1	3.8	3.7	3.2
265	5.0	4.5	4.1	3.8	3.6	3.2
270	4.9	4.5	4.0	3.7	3.6	3.1
275	4.9	4.5	4.0	3.7	3.5	3.1
280	4.9	4.4	4.0	3.6	3.5	3.0
285	4.9	4.4	3.9	3.6	3.5	3.0
290	4.9	4.4	3.9	3.6	3.4	2.9

The lower panel of Table 5–2 projects the P&L of the maturity cross-hedge. The hedge's P&L equals the final basis (see upper panel entries) minus the initial basis (−2.82) plus the reinvested value of the two-month holding period's dividend inflows (here, 2.03). This hedge P&L reveals two sources of basis risk in the maturity cross-hedge. The first relates to the level of financing rates, the second, to the cash stock index level.

Financing rate risk in this maturity cross-hedge is unavoidable. The hedge benefits from a fall in rates since the final basis will strengthen with lower rates. Conversely, the hedge is hurt by a rise in rates since the final basis will weaken with higher rates.

Final cash stock index price levels also determine the hedge's P&L. Here the final index level matters since the carry until contract maturity (measured in index points) is a function of the value of the index portfolio that must be financed.

However, this cash index level component of the hedge's basis risk can be reduced with an adjustment to the hedge ratio. Note that the fair final basis can be expressed as

$$\text{Final Basis} = \text{Dividends} - (1 + [\text{Rate}(1/1200)]) \text{ Cash Index}$$

The source of the cash index level risk in the final basis is the financing factor multiple. Because this multiple is greater than 1.0, the final basis moves more than 1- to-1 for any cash index shift. Underhedging by a factor equal to its inverse will offset this multiple. Using the one-month forward interest rate of 9.375% (implicit from the current two- month rate of 8.0% and the three-month rate of 8.50%), a hedge ratio of 0.9922 ($= 1/[1 + (9.375/1200)]$) is appropriate.

Table 5–3 presents results for this financing factor adjusted hedge. Here, the hedge basis is defined as the cash price minus 0.9922 times the futures price. The upper panel presents the final hedge basis as a function of index level and financing rates. The lower panel presents the hedge P&L as a function of the same variables. The hedge P&L equals the final hedge basis (see table entries) minus the initial hedge basis (here, −0.67) plus the reinvested dividend inflows (2.03 index points).

While the hedge's P&L is still risky, the cash index component of the hedge's basis risk has been reduced by the new hedge ratio choice. This index level-related risk is eliminated completely if the hedge-lifting date's financing rate turns out to be 9.375% (the forward rate used to guess the appropriate financing factor).

Table 5–3. The Hedge-Lifting Date Basis (Hedge Ratio = 0.9922).

Months-to-maturity: 1
Dividends: 1.00 Index Points Per Month
Final Basis = Cash Price − (0.9922 × Futures Price)

	Financing Rate (%)					
	4	6	8	9.375	10	12
Cash Price						
260	2.2	1.7	1.3	1.0	0.9	0.4
265	2.2	1.7	1.3	1.0	0.9	0.4
270	2.2	1.8	1.3	1.0	0.9	0.4
275	2.2	1.8	1.3	1.0	0.9	0.4
280	2.2	1.8	1.3	1.0	0.9	0.4
285	2.3	1.8	1.3	1.0	0.9	0.4
290	2.3	1.8	1.3	1.0	0.9	0.4

The Maturity Cross-Hedge P&L (Hedge Ratio = 0.9922).

Months-to-maturity: 1
Dividends (two month's): 2.01
Initial Hedge Basis: −2.82 [= 275 − (0.9922 × 277.82)]
Hedge P&L = Final Hedge Basis − Initial Hedge Basis + Dividends.

	Financing Rate (%)					
	4	6	8	9.375	10	12
Cash Price						
260	4.8	4.4	4.0	3.7	3.5	3.1
265	4.9	4.4	4.0	3.7	3.5	3.1
270	4.9	4.4	4.0	3.7	3.5	3.1
275	4.9	4.4	4.0	3.7	3.5	3.1
280	4.9	4.5	4.0	3.7	3.5	3.1
285	4.9	4.5	4.0	3.7	3.5	3.1
290	5.0	4.5	4.0	3.7	3.5	3.1

Tables 5–2 and 5–3 provide some understanding of the carry-related origins of basis risk for futures hedges of the underlying asset. However, such hedges typically contain other sources of cash-futures price slippages. Without specific equilibrium explanations, excess variation in the basis is defined to represent market "mispricing." Extended periods of basis mispricing—such as those observed in the stock index futures basis market between 1982 and 1984—is indicative of an under-developed arbitrage sector.

Tailing the Position

This maturity cross-hedge must also be tailed to offset variation margin effects. Multiplying the untailed hedge ratio (0.9922) by the present value factor for the initial two-month length of the hedging period (0.9871) will produce the properly tailed hedge ratio (0.9794). This hedge ratio incorporates the same present value-related tailing adjustments as in the hold-to-maturity hedge in the first example. Thus, the total underhedging adjustment consists of two components. The pure underhedging component is based on the equilibrium relationship between the riskiness of the longer-dated futures relative to the riskiness of the cash index at some earlier hedge-lifting date. The second underhedging factor is related to the initial compounding period for the first day's variation margin flow.

Fortunately, a simple rule emerges to guide maturity cross-hedging: Compute a properly tailed hedge ratio as if the hedge were to be held to contract maturity. To hedge *any* holding period, underhedge by the present value tail factor to the contract's maturity date. Thus, to hedge a cash market position with a 90-day-to-maturity contract, an 89-day present value factor (reflecting, less one day, the three-month time-to-expiration of the date T expiration futures as of the hedge's date 0 inception) is initially appropriate. For a constant interest rate, the appropriate hedge ratio rises with the passing of each day, reflecting the shrinking compounding period for the daily variation margin.

Measures of Hedge Performance

How should hedge performance be evaluated? Certainly, one could judge a particular hedge's success by comparing the variability of its returns to the variability of the unhedged cash security's returns. The standard deviation of returns is the classic measure of portfolio return dispersion. Thus, it is useful to compare estimates of return standard deviation or return variance (the standard deviation squared) of both hedged and unhedged returns. An in-sample estimate of the return variance for a return sample consisting of J observations is computed as

$$\text{Var}(R^v) = \frac{1}{J-1} \sum_{t=1}^{J} (R_t^v - \overline{R}^v)^2$$

where $\overline{R}^v$ denotes the in-sample average of observed hedge returns. For the hedge ratio, h, specified under a given hedging rule, these returns are defined as

$$R_t^v = R_t^p - hR_t^f$$

and the sample's average hedge return can be written as

$$\overline{R}^v = (1/J) \sum_{}^{J} (R_t^p - hR_t^f)$$

where:

$$R_t^p = (P_t - P_0)/P_0$$

and

$$R_t^f = (F_t - F_0)/P_0$$

As an illustrative example, Table 5–4 presents comparative statistics for returns to hedges of the cash S&P 500 stock index portfolio based on daily close-to-close price changes over the January 3, 1985 to March 31, 1986. The returns for five alternative hedge ratios ($h = 0.0, h = 0.5, h = 0.8, h = 0.98, h = 1.0$ and $h = 1.2$) are computed. For each hedge ratio choice, the appropriate position in near contract S&P 500 futures contracts is used.

The $h = 0.98$ hedge ratio choice approximates the basic analytical hedging strategy for these one-day nearby contract hedges.[2] The $h = 0.0$ case examines the unhedged cash S&P 500 stock portfolio. The $h = 1.0$ case represents the naive answer. The remaining choices were arbitrary. For each hedge ratio choice, the hedge portfolio's return standard deviation, the fraction of the unhedged return's variance that is eliminated by the hedge, and the hedge portfolio's average return are reported.

These data show that S&P 500 futures hedges are able to reduce a substantial proportion of the risk to daily returns on the S&P 500 stock portfolio. The best performing hedge ($h = 0.80$) eliminates 83% of the variance of daily S&P 500 returns. Furthermore, hedging lowers the investor's average portfolio return. The unhedged return (capital gains only) on the S&P 500 stock portfolio during this "bull market" period sampled equalled 0.123% per day (about 31.0% when annualized over

---

2. At an assumed interest rate of 9%, one-day hedges for nearby futures would entail a hedge ratio path running between 0.978 (when the contract becomes the nearby) and 1.0 (the day before expiration). Our choice of a constant $h = .98$ ratio approximates this solution.

Table 5–4. A Comparison of Alternative S&P 500 Index Futures Hedges
Daily Return Data: January 3, 1985–March 31, 1986.

Hedge Ratio (h)	Hedge Return Standard Deviation	Fraction of Variance Eliminated	Average Hedge Return	Maximum Hedge Return	Minimum Hedge Return
$h = 0.00$	0.688%	—	0.123%	2.28%	−2.73%
$h = 0.50$	0.368%	.71	0.062%	1.18%	−1.01%
$h = 0.80$	0.283%	.83	0.025%	1.03%	−1.37%
$h = 0.98$	0.317%	.79	0.003%	0.94%	−1.63%
$h = 1.00$	0.324%	.78	0.001%	0.93%	−1.66%
$h = 1.20$	0.424%	.62	−0.024%	1.65%	−1.94%

a 252-trading day year). Hedging with the best risk-reducing hedge ratio lowered the average portfolio return to just 0.025% per day (about 6.30% per trading year, excluding dividends).

These particular stock return estimates, like all portfolio risk and return estimates from market data samples, must be interpreted with care. First, the sample period chosen lies within the great bull market which started in 1982, continued through August 1987, and ended abruptly with the October 19, 1987 crash. Thus, the average return difference between unhedged and hedged portfolios of about 24.7% per year should be viewed as the *realized* average cost of hedging over this specific time period. It should not be used to extrapolate the *expected* average cost of hedging in any future sample period. (Even more misleading would be inferences about average hedging costs derived from studying the returns from S&P 500 futures hedges over an August 1987 to November 1987 sample period. In this sample period, the large negative average return of the unhedged S&P 500 portfolio would seemingly imply that hedging both reduces portfolio risk *and increases* portfolio returns.)

In contrast, conclusions about relative variance reduction through hedging, while not completely invariant to the sample period studied, are not greatly affected by price "trends" induced by arbitrary selection of the beginning and ending points of a specific sample.[3]

However, the results in Table 5–4 reveal an important surprise: The best performing hedge ($h = 0.80$) is not the one predicted by the basis equals carry pricing model ($h = 0.98$). At least for hedging day-to-day

---

3. However, the next chapter presents evidence showing how the hedging effectiveness of the S&P 500 index futures market has improved as trading volume in this market has grown.

stock return risk, other factors enter futures pricing which the hedger must consider while constructing hedges. Thus, in order to construct the best possible hedge, the prospective hedger should assess the performance of alternative hedging rules through careful empirical analysis whenever possible. Regression analysis, a statistical technique applied in many empirical hedging studies, is discussed in Chapter 6.

Arbitrage and Expected Hedge Returns

Arbitrage pressures are continually at work in the market. If a contract is overpriced at a hedge's inception, the hedger should expect that at least part (if not all) of this initial overpricing will be eliminated by the hedge-lifting date. Other things being equal, there will be a tendency for the basis to increase. Likewise, initial futures contract underpricings also should be partly (if not completely) reversed by the hedge-lifting date. Other things being equal, there will be a tendency for the basis to shrink.

Of course, by the hedge-lifting date, some new source of futures market disturbance could arrive and lead to a further (and unexpected) change in the basis. Nevertheless, on average, the hedger should expect some degree of mispricing reversal.

How much of an initial date's mispricing should be eliminated by the hedge-lifting date? It depends on the length of the hedging period, the nearness of the hedge-lifting date to the futures contract's expiration (delivery) date, and the particular market under study. The longer the hedging period, the greater the chance that more of the initial mispricing will have been reversed. Furthermore, the fair futures pricing relation tends to hold better the closer the contract is to its expiration (deliver) date. Obviously, if the hedge-lifting date corresponds to a contract expiration date, a complete reversal of the initial mispricing must occur for cash settlement contracts.

Some futures markets have experienced long periods of persistent overpricing or underpricing (e.g., stock index futures in the early years of trading), while others rarely exhibit persistent mispricing patterns. In any case, the prospective hedger should have a firm understanding of the speed and predictability with which any initial mispricing typically will be eliminated. The properties of the movements of futures contract mispricings are crucial in evaluating expected hedge returns and for analyzing realized hedge return performance.

Why Hedge When Futures Are Mispriced?

The prospective hedger is always faced with the decision to make her desired portfolio reallocation by cash market transactions or futures markets trades. Futures contract markets offer some distinct transactional advantages over cash markets. The most important of these advantages are better liquidity and lower direct transactions costs.

Recall that through its own profit-seeking behavior, the arbitrage sector helps to keep futures in line with carry-adjusted cash market prices. Absolute deviations from fair pricing may regularly exceed transactions cost levels of arbitragers in some markets. However, such deviations from fair pricing may not be larger than the difference between cash and futures market transactions costs for ordinary hedgers. For example, suppose that the initial futures price lies at a discount to its fair minimum transactions cost-adjusted level. In particular, assume that arbitrager transactions costs equal 1% of the cash price, but that the current price discount from its fair value is equal to 2.5% of the cash index. At least in the case of cash settlement contracts, hedgers know that the entire 2.5% futures discount will be closed by the contract's terminal date. They also suspect that, within a short period of time, the discount will drift up by 1.5% to the 1% discount level supported by the arbitrager transactions cost levels. This upward drift will work against the short hedger.

Nevertheless, hedgers may still find selling "underpriced" futures an attractive alternative to liquidating the cash asset position. Suppose that hedgers are subject to relatively high transactions costs (especially on the cash market side) or that the short-term interest rate at which they can invest the funds from cash asset sales is lower than that of arbitragers. For example, selling the underpriced futures would still be the better alternative for hedgers if their direct transactions costs were at least 1.25% higher and their riskless investment rate were 0.25% lower than those faced by the arbitrage sector.

Furthermore, expecially during chaotic times, the liquidity offered by the futures markets is worth the extra cost implied by trading at otherwise unattractive prices. During the stock market crash of 1987, stock index futures contracts traded at otherwise unthinkably deep discounts to their cost of carry values. Apparently, the risks associated with price changes in the face of possible cash market execution delays during this volatile period kept dramatically low futures prices acceptable for sellers.

Strip Hedges

A *strip* of contracts refers to a portfolio of individual positions in contracts with successively more distant maturity dates. Strips can be either bought or sold. Furthermore, the number of contracts of each maturity in the strip need not be the same. The appropriate strip position must be tailored to solve the particular problem faced by the investor.

Eurodollar Strips

Financial institutions with money market risk exposure use Eurodollar futures contract strips in a variety of ways. By buying a strip of Eurodollar futures to hedge against falls in money market reinvestment rates, a portfolio manager synthetically extends the maturity of a short-term money market investment. By selling a strip of Eurodollar futures contracts to hedge the coupon reset risk of floating rate note, a corporate treasurer transforms floating-rate funding into fixed-rate funding.

A key reason the Eurodollar futures market attracts strip strategy users is its unusually large "back month" trading. For example, on October 4, 1988, while the two front contracts (DEC 88 and MAR 89) accounted for 284,470 contracts of the Eurodollar market's total open interest, 8 of the remaining 10 back month contracts had individual open interests of at least 10,000 contracts.

Extending Investment Maturities

Eurodollar strips can synthetically extend the maturity of a LIBOR-based short-term Eurodollar deposit or a money market instrument such as a Euro Certificate of Deposit (CD). This section presents a detailed example of such strip strategies based on opportunities available August 19, 1988.[1]

On August 19, 1988, the one-month LIBOR was 8.375%, the three-month LIBOR was 8.6875%, the six-month LIBOR was 9%, the nine-month LIBOR was 9.125% and the one-year LIBOR was 9.25%. Rates for the following maturities could be interpolated: the four-month LIBOR at 8.792%; the seven-month LIBOR at 9.042%; and the ten-month LIBOR at 9.167%.[2]

---

1. In the examples below, each investment studied returns LIBOR. Deposits or CDs quoted as a fixed spread off LIBOR could be handled easily. All rates are expressed using an actual/360 money market convention.

2. Simple linear interpolation was used here for illustrative purposes.

At the same time, 12 different Eurodollar futures contract maturities were trading (September 1988 through June 1991). Prices and implied futures rates for the front four contracts are presented here: the September 1988 Eurodollar contract was priced at 91.25 (implied rate of 8.75%); the December 1988 contract was priced at 90.78 (9.22%); the March 1989 contract was priced at 90.76 (9.24%); and the June 1989 contract was priced at 90.63 (9.37%).

A One-Contract/Rollover Strategy

As an alternative to buying a *122-day (four-month)* Euro CD, an investor could buy a 31-day CD and buy 102 $1 million face value September Eurodollar futures contracts. The long September Eurodollar futures position hedges the reinvestment rate risk of the September 19 CD rollover into a new 91-day CD. This futures position could be classified as an "anticipatory long hedge."

Why buy 102 contracts? These 102 September contracts are bought since (1) $100,721,181(= \$100,000,000 \times [1 + 0.08375(31/360)])$ needs to be reinvested on September 19, 1988 and (2) a futures to cash hedge ratio of (91/90) is used to adjust for the different price values of a basis point yield change for the 91-day CD versus the 90-day Eurodollar futures contract.[3] (Actually, the exact number of futures contracts bought should be scaled down—"tailed"— by a present value discount factor. See below.)

On September 19, 1988, the original CD matures and the $100,721,181 must be reinvested for 91 days at the then prevailing three-month LIBOR.[4] Suppose the three-month LIBOR on September 19 were 8.65%. Thus, the reinvestment rate is low relative to the initial August 19, 1988 rate structure. The final end-of-period value (in December) of the rolled-over deposit CD would accumulate to $102,923,477. However, the 102 long September Eurodollar futures contract position, cash settled on this contract's September 19 expiration date at a final price of 91.35 (= 100 − 8.65), shows a profit of $25,500(= 102 \times \$2500 \times [91.35 − 91.25])$.[5] Thus, the total December 19, 1988 value of this investment plan would be $102,949,027, implying a 122-day money

---

3. Specifically, $100,721,181 \times (91/90) = \$101,840,305$, which rounds to 102 $1 million face value contracts.

4. We could easily build in a CD rate which was a fixed spread off LIBOR.

5. The contract's value is $25 per basis point, which implies $2,500 per percentage point.

market-equivalent yield of 8.75%. Furthermore, the end-of-period value of this rolled-deposit/long futures position would be the same regardless of the three-month LIBOR that might occur.

Why does the hedge work? The amount to be reinvested on September 19 equals $100,721,181. The investor obtains the actual three-month LIBOR on this rollover date. Denote this (decimal) rate by $R_{1,4}$. Thus, the rolled CD maturity value will be $100, 721, 181(1 + R_{1,4}[91/360])$.

The chosen 102 contract long September futures position approximates a position worth $[\$100, 721, 181 \times (91/90)]$ in face value. Such a position's cash settlement payoff can be expressed as $100, 721, 181(91/90)[R^f_{1,4} - R_{1,4}](90/360)$, where the initial futures rate is denoted as $R^f_{1,4}$.[6]

The investor's total portfolio value at the maturity of the rolled position is $100, 721, 181\{(1 + R_{1,4}[91/360]) + (91/90)[R^f_{1,4} - R_{1,4}](90/360)\}$, which simplifies to $100, 721, 181(1 + R^f_{1,4}[91/360])$. Expressing the $100,721,181 in terms of the initial 31-day CD rate, $R_{0,1}$, the synthetic 122-day deposit can be rewritten as shown in the following expression $100, 000, 000(1 + R_{0,1}[31/360])(1 + R^f_{1,4}[91/360])$.

The Money Market-Equivalent Rate

The return on this synthetic four-month investment can be expressed as

$$\left(1 + R^s_{0,4}\frac{122}{360}\right) = \left(1 + R^s_{0,1}\frac{31}{360}\right)\left(1 + R^f_{1,4}\frac{91}{360}\right)$$

where: $R^s_{0,4}$ is the effective four-month money market-equivalent rate of return, $R^s_{0,1}$ is the date 0 (August 19, 1988) one-month spot deposit rate, and $R^f_{1,4}$ is the implied futures rate quoted at date 0 for a three-month deposit to be issued in one month (i.e., a deposit that is issued one month from date 0 and matures four months from date 0). For the four-month synthetic deposit, this effective rate can be solved as

$$\left(1 + R^s_{0,4}\frac{122}{360}\right) = \left(1 + 0.08375\frac{31}{360}\right)\left(1 + 0.0875\frac{91}{360}\right)$$

or,

$$R^s_{0,4} = \frac{360}{122}\left\{\left(1 + 0.08375\frac{31}{360}\right)\left(1 + 0.0875\frac{91}{360}\right) - 1\right\} = 0.08702$$

This projected 122-day rate of 8.702% equals the actual return.

---

6. This is equivalent to $102 \times \$25$ per basis point.

Note that the 8.702% synthetic four-month rate is nine basis points lower than the four-month rate of 8.792% interpolated from the August 19, 1988 cash LIBOR curve. Thus, the rolled short deposit/long September futures synthetic four-month LIBOR investment yields less than the corresponding four-month cash LIBOR.[7]

A Two-Contract Strip

As an alternative to buying a *206-day (seven- month)* $100 million Euro CD maturing on March 13, 1989, the investor could buy a 31-day $100 million Euro CD and buy the following *strip* of Eurodollar futures contracts: 102 September futures contracts and 96 December futures contracts. The logic behind the choice of 102 September contracts is the same as before. The 96 December contract positon is chosen because the reinvested value of the hedged/rolled Eurodollar deposit position is scheduled to accumulate to $102,948,937 by December 19, 1988 and the day-count scaling factor for the 84-day reinvestment period is $(84/90)$.[8]

The accumulated value of this investment plan—once each futures expires and the deposits are rolled over at their hedged reinvestment rates—can be written as

$$\left(1 + R_{0,7}^s \frac{206}{360}\right) = \left(1 + R_{0,1}^s \frac{31}{360}\right)\left(1 + R_{1,4}^f \frac{91}{360}\right)\left(1 + R_{4,7}^f \frac{84}{360}\right)$$

where $R_{4,7}^f$ is the date 0 price of a futures contract expiring in 122 days (four months) and written on a three-month deposit, and $R_{0,7}^s$ is the money market-equivalent rate on this synthetic 206-day investment.

The Strip Rate

This money market-equivalent rate, $R_{0,7}^s$, is generally referred to as the 206-day "strip rate."[9] It is the rate that can be locked-in at date 0 on a

---

7. This shortfall could also be expressed in terms of the forward rate/futures rate relation. The August 19, 1988 implied September futures rate of 8.75% is lower than the same date's implied forward rate of 8.869%. Thus, August 19, 1988 September Eurodollar futures price at 91.25 is expensive relative to a corresponding IMM-type quote from the forward curve of 91.13.

8. Specifically, $(84/90) \times \$102,948,937 = \$96,085,675$. This amount rounds to 96 $1 million face Eurodollar futures contracts.

9. The Euro CD-equivalent rate for the single contract rollover example above could be viewed as the strip rate for a "strip" of one contract.

synthetic 206-day investment created by buying the 31-day deposit and rolling into three-month deposits at reinvestment rates effectively locked-in through the long positions in September 1988 and December 1988 Eurodollar futures contracts. For this 206-day synthetic deposit, the strip rate is implied by the compounded total reinvested return relationship expressed above, and is calculated as

$$R^s_{0,7} = \frac{360}{206}\left\{\left(1 + R_{0,1}\frac{31}{360}\right)\left(1 + R^f_{1,4}\frac{91}{360}\right)\left(1 + R^f_{4,7}\frac{84}{360}\right) - 1\right\}$$

or

$$R^s_{0,7} = \frac{360}{206}\left\{\left(1 + [0.08375]\frac{31}{360}\right)\left(1 + [0.0875]\frac{91}{360}\right)\right.$$

$$\left.\times \left(1 + 0.0922\frac{84}{360}\right) - 1\right\} = 0.09024$$

A Three-Contract Strip

Finally, as an alternative to buying a 304-day (10-month) CD maturing on June 19, 1989, the investor could buy a 31-day CD and buy a strip of 102 September 1988 futures contracts, 96 December 1988 contracts and 115 March 1989 contracts. The long 115 March contract position reflects the $105,163,712 in funds that need to be reinvested as of the March 13, 1989 Eurodollar contract expiration date multiplied by the (98/90) adjustment factor.[10] The 304-day return on this rolled deposit strip can be expressed as

$$\left(1 + R^s_{0,10}\frac{304}{360}\right) = \left(1 + R_{0,1}\frac{31}{360}\right)\left(1 + R^f_{1,4}\frac{91}{360}\right)\left(1 + R^f_{4,7}\frac{84}{360}\right)$$

$$\times \left(1 + R^f_{7,10}\frac{98}{360}\right)$$

In turn, the 10-month strip rate on August 19, 1988 can be calculated as

---

10. The March 13, 1989 accumulated value of $105,163,712 reflects the initial $100 million and compounded returns of 8.375% for 31 days, 8.75% for 91 days, and 9.22% for 84 days. Actual funds on hand for reinvestment will be slightly different because of integer constraints on the number of futures contracts which can be bought.

$$R_{0,10}^s = \frac{360}{304}\left\{\left(1 + 0.08375\frac{31}{360}\right)\left(1 + 0.0875\frac{91}{360}\right)\left(1 + 0.0922\frac{84}{360}\right)\right.$$

$$\left.\times\left(1 + 0.0924\frac{98}{360}\right) - 1\right\}$$

This 9.247% 304-day Euro CD-equivalent rate is 8.0 basis points greater than the 9.167% 10-month rate implied by the LIBOR cash curve. Thus, on August 19, 1988, this Eurodollar strip synthetic 304-day CD is more attractive than the 10-month LIBOR.

Strip Maturities Longer Than One-Year

For strip maturities exceeding one year, the strip rate is quoted on an annually compounded basis. For example, the four-contract, 13-month strip rate on August 19, 1988 can be calculated from the relation

$$\left(1 + R_{0,13}^s\frac{365}{360}\right)\left(1 + R_{0,13}^s\frac{30}{360}\right) = \left(1 + R_{0,1}\frac{31}{360}\right)\left(1 + R_{1,4}\frac{91}{360}\right)\left(1 + R_{4,7}\frac{84}{360}\right)$$

$$\times\left(1 + R_{7,10}\frac{98}{360}\right)\left(1 + R_{10,13}\frac{91}{360}\right)$$

Substituting for the observed rate values implies a 13-month compounded investment value of 1.1036:

$$\left(1 + 0.08375\frac{31}{360}\right)\left(1 + 0.0875\frac{91}{360}\right)\left(1 + 0.0922\frac{84}{360}\right)$$

$$\times\left(1 + 0.0924\frac{98}{360}\right)\left(1 + 0.0937\frac{91}{360}\right) = 1.1036$$

Thus,

$$\left(1 + R_{0,13}^s\frac{365}{360}\right)\left(1 + R_{0,13}^s\frac{30}{360}\right) = 1.1036$$

$$R_{0,13}^s = 0.09377$$

The 13-month (395-day) strip rate equals 9.377%.[11]

Table 5–5 summarizes the strip rate calculations for each of the 12 possible maturities available on August 19, 1988. The 12-contract strip begun on this date would mature on September 16, 1991 (three years and 28 days later). Strip rates are quoted both in annually compounded 360-day and bond-equivalent yield terms.

---

11. Note that this equation is a quadratic expression in $R_{0,13}^s$ that can be solved via the quadratic formula.

Table 5-5. Eurodollar Futures Strip Rates.

Pricing Date: 08/19/88

Contract Number	Contract Expiration		Price	Rate	Strip Rate	Bond Equiv. Yield	Number of Days	
	Month	Date					To Next Rollover	To Strip's End
0	—	—	—	8.375	—	—	31	—
1	SEP88	09/19/88	91.25	8.75	8.702	8.887	91	122
2	DEC88	12/19/88	90.78	9.22	9.024	9.123	84	206
3	MAR89	03/13/89	90.76	9.24	9.247	9.235	98	304
4	JUN89	06/19/89	90.63	9.37	9.377	9.322	91	395
5	SEP89	09/18/89	90.52	9.48	9.411	9.398	91	486
6	DEC89	12/18/89	90.42	9.58	9.487	9.466	91	577
7	MAR90	03/19/90	90.35	9.65	9.584	9.526	91	668
8	JUN90	06/18/90	90.28	9.72	9.658	9.580	91	759
9	SEP90	09/17/90	90.21	9.79	9.681	9.630	91	850
10	DEC90	12/17/90	90.13	9.87	9.732	9.678	91	941
11	MAR91	03/18/91	90.05	9.95	9.802	9.726	91	1032
12	JUN91	06/17/91	89.97	10.03	9.862	9.772	91	1123

Tailing the Strip

Gains and losses to the futures positions considered above are settled in full by each respective CD roll date in the strip. For a 12-contract strip entered on August 19, 1988, the cash flows from the futures side of the strip occur from between three and 37 months before the coupon payment on the rolled CDs. A minimum acceleration of three months occurs since the futures' expiration date is three months before the maturity of the new three-month CD purchased on that date. Furthermore, mark-to-market daily settlement means that cash flows may occur each day on all contracts. Thus, a change in the price of the June 1991 contract between August 19 and August 20, 1988 generates a futures position profit or loss 37 months earlier than the September 16, 1991 maturity of the final three-month CD rolled on June 19, 1991. Of course, losses entailed on the futures side must be financed until the appropriate CD's maturity date. Conversely, profits made on the futures position can be invested until that date. Thus, unless corrected, the futures strip positions outlined above will exaggerate the cash flows necessary to hedge each CD rollover.

The proper number of contracts for each maturity included in the strip should be tailed to mitigate these compounding effects. In particular, each position should be scaled down by a present value factor to offset the effects of compounding interest. The appropriate present value factor for each contract maturity depends on the current time until the relevant CD maturity (three months past the contract's maturity date) and the interest rate relevant for that horizon.

To determine the number of contracts for, say, March 1989, the third futures maturity in the strip, first solve for the reinvestment amount by multiplying the original deposit size (say, $100,000,000) times the strip rate factor for the period ending on the third contract's expiration date (i.e., one plus the product of the strip rate times the fraction of a year covered by the strip ending after the first two contracts) times the day scaling factor for the 98-day period between March 13, 1989 and June 19, 1989 ($1.089 = 98/90$). This strip rate factor equals 1.0516 ($= 1 + [0.09024 \times (206/360)]$). Thus, as above, the "untailed" number of contracts would equal $114.52 = 100 \times 1.0516 \times 1.089$, or 115.

However, as of August 19, 1988, there are 304 days until the June 19, 1989 maturity of the CD which will be purchased on March 13, 1989. Thus, the next day's variation margin profit or loss will compound for

303 days. For simplicity, use the current 304-day strip rate (9.247%) as a forecast of the next day's 303-day term rate.[12] Then, the August 19, 1988 present value tailing factor to apply to the March 1989 contract position equals

$$1/(1 + [0.09247 \times (303/360)]) = 0.9278$$

Thus, on August 19, 1988, the properly tailed March 1989 contract position equals 98 contracts ($=0.9278 \times 105.16 = 97.57 \approx 98$). Since, as time passes, the compounding period out to March 13, 1989 shrinks, the tail must be appropriately adjusted. For example, on March 12, 1989, the compounding period would equal 97 ($=98 - 1$) days.

The proper tailed positions for Eurodollar strips as of August 19, 1988 are presented in Table 5–6:

Table 5–6.   Tailing a Eurodollar Futures Strip.

Contract Number	Contract Expiration		Tail Factor	Number of Contracts	
	Month	Date		Untailed	Tailed
1	SEP88	09/19/88	.971	102	99
2	DEC88	12/19/88	.951	96	91
3	MAR89	03/13/89	.928	115	106
4	JUN89	06/19/89	.906	112	99
5	SEP89	09/18/89	.885	112	99
6	DEC89	12/18/89	.864	114	99
7	MAR90	03/19/90	.843	117	99
8	JUN90	06/18/90	.823	120	99
9	SEP90	09/17/90	.803	123	99
10	DEC90	12/17/90	.784	126	99
11	MAR91	03/18/91	.765	129	99
12	JUN91	06/17/91	.746	132	99

Mismatched Rollovers

Each of the strip examples above assume that the underlying CD rollover dates correspond precisely to the IMM Eurodollar futures contract's expiration dates. However, the investor may wish to hedge the rollover

---

12. Note the inherent risk: to properly tail, the investor must forecast the *next day's* term rate.

risk of short-term deposits maturing on non-IMM dates. Suppose that the first rollover will occur on October 21 (between the September 19 and December 19 IMM dates). Since no October 21 expiration Eurodollar contract is traded, hedges combining the September and December contracts might be contemplated. To hedge the October roll, buy both September and December contracts and, upon expiration of the September contracts on September 19, replace the expiring position with additional December contracts.

Pitts and Kopprasch (1984) suggest a simple scheme by which to weight the contracts surrounding the rollover date. They use positions based upon the relative place of the actual contract rollover date on a time line between each contract expiration date. For example, there are 32 days between September 19 and October 21, and 59 days between October 21 and December 19. Thus, the combination hedge position would use a 64.8% weight (59/91) in September contracts and a 35.2% weight (32/91) in December contracts. If 100 contracts were needed, 65 September contracts and 35 December contracts would be bought. Upon expiration of the September contracts, 65 more December contracts would be bought.

Quantity Risk: A Currency Futures Hedging Example[13]

Each hedging example thus far has assumed a predetermined size for the cash position to be hedged. Interesting complications to the standard hedging problem arise when the size of the cash position is subject to uncertainty. Rolfo (1980) addresses this problem in the context of commodity hedging where the quantity of a future harvest is subject to random shocks. However, the quantity risk problem also appears in certain financial market settings.

In particular, foreign investors face a quantity risk in currency futures hedges of risky US dollar investments. The foreign investor buys foreign currency futures contracts to hedge against the possible depreciation of the dollar during the period in which the dollar investment is held. At the initial futures exchange rate, currency futures contracts will hedge the forward exchange of a fixed amount of US dollars. The

---

13. This section draws heavily from "Hedging the Currency Risk of US Treasury Investments: Strategies for the Japanese Investor," Derivative Products Research Group, Shearson Lehman Hutton (August 1989), written in collaboration with Munir Dauhajre and Sanjiv Sharma.

quantity risk arises because the future dollar value of the investment varies with securities prices. The following section describes how a Japanese investor can use yen futures to hedge the foreign exchange risk incurred when investing in the U.S. Treasury markets.

Currency Risks versus Treasury Market Risks

A Japanese investor likes the prices of U.S. Treasuries and is considering investing in the Treasury market. If Treasury yields do fall, he will make a profit on his dollar investment. However, his performance in yen will be exposed to *foreign exchange* risk. Even if this Japanese investor correctly anticipates a fall in U.S. Treasury yields, his performance will be adversely affected by a rise in the dollar/yen exchange rate.

To highlight the currency versus yield level aspects of the Japanese investor's risks, consider an example from October 1985. Assume that a Japanese investor bought the 11.25% 2/15/2015 Treasury bond on October 1, 1985. The investor felt that U.S. interest rates had peaked by the end of September 1985 and believed that a rally in the U.S. Treasury market was likely.

On October 1, 1985, the price of the bond plus accrued interest was about 107-10 (points and 32nds), or 107.3125% of par. The spot dollar/yen exchange rate was $4,619 per ¥ 1 million. Finally, assume that the Japanese investor desired to buy $100 million in par value of this issue (¥ 23.235 billion).

Table 5–7 presents the Treasury position's final *dollar* value and percentage dollar return (Panel A), its final *yen* value (Panel B), its final yen P&L (Panel C), and its final percentage yen return (Panel D) for various shifts in Treasury market values and the dollar/yen exchange rate. First, consider the stable exchange rate case (dollar/yen remains at $4,619 per million yen). Here, the percentage yen return exactly reflects the percentage return to the dollar investor. These returns are given in the 4,619 dollar/yen exchange rate row of Panel D in Table 5–7.

The remaining rows of each panel show how shifts in the dollar/yen exchange rate affect the Japanese investor's position. For example, the foreign exchange losses generated by a rise in the dollar/yen exchange rate from 4,619 to 6,000 would more than offset the Treasury position gains of a market move from 107-10 to 130. Of course, should the dollar strengthen, the yen return for any Treasury market move would be enhanced. Indeed, if the Treasury market remained stable, the yen return to the Treasury position would be a pure currency play. The 107-10

Table 5-7. Currency vs Treasury Market Risks for Yen Investor

Initial Investment: 23,235 million Yen ($107.3 million)
Treasury Face Amount: $100 million US
Initial Treasury Value: 107.3 (Decimal)
Initial Spot $/Yen Exchange Rate: $4,619 per million Yen
Pricing Date: October 1, 1985

A. Dollar position as a Function of Treasury Market Levels

Value	80	90	100.0	107.3	120	130	139.4
Return	−25.5%	−16.1%	−6.8%	0.0%	11.8%	21.1%	29.9%

B. Yen Value as a Function of Treasury Market and Currency Levels

$/Yen	80	90	100.0	107.3	120	130	139.4
3000	26669	30003	33336	35774	40004	43337	46471
3500	22859	25717	28574	30664	34289	37146	39832
4000	20002	22502	25002	26831	30003	32503	34853
4500	17779	22224	22224	23849	26669	28892	30981
4619	17321	19487	21652	23235	25982	28147	30182
4721	16947	19066	21184	22733	25421	27539	29530
5000	16001	18002	20002	21464	24002	26002	27883
5690	14061	15819	17576	18862	21092	22849	24501
6000	13335	15001	16668	17887	20002	21669	23235

Table 5-7. (continued)

C. Yen P&L as a Function of Treasury Market and Currency Levels

$/Yen	80	90	100.0	107.3	120	130	139.4
3000	3434	6768	10101	12539	16769	20102	23236
3500	-376	2482	5339	7429	11054	13911	16597
4000	-3233	-733	1767	3596	6768	9268	11618
4500	-5456	-3233	-1011	614	3434	5657	7746
4619	-5914	-3748	-1583	0	2747	4912	6947
4721	-6288	-4169	-2051	-502	2186	4304	6295
5000	-7234	-5233	-3233	-1771	767	2767	4648
5690	-9174	-7416	-5659	-4373	-2143	-386	1266
6000	-9900	-8234	-6567	-5348	-3233	-1566	0

D. Yen Return as a Function of Treasury Market and Currency Levels

$/Yen	80	90	100.0	107.3	120	130	139.4
3000	14.8%	29.1%	43.5%	54.0%	72.2%	86.5%	100.0%
3500	-1.6%	10.7%	23.0%	32.0%	47.6%	59.9%	71.4%
4000	-13.9%	-3.2%	7.6%	15.5%	29.1%	39.9%	50.0%
4500	-23.5%	-13.9%	-4.3%	2.6%	14.8%	24.3%	33.3%
4619	-25.5%	-16.1%	-6.8%	0.0%	11.8%	21.1%	29.9%
4721	-27.1%	-17.9%	-8.8%	-2.2%	9.4%	18.5%	27.1%
5000	-31.1%	-22.5%	-13.9%	-7.6%	3.3%	11.9%	20.0%
5690	-39.5%	-31.9%	-24.4%	-18.8%	-9.2%	-1.7%	5.5%
6000	-42.6%	-35.4%	-28.3%	-23.0%	-13.9%	-6.7%	0.0%

Treasury market value column shows the pure exchange risk component of the position.

The Dollar/Yen Exchange Rate versus Treasury Yields: The Historical Record

The payoffs in Table 5–7 reveal how yen returns on Treasury investments depend crucially on the relationship between Treasury yield and exchange rate shifts. Some insight into the nature of this relationship is gained through an analysis of historical data.

Figure 5–1 depicts the actual historical relationship between 30-year U.S. Treasury bond yields and the dollar/yen spot exchange rate. This evidence suggests that the relationship between Treasury yields and the dollar/yen exchange rate has behaved quite differently over different time periods:

- Between mid-1983 and mid-1984, the Treasury bond yield rose by about 350 basis points, while the exchange rate remained relatively constant.

Figure 5–1.   30-Year Treasury Yield versus $/¥ Exchange Rate.

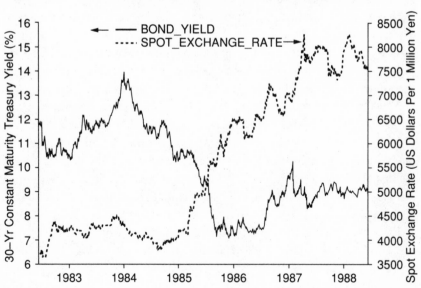

- Between mid-1984 and early 1985, the Treasury bond yield and the dollar/yen exchange rate fell together.
- Between early 1985 and the end of 1986, the Treasury bond yield continued its sharp fall, but the dollar/yen exchange rate began to rise.
- From the end of 1986 through the October 1987 stock market crash, both the Treasury bond yield and the dollar/yen exchange rate rose.
- Finally, from October 1987 through the last date plotted (in April 1989), Treasury yields fluctuated in a narrow range while the dollar/yen exchange rate was more volatile.

The episodic nature of the relationship between Treasury bond yields and the dollar/yen exchange rate makes U.S. Treasury investments problematic for the Japanese investor. Thus, the Japanese investor may wish to explore ways of limiting his dollar/yen exchange rate exposure over some time horizon.

Locking in the Futures Exchange Rate: Hedging with Yen Futures Contracts

The Japanese yen futures contract gives the buyer the right and obligation to purchase a fixed amount of yen with U.S. dollars at a predetermined exchange rate on the contract delivery date. The predetermined exchange rate is set by the initial price of the futures contract. The price of the futures contract on its last trading date will equal the *spot* exchange rate on the date. Full convergence of the spot and futures exchange rates on the contract delivery date is ensured by arbitrage forces.

Yen futures contracts are quoted in U.S. dollars per 1 million yen. A quote of 4,721 implies an exchange rate of $4,721.00 per ¥ 1 million (211.8 yen/dollar). To protect a Treasury investment from a weaker dollar, a Japanese investor buys this futures contract. As the dollar weakens against the yen, the price of this contract increases (since it takes more dollars to purchase ¥ 1 million). The Chicago Mercantile Exchange's ¥ futures contract has a size of yen 12.5 million per contract.

How many contracts should the Japanese investor buy in order to limit his exchange rate exposure? The investor needs to ensure that losses or gains generated by changing exchange rates are offset by gains or losses on its futures position. To hedge the exchange rate exposure of a known future dollar amount viewed at the futures contract's delivery date, the investor should buy the number of contracts that can be funded at the yen futures contract price. For example, if the precise future dollar value of the position to be exchanged for yen were \$100 million, the hedger would buy 1,695 contracts to hedge this pure currency exposure $(1,695 = \$100,000,000/[12,500,000 \times (4721/1,000,000)])$.[14]

Hedging Risky Dollar Investments

Treasury securities entail some degree of investment risk, as the market value of a fixed-income security depends on shifts in its yield. Hedging the currency component of risky dollar investments is not so straightforward. The Japanese investor *can* hedge a particular dollar amount— say, the *initial* value or the *forward* value of the investment— against currency shifts.

For instance, return to the October 1985 example discussed in the previous section. Recall that on October 1, 1985, the price of the bond plus accrued interest was about 107-10. Thus, the initial market value of the position was \$107.3 million (¥ 23.235 billion). The spot dollar/yen exchange rate was \$4,619 per ¥ 1 million. Finally, the March 1986 yen futures contract was priced at \$4,721 per ¥ 1 million on the same date.

Suppose that the Japanese investor decides to hedge the currency exposure on the initial \$107.3 million market value of Treasury position. As above, assume a hedging horizon ending on the futures contract's delivery date. To hedge the exchange risk on this quantity of dollars, the Japanese investor would buy 1,819 yen futures contracts (i.e., $1,819 = \$107,312,500/[12.50 \times 4,721]$).[15]

The P&L of the futures will equal \$12.50 times the difference between the final futures price and the initial futures price. Since the hedge is lifted on the contract's delivery date, full "convergence" of the futures price to the spot dollar/yen exchange rate will occur.[16] In particular, the

---

14. However, see the discussion on "tailing" below.

15. "Tailing" is ignored here for simplicity.

16. Positions unwound prior to a contract maturity date are subject to "basis" risk. The actual convergence cost realized on the trade may differ from what was anticipated. Prior to delivery, the yen futures basis will vary as a function both of relative short-term interest rates in the US and Japan, and of spot exchange rate levels. Finally, in the case that the investment horizon lasts beyond a contract's last trading date, any long or short futures positions must be "rolled" into the next futures contract listed in the exchange. The roll is executed as a spread trade. The roll could have a significant impact on the efficiency of the hedging strategy being placed.

futures-cash spread, initially 102 ($= 4,721 - 4,619$), will fall to 0 on the delivery date. Thus, the hedger will lose $1,275 ($= \$12.50 \times 102$) per contract in convergence costs.

Table 5–8 presents an analysis of the expected cash flows on the yen futures positions. For the range of possible final exchange rates, the per contract and total 1,819 contract position P&Ls are reported. Should the dollar/yen exchange rate rise to 5,000 ($5,000 per ¥ 1 million), the futures position will show a profit of $6 million ($3,488 per contract). This $6 million profit will hedge the exchange rate losses on the initial $107.3 million market value of Treasury position. In contrast, should the dollar/yen rate fall to 4,500, the futures position will lose $5 million ($2,763 per contract). These futures losses can be funded out of the exchange rate gains on the Treasury position.

Table 5–9 presents the potential set of outcomes (in both dollar and yen terms) for this hedge as a function of Treasury market and dollar/yen exchange rate moves. Panel A presents the final dollar position of the hedge, which includes both the value of the Treasury bonds and the gain or loss on the yen futures contracts. Panel B presents the final position values in yen, converting each dollar position at the appropriate final exchange rate. Panel C presents the associated yen P&L to the position (subtracting out the initial ¥ 23.235 billion investment value). Finally, Panel D computes the realized yen rate of return on the initial investment.

Table 5–8. Futures Component of Hedge P&L in U.S.$ (1,819 Contract Base Position).

Final Offset Date: March 17, 1986
Initial Futures Price: 4,721

$/Yen	P&L per Contract	Hedge P&L ($ Million)
3000	−$21,513	−39
3500	−$15,263	−28
4000	−$9,013	−16
4500	−$2,763	−5
4619	−$1,275	−2
4721	$0	0
5000	$3,488	6
5690	$12,113	22
6000	$15,988	29

Table 5–9. Components of the Hedged Return.

A. Final March 17, 1986 Dollar Value of Hedged Position

$/Yen	80	90	100.0	107.3	120	130	139.4
3000	41	51	61	68	81	91	100
3500	52	62	72	80	92	102	112
4000	64	74	84	91	104	114	123
4500	75	85	95	102	115	125	134
4619	78	88	98	105	118	128	137
4721	80	90	100	107	120	130	139
5000	86	96	106	114	126	136	146
5690	102	112	122	129	142	152	161
6000	109	119	129	136	149	159	168

B. Final Yen Value of Hedged Position

$/Yen	80	90	100.0	107.3	120	130	139.4
3000	13628	16962	20295	22733	26963	30296	33430
3500	14929	17786	20644	22773	26358	29216	31902
4000	15904	18404	20905	22733	25095	28405	30756
4500	16663	18885	21108	22733	25553	27775	29864
4619	16819	18985	21150	22733	25480	27645	29680
4721	16947	19066	21184	22733	25421	27539	29530
5000	17270	19270	21270	22733	25271	27271	29151
5690	17932	19690	21448	22733	24963	26721	28373
6000	18180	19847	21514	22733	24848	26515	28081

Table 5–9. Components of the Hedged Return.

C. Yen P&L on Hedged Position

$/Yen	80	90	100.0	107.3	120	130	139.4
3000	−9607	−6273	−2940	−502	3728	7061	10195
3500	−8306	−5449	−2591	−502	3123	5981	8667
4000	−7331	−4831	−2330	−502	2670	5170	7521
4500	−6572	−4350	−2127	−502	2318	4540	6629
4619	−6416	−4250	−2085	−502	2245	4410	6445
4721	−6288	−4169	−2051	−502	2186	4304	6295
5000	−5965	−3965	−1965	−502	2036	4036	5916
5690	−5303	−3545	−1787	−502	1728	3486	5138
6000	−5055	−3388	−1721	−502	1613	3280	4846

D. Yen Return on Hedged Position

$/Yen	80	90	100.0	107.3	120	130	139.4
3000	−41.3%	−27.0%	−12.7%	−2.2%	16.0%	30.4%	43.9%
3500	−35.7%	−23.5%	−11.2%	−2.2%	13.4%	25.7%	37.3%
4000	−31.6%	−20.8%	−10.0%	−2.2%	11.5%	22.3%	32.4%
4500	−28.3%	−18.7%	−9.2%	−2.2%	10.0%	19.5%	28.5%
4619	−27.6%	−18.3%	−9.0%	−2.2%	9.7%	19.0%	27.7%
4721	−27.1%	−17.9%	−8.8%	−2.2%	9.4%	18.5%	27.1%
5000	−25.7%	−17.1%	−8.5%	−2.2%	8.8%	17.4%	25.5%
5690	−22.8%	−15.3%	−7.7%	−2.2%	7.4%	15.0%	22.1%
6000	−21.8%	−14.6%	−7.4%	−2.2%	6.9%	14.1%	20.9%

These results highlight a number of important issues concerning hedging the currency exposure of Treasury investments:

- The yen futures hedge dramatically changes the Japanese investor's payoff profile relative to the unhedged position (given in Table 5-7). The position's exposure to shifts in the dollar/yen exchange rate is greatly reduced. (The breakeven points for the hedged position no longer lie along the diagonal line in the dollar/yen versus Treasury market level payoff matrix.) Instead, the investment performance is determined mainly by the movement of Treasury prices.

- As explained above, the delivery date "convergence" of the futures price to the spot exchange rate is an explicit cost of hedging. Thus, even if the Treasury market remains unchanged, the Japanese investor loses ¥ 502 million in convergence costs. The convergence cost is a key difference in the Treasury market payoff profiles for the Japanese investor versus a US (domestic) investor.

- Some sensitivity of the hedged investor's yen P&L to shifts in the dollar/yen exchange rate remains due to the effects of "quantity risk."

Assessing Quantity Risk

The "quantity risk" of the hedged position derives from the fact that the number of yen futures contracts purchased was determined prior to knowing the exact final dollar value of the investment. In this example, the initial dollar value was used to construct the hedge. However, the realized final dollar value of the security position most likely will differ from the investment's initial value (or, for that matter, its forward value).[4]

The difference between the initially hedged dollar value of the security and its final market value represents the quantity risk of the Japanese investor's position. Quantity risk produces a secondary foreign currency exposure that becomes important for large Treasury market moves. Indeed, Panels C and D of Table 5-9 document that the exchange rate sensitivity of the hedge is greater the larger the Treasury market move (up or down).

---

4. Indeed, the bullish Japanese investor believes that dollar values will rise.

Panel A of Table 5–10 presents the precise number of contracts necessary (ex-post) to hedge the currency exposure of the Treasury position's realized final dollar value. For example, a market rally to 130 would leave the Japanese investor with 1,819 yen contracts about 384 contracts too short of the actual 2,362 contract position needed to hedge the final $139.4 million value of the investment. In contrast, a market drop to 80 would leave this investor about 463 yen contracts too long to hedge the final $80 million value of the investment.

Re-Weighting the Hedge to Reduce Quantity Risk

A quantity risk exposure will occur under any "static" hedging approach—that is, any approach that keeps the number of currency contracts constant regardless of ongoing market moves. In contrast, dynamic hedging approaches could be used in order to reduce the net impact of quantity risk on the overall performance of the hedging strategy.

Panel B of Table 5–10 presents a matrix of desired yen futures contract positions computed for alternative Treasury market and yen futures prices. The center cell—based on the current 4,721 futures and current 107-10 (107.3) Treasury prices—determines the initial 1,819 futures contract position. However, if the yen futures price or the Treasury price changes, the hedger should re-weight the yen futures position. For example, suppose that after entering the initial Treasury and yen futures position, the yen futures price falls to 4,619 and the Treasury market moves to 120. Reading off of the weighting matrix in Panel B of Table 5–10, the target futures position increases to 2,079 contracts. To remain hedged, the Japanese investor would update the futures position by buying 260 additional contracts (for a new total of 2,079).

The grid used in the matrix of contract weightings illustrated in Table 5–10 is too coarse for daily trading purposes. In practice, the re-weighting matrix would be constructed with a much finer grid of yen futures and Treasury prices. The trader would then be able to trigger re-weightings if market moves caused his position to differ from its target by more than some predetermined amount.

Of course, to offset the compounding effects on the futures' daily settlements, the number of contracts used in the hedge is scaled down ("tailed") by a present value discount factor. With five months to expiration and an 8% financing rate, the tailed position would equal 96.77% of the untailed position. Thus, in the example above, the hedge would be initiated by selling 1,760 March 1986 contracts (i.e., $= .9677 \times 1,819$).

Table 5–10. Quantity Risk and Futures Contract Choice

A. Static Strategy Errors Due to Treasury Market Risk

	80	90	100.0	107.3	120	130	139.4
Actual Need	1356	1525	1695	1819	2034	2203	2362
Number Used	1819	1819	1819	1819	1819	1819	1819
Ex-post Error	463	293	124	0	−215	−384	−544

B. Re-weighted Futures Positions as a Function of Treasury and Currency Levels

$/Yen	80	90	100.0	107.3	120	130	139.4
3000	2134	2400	2667	2862	3200	3467	3718
3500	1829	2057	2286	2453	2743	2972	3187
4000	1600	1800	2000	2146	2400	2600	2788
4500	1422	1600	1788	1908	2134	2311	2478
4619	1386	1559	1732	1859	2079	2252	2415
4721	1356	1525	1695	1819	2034	2203	2362
5000	1280	1440	1600	1717	1920	2080	2231
5690	1125	1265	1406	1509	1687	1828	1960
6000	1067	1200	1333	1431	1600	1733	1859
6500	985	1108	1231	1321	1477	1600	1716
7000	914	1029	1143	1227	1372	1486	1593

The necessary tailing adjustment is reduced by the passage of time since the compounding period to contract maturity shrinks.

Hedge Results

Figures 5–2 and 5–3 present the actual historical results of both currency-hedged and unhedged (naked) versions of the trade for the period ending March 17, 1986. For the purposes of this example, the futures position is re-weighted each day at the close of trading. The market value of the Treasury security rose from $107.3 million on October 1, 1985, to approximately $139.4 million on March 17, 1986 (a 29.9% *gain* in dollar terms).

Figure 5–2 shows the change in value of, the naked and hedged positions in yen. (A plot of the spot dollar/yen exchange rate is also provided for convenience.) After translating the market value of the position into yen, the initial investment of ¥ 23,235 million (JY_Naked) rose to ¥ 24,501 million by March 17, 1986 (a 5.5% *gain* in yen). This small ¥ 1,266 million increase in the *naked* position was due to the rise in the dollar/yen exchange rate over the same time period. The exchange rate rose from $4,619 per ¥ 1 million to $5,690 dollars per ¥ 1 million. For a *hedged* investor, the long yen futures position realized profits. With these futures profits, the net value of the hedged position rose by ¥ 5,606 million to ¥ 28,841 million (a 24.1% *gain* in yen).

Figure 5–3 compares the rates of return of the dollar investor with both the naked and hedged returns to the yen investor. The currency-hedged Japanese investor underperforms the 29.9% pure dollar return by 5.8% both because of the initially projected convergence costs (2.2%) and some degree of ex-post underhedging of the currency position in a rising dollar/yen exchange rate environment (3.6%).

The yen futures hedge substantially reduces, but does not completely eliminate, the currency risk of the position. Interestingly, the dynamic re-weighting of the futures position improves upon a static hedging approach. The static hedging approach (using 1,819 contracts without any updating) would have generated a final value of ¥ 28,373 million to return only 22.1% in yen. Thus, the static approach would have lost 2.0% because of increased quantity risk.

Summary

Hedgers use futures contract positions to adjust the risk structure of a cash market portfolio. Thus, futures hedges are entered because the

Figure 5–2. Yen Profit & Losses on Treasury Bond Position versus Spot $/¥ .

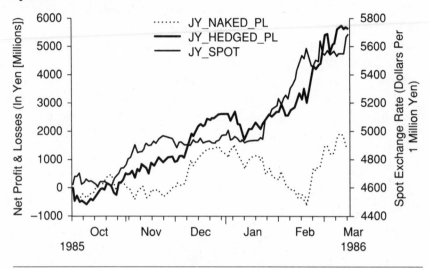

Figure 5–3. Rates of Return Comparison U.S. Naked versus Yen Naked and Hedged Positions.

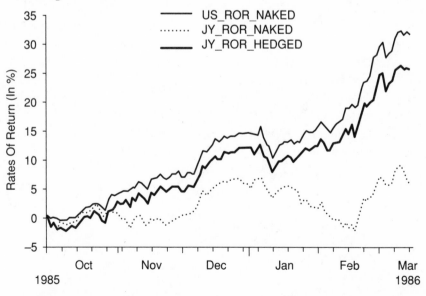

investor is dissatisfied with at least one aspect of her initial portfolio. Furthermore, hedging is done by degree. Whether the investor hedges fully, partially, or not at all depends on her current perception of future unhedged returns and her risk/reward tradeoff.

This chapter explained the concept of the hedger's basis. Hedging was analyzed from a basis equals carry pricing perspective stressing the relationship between arbitrage activity and hedging performance. Furthermore, a strip hedge geared to offsetting the risk of a series of cash market exposures was discussed. Finally, quantity risk was discussed in the context of foreign exchange risk hedging.

CHAPTER 6

Estimating Hedge Ratios: Applications to Stock Index Futures

"Never trust a fact unsupported by a theory."

Regression analysis is an empirical method which provides guidance for hedge ratio selection.[1] This method stresses careful study of the historical co-movement between cash and futures price changes. In contrast to the basis analytics approach, regression analysis simply measures past cash and futures price change relationships on the premise that these measurements will be useful in formulating future hedges. This empirical method is especially applicable in the context of hedging cash market positions with futures contracts written on a related, but not identical, security.

Regression Analysis for Minimum Variance Hedges

Regression analysis is a statistical technique that lends itself to historically-based studies of hedge construction and performance. As applied to a time series of observations, the generic linear regression model assumes that the relationship between two variables, Y_t and X_t, can be

---

1. Ederington (1979) is the first published paper to apply regression analysis to a financial futures hedging problem. Numerous related applications to a number of different markets have followed: e.g., Figlewski (1984) and Merrick (1988) for stock index futures, and Hill and Schneeweis (1982) and Toevs and Jacob (1986) for bonds.

broken down into two parts. The first part is a fixed, nonrandom *linear* relationship between Y_t and X_t of the form:

$$Y_t = a + bX_t$$

In this expression, Y_t is termed the "dependent" variable, while X_t is termed the "independent" variable. The parameter a is the "intercept" and the parameter b is the "slope."

The second component of the relationship between Y_t and X_t is a random residual, e_t. This residual represents the component of Y_t that is not explained by variation in X_t. Specifically, the full relationship between Y_t and X_t is assumed to be

$$Y_t = a + bX_t + e_t$$

The regression model selects the parameters a and b to minimize the statistical variance of the residual e_t. In order to minimize residual variance, the regression model chooses

$$b = \mathrm{Cov}(Y,X)/\mathrm{Var}(X)$$
$$a = EY - bEX$$

where $\mathrm{Cov}(Y,X)$ is the covariance between Y_t and X_t, $\mathrm{Var}(X)$ is the variance of X, and EY and EX are, respectively, the unconditional means of Y_t and X_t. An important restriction of the regression model is that

$$\mathrm{Cov}(e_t, X_t) = 0.$$

The model is implemented using an actual historical sample of data for Y_t and X_t. Estimates of the coefficients a and b are derived from sample estimates of the mean, variance and covariance parameters. The estimation usually proceeds under the assumption that the regression parameters are identical for each observation in the sample. Numerous statistical computer program packages capable of regression parameter calculations are available.[2]

The regression model sketched above may not seem relevant for guiding futures market hedge construction and performance measurement. However, the usefulness of the regression model for hedging analysis

---

2. The most widely accessible regression programs are those contained in popular personal computer spreadsheet programs.

becomes clear if the generic variables Y_t, X_t and e_t and the coefficients a and b are reinterpreted.

Interpret the dependent variable, Y_t, to be the cash asset return, $R_t^c = (P_t - P_0)/P_0$. Interpret the independent variable, X_t, to be the futures contract return, $R_t^f = (F_t - F_0)/P_0$. Interpret the slope coefficient, b, as the risk-minimizing futures hedge ratio, h. Interpret the intercept coefficient, a, as the mean return on the risk-minimizing hedge. Then, the regression residual, e_t, can be interpreted as the deviation of the hedge portfolio's actual return from its mean value.

To understand this interpretation, define the hedge return over the date 0 to date t interval as

$$R_t^v = R_t^c - hR_t^f.$$

Decompose R_t^v into its mean component, ER^v, and a deviation from mean component, $R_t^v - ER^v$. Then, following the regression model outline, the minimum variance return hedge portfolio can be constructed from regression estimates of the equation:

$$R_t^c = a + bR_t^f + e_t.$$

In particular,

$$b = \mathrm{Cov}(R^c, R^f)/\mathrm{Var}(R^f)$$

and

$$a = ER^v = ER^c - bER^f$$

The actual hedge return for each observation period can be written as

$$R_t^v = R_t^c - bR_t^f = a + e_t$$

The residual e_t is the sole risky component of the hedge return. Thus, the variance of the hedge return equals the variance of e_t. Since the regression model chooses the slope parameter b in a way which minimizes the residual variance, a hedge portfolio constructed with a futures to cash hedge ratio equal to b will minimize hedge return variance. In practice, the estimated slope coefficient (b) identifies the hedge ratio which would have minimized the sample variance of hedge returns around the sample mean. The estimated intercept coefficient (a) computes the average return that this risk-minimizing portfolio would have earned had it been held over the sample period.

Most regression packages compute not only the slope and intercept estimates, but also a number of statistics summarizing the behavior of the regression's residuals. The two most widely computed residual statistics are the coefficient of determination (r^2) and the standard error of the regression (usually denoted as SER). These statistics provide insight concerning the variation of the estimated residual series both on an absolute basis (SER) and in comparison to the total variation of the dependent variable (r^2). Finally, regression output usually includes an estimate of the individual standard errors of the intercept and slope coefficients.

The regression's r^2 computes the proportion of the unhedged cash return's variance that would have been eliminated through futures hedging, had the regression-selected hedge ratio been used over the historical sample period. To see this, define $\text{Corr}(R^c, R^f)$ as the correlation coefficient between R^c and R^f,

$$\begin{aligned} \text{Var}(R^v) &= \text{Var}(e_t) \\ &= [1 - \text{Corr}(R^c, R^f)^2]\text{Var}(R^c) \\ \text{Var}(R^v) &= [1 - r^2]\text{Var}(R^c) \end{aligned}$$

Thus, the variance of the hedged return is some proportion of the variance of the unhedged cash return. This proportion equals $1 - r^2$, where r^2, the coefficient of determination, equals the square of the correlation coefficient between cash and futures returns. The proportion of the unhedged cash return variance that is eliminated by the hedge is

$$[\text{Var}(R^c) - \text{Var}(R^v)]/\text{Var}(R^c) = r^2$$

Thus, a regression estimate of $r^2 = 0.89$ implies that the hedge portfolio's variance would have been only 11% ($= 100\% - 89\%$) of the unhedged portfolio's variance had the estimated hedge ratio (say, $b = 0.77$) been used to routinely hedge throughout the historical sample period.

The computed standard error of the regression (SER) helps to pin down the variation of hedge returns. If returns are normally distributed, 95% of the actual hedge returns will lie within two SERs of the average hedge return (a). Likewise, the coefficient standard errors permit probability statements about the location of the true intercept and slope parameters. Under the assumption that returns are normally distributed, there is 95% confidence that the true population hedge ratio lies within two standard errors of the coefficient's point estimate.

Example 1: Hedging a Stock Index Portfolio

Apply the regression method to hedge a $50 million stock portfolio with the S&P 500 futures contract. To implement the analysis, a series of choices which fully specify the nature of the hedging problem must be made.

First, identify the exact cash market stock portfolio that must be hedged. Assume that the portfolio mirrors the actual value-weighted S&P 500 index portfolio. In truth, except for index fund managers, this particular choice will not represent the typical portfolio manager's stock position. Instead of the index portfolio, a particular manager might be, say, overweighted in industrials and underweighted in consumer stocks. Of course, regression-based hedging analysis is also directly applicable to any particular non-index stock position. It is only necessary to use the specific non-index portfolio's returns as the regression's dependent variable.

Second, specify the anticipated holding period for the hedge. Choosing a particular hedging period is important since it establishes the particular return distribution to be altered (e.g., hourly, daily, weekly, monthly, quarterly, or annual returns). Typically, this choice is natural given various institutional constraints. For example, security marketmakers turn over their cash market positions frequently and might measure their hedging horizons in minutes or hours. In contrast, portfolio managers might judge themselves (or be judged) on a quarterly basis. Thus, portfolio managers would be free to ignore variations in stock prices within a given day. Such variation would be crucial for the director of an equity block trading desk. For the current example, choose a hedge horizon of one day. This choice implies that daily return fluctuations matter most.

Choose the nearby S&P 500 futures contract as the hedging instrument. For the assumed one-day hedging horizon, the choice of the nearby contract is natural since its expiration date corresponds most closely to the hedge-lifting date. Furthermore, especially for the S&P 500 stock index contracts of this example, trading in the nearby contract month tends to be substantially more liquid than that in the deferred contract months. Thus, on liquidity cost grounds, using the nearby contract might still make sense for sizable positions even if the anticipated hedging period were five or six months.

Finally, choose a sample of data upon which to estimate the parameters of the regression model. Assume that the real-time hedging problem is to structure a sequence of one-day hedges for the April-May 1986 period. Since it is reasonable to analyze a recent sample of data, select daily cash and futures return data beginning January 3, 1985 and ending March 31, 1986. The underlying assumption of the analysis is that the parameters of the model are constant over this 15-month historical period.

In line with the R_f^c definition above, the dependent cash index return variable measures the close-to-close percent change in the S&P 500 stock index. The dividend return is excluded from R_f^c since, over very short-term horizons such as a day or a week, dividends are predetermined (i.e., dividends are variable, but not risky). Define the independent futures return variable as the close-to-close change in the near S&P 500 futures price expressed as a percent of the initial cash S&P 500 index close.

Table 6-1 presents the output from the regression of daily cash index returns on an intercept and daily futures returns over the historical sample period. Estimates of the slope and intercept coefficients, the slope coefficient standard error, the coefficient of determination and the standard error of the regression are reported.

For hedging purposes, interpret this output as follows: First, from the estimate of the slope coefficient (b), a futures to cash hedge ratio of 0.8 would have minimized one-day hedge return variance over the specific January 3, 1985 to March 31, 1986 historical sample period. Second, from the computed r^2, 83% of the unhedged cash index return's sample variance would have been eliminated had the estimated 0.8 hedge ratio been used over this historical period. Third, from the estimated intercept (a), the average return (net-of-dividends) on this risk-minimizing hedge would have been 0.025% per day. Fourth, given the estimated SER and assuming normally distributed returns, the 95% confidence range for a given day's hedge return is bounded by 0.593% and -0.543% $[= 0.025 +/- (2[.284])]$. Finally, given the standard error of the estimated slope coefficient, there is a 95% probability that the true risk-minimizing hedge ratio for the 15-month period was between .76 and .84 $[= .80 +/- (2[.02])]$.

Turning the Estimates into a Trade

With this statistical work completed, one may move towards actually putting on a futures market position. There are four steps to turning the regression estimates into a trade.

**Table 6–1.   Stock Index Futures Regression Param-
eter Estimates for Equation of the Form:**

$$R^c = a + bR^f + e_t$$

Daily return data: January 3, 1985–March 31, 1986

Coefficient	Estimate
Intercept (a)	0.025
Slope (b)	0.800
	[.020]*
Coefficient of Determination (r^2)	0.83
Standard Error of Regression (SER)	0.284

*Coefficient standard error in [.]

Step 1: Position Size.

First, in selecting the proper number of futures contracts, allow for both the magnitude of the cash stock position and the fact that the S&P 500 contract is valued at $500 per index point. On March 31, 1986 the S&P 500 index closed at 238.90. At $500 per index point, the size of the S&P 500 futures contract equalled $119,450 (= $500 × 238.90). Thus, for a prospective hedge beginning March 31, 1986, the number of futures contracts that matches the size of the $50 million stock position is 418.59 (= $50,000,000/[$500 × 238.90]). This would be the number of contracts to sell to hedge the $50 million stock portfolio *if* a hedge ratio of 1.0 were desired.

Step 2: Hedge Ratio.

The regression analysis showed that a hedge ratio of 1.0 did not balance the risks of one-day changes in the hedge portfolio over the particular historical period. Specifically, because a given one-day change in S&P 500 futures prices predictably is associated with a stock portfolio change of smaller magnitude, scale the futures position down to reflect this relationship. The estimated hedge ratio from the daily return regression slope estimate in Table 6.1 is 0.80. Thus, the proper number of futures contracts to sell is 334.87 (= .80 × 418.59).

Step 3: The Tail.

The hedge's tail should be set to counteract time value of money effects which are caused by mark-to-market daily settlement of the futures. Here, the tail adjustment equals the present value factor for the time period equal to the horizon of the hedge less one day. No tail is necessary since the hedge horizon is exactly one day.

Step 4: Rounding. Fractions of a contract cannot be traded. Any fractional number of contracts must be rounded into an integer. Thus, the final answer for the problem is 335 contracts. The hedger should sell 335 contracts to place a risk-minimizing hedge for the $50 million stock portfolio over the one-day period between the close of trading on March 31, 1986 and the close of trading on April 1, 1986.

A Sequence of Real-Time Stock Index Portfolio Hedges

Table 6–2 presents the cash flows from a sequence of 43 consecutive daily hedges. For each date, Table 6-2 lists (1) the date ending the daily holding period, (2) the closing near S&P 500 futures price, (3) the closing S&P 500 stock index, (4) the percent change in the stock index over the previous day, (5) the dollar change in the stock portfolio, (6) the number of index futures contracts sold to start the hedge at the close of trading on the previous day, (7) the dollar change in the value of those contracts, (8) the dollar change in the total hedged portfolio [i.e., (5) + (7)], (9) the percent change in the total portfolio's value over the previous trading day, and (10) the end-of-day dollar value of the hedged portfolio.

The first position reported in Table 6–2 is entered at the close of trading on March 31, 1986 and unwound at the close of trading on April 1, 1986. It consists of an index-weighted $50,000,000 stock portfolio hedged by the sale of 335 June 1986 S&P 500 futures contracts. By the close of trading on April 1, the S&P 500 index fell by 3.76 index points, while the futures price fell 4.50 index points. This 1.57% fall in the stock index translates into a $786,940 capital loss on the initial $50,000,000 stock position. However, the 335 contract short futures position gains $753,750 (= 335 × 4.50 × $500). Thus, the total hedged portfolio has a loss of only $33,190 or 0.07%.[3] The value of the portfolio at the close of trading on April 1, 1986 is $49,966,810.

The second position is entered at the close of trading on April 1, 1986 and is unwound at the close of trading on April 2, 1986. Reflecting the fall in the futures contract's value (now, $117,570 = $500 × 235.14)

---

3. For simplicity, these numbers exclude daily dividend inflows, which, if reinvested, would change the size of the portfolio. Transactions costs are also ignored.

and the new initial value of the stock position (now, $49,966,810),
340 futures contracts are sold to start the hedge (i.e., 0.8 ×
[$49,966,810/($500 × 235.14)]). The remaining 41 hedges follow in
a similar manner.

The statistics reported at the bottom of Table 6–2 summarize the performance of this sample of daily hedges. On average, each hedged position earned $15,078 (0.03%) net of dividends. The standard deviation of
these daily hedged returns was $111,945 (0.22%). The maximum return
was a profit of $238,672 (0.48%) earned on April 24. The minimum
return was a loss of $205,926 (−0.41%) suffered on April 23. Of the
43 daily returns in the sample, only these two days generated returns
greater than 0.4% (about $200,000) in absolute magnitude.

In contrast, an unhedged stock index portfolio (from column 4) gained
an average of 0.09% a position. These unhedged returns had a sample
standard deviation of 0.94%. The maximum unhedged return was a gain
of 2.14% on April 8. The minimum unhedged return was a loss of 2.07%
on April 30. The returns on the unhedged stock portfolio exceeded 0.4%
in magnitude on 24 out of the 43 days in the sample.

Comparing Hedged and Unhedged Returns

A comparison of the hedged and unhedged returns shows that hedging
substantially reduced the variability of daily portfolio returns. Using
the percent reduction in unhedged portfolio return variance as the measure for hedging effectiveness, the hedges were 94.5% (= 100[1.00
− ([0.0022]^2/[0.0094]^2)]) effective. These hedges were more effective
in the real-time April-May 1986 period than during the historical sample period. Recall that our Table 6-1 estimate for the regression's r^2
was 0.83, suggesting that only 83% of one-day S&P 500 stock return
variance could be hedged away.

The average hedging effectiveness for this sequence of 43 daily hedges
may be of little relevance to a position manager who places only one
such hedge in this two-month period. Using an alternative standard of
maximum sustained loss, the performance of the futures hedging strategy
also was impressive. The largest one-day loss suffered by the unhedged
stock position was 2.14%. The largest loss for the futures hedge was
0.41% (less than one-fifth that of the unhedged position).

Futures hedging "failed" on six of the 43 days (April 7, 9, 15, 23,
24, and May 1). Over each of these days, the futures price moved in the
direction opposite that of the stock index. For example, on April 7, the

Table 6–2. A Sequence of One-Day Hedges of a Stock Portfolio Position.

Start: March 31, 1986   End: May 30, 1986

Hedge Date	Near Futures Price	Cash S&P 500 Index	Stock Portfolio Return Over Previous Day		Futures Contract Short	Dollar Return to Futures Position	Portfolio Value Change		End Portfolio Value
			Percent	Dollars			Dollars	Percent	
60331	241.00	238.90							
60401	236.50	235.14	−1.57%	(786,940)	335	753,750	(33,190)	−0.07%	49,966,810
60402	237.45	235.71	0.24%	121,123	340	(161,500)	(40,376)	−0.08%	49,926,434
60403	232.75	232.47	−1.37%	(686,270)	339	796,650	110,376	0.22%	50,036,810
60404	228.90	228.69	−1.63%	(813,598)	344	662,200	(151,407)	−0.30%	49,885,403
60407	229.30	228.63	−0.03%	(13,088)	349	(69,800)	(82,888)	−0.17%	49,802,515
60408	235.60	233.52	2.14%	1,065,194	349	(1,099,350)	(34,160)	−0.07%	49,768,355
60409	235.35	233.75	0.10%	49,020	341	42,625	91,643	0.18%	49,859,998
60410	238.05	236.44	1.15%	573,809	341	(460,350)	113,440	0.23%	49,973,438
60411	236.65	235.97	−0.20%	(99,341)	338	236,600	137,262	0.27%	50,110,700
60414	239.05	237.28	0.56%	278,200	340	(408,000)	(129,808)	−0.26%	49,980,892
60415	238.85	237.73	0.19%	94,792	337	33,700	128,488	0.26%	50,109,380
60416	244.20	242.22	1.89%	946,447	337	(901,475)	44,939	0.09%	50,154,320
60417	244.80	243.03	0.33%	167,723	331	(99,300)	68,419	0.14%	50,222,739
60418	243.30	242.38	−0.27%	(134,327)	331	248,250	113,926	0.23%	50,336,665
60421	246.25	244.74	0.97%	490,124	332	(489,700)	417	0.00%	50,337,082
60422	242.90	242.42	−0.95%	(477,170)	329	551,075	73,907	0.15%	50,410,989
60423	243.30	241.75	−0.28%	(139,327)	333	(66,600)	(205,926)	−0.41%	50,205,063
60424	242.20	242.02	0.11%	56,072	332	182,600	238,672	0.48%	50,443,735
60425	243.45	242.29	0.11%	56,276	333	(208,125)	(151,849)	−0.30%	50,291,886
60428	244.70	243.08	0.33%	163,980	332	(207,500)	(43,521)	−0.09%	50,248,365
60429	240.45	240.51	−1.06%	(531,261)	331	703,375	172,117	0.34%	50,420,482
60430	234.80	235.52	−2.07%	(1,046,097)	335	946,375	(99,728)	−0.20%	50,320,754

60501	234.95	235.16	−0.15%	(76,918)	342	(25,650)	(102,567)	−0.20%	50,218,187
60502	234.75	234.79	−0.16%	(79,015)	342	34,200	(44,813)	−0.09%	50,173,374
60505	237.85	237.73	1.25%	628,273	342	(530,100)	98,162	0.20%	50,271,536
60506	237.25	237.24	−0.21%	(103,620)	338	101,400	(2,218)	0.00%	50,269,318
60507	236.95	236.08	−0.49%	(245,800)	339	50,850	(194,945)	−0.39%	50,074,373
60508	237.20	237.13	0.44%	222,718	339	(42,375)	180,338	0.36%	50,254,711
60509	238.30	237.85	0.30%	152,592	339	(186,450)	(33,861)	−0.07%	50,220,850
60512	237.25	237.58	−0.11%	(57,010)	338	177,450	120,441	0.24%	50,341,291
60513	236.50	236.41	−0.49	(247,918)	339	127,125	(120,789)	−0.24%	50,220,503
60514	237.15	237.54	0.48%	240,050	340	(110,500)	129,546	0.26%	50,350,048
60515	233.40	234.43	−1.31%	(659,222)	339	635,625	(23,585)	−0.05%	50,326,463
60516	232.20	232.76	−0.71%	(358,518)	343	205,800	(152,709)	−0.30%	50,173,755
60519	232.80	233.20	0.19%	94,849	345	(103,500)	(8,654)	−0.02%	50,165,101
60520	236.85	236.11	1.25%	626,008	344	(696,600)	(70,612)	−0.14%	50,094,489
60521	236.40	235.45	−0.28%	(140,033)	339	76,275	(63,754)	−0.13%	50,030,735
60522	241.60	240.12	1.98%	992,353	340	(884,000)	108,328	0.22%	50,139,063
60523	242.45	241.35	0.51%	256,841	334	(141,950)	114,884	0.23%	50,253,947
60527	246.35	244.75	1.41%	707,967	333	(649,350)	58,599	0.12%	50,312,545
60528	247.85	246.63	0.77%	386,474	329	(246,750)	139,716	0.28%	50,452,262
60529	248.85	247.98	0.55%	276,171	327	(163,500)	112,665	0.22%	50,564,927
60530	247.55	247.35	−0.25%	(128,464)	326	211,900	83,438	0.17%	50,648,365
Mean			0.09%	42,398		(27,316)	15,078	0.03%	
Standard Deviation			0.94%	471,076		455,567	111,945	0.22%	
Maximum			2.14%	1,065,194		946,375	238,672	0.48%	
Minimum			−2.07%	(1,046,097)		(1,099,350)	(205,926)	−0.41%	

futures rose 0.40 points, while the stock index fell 0.06 points. Short futures positions on these six days moved in the same direction as the long stock position. Consequently, the futures position's contribution to the hedge portfolio exacerbated the riskiness of the stocks. For example, the $13,088 loss on the stock position on April 7 was compounded by a $69,800 loss on the short futures position. Not surprisingly, the two extreme returns on the hedge occurred on days in which hedging failed (April 23 and April 24). However, in general, stock and stock index futures prices tend to move in opposite directions only on quiet days when the magnitudes of both changes are small.

Over this two-month period, the unhedged portfolio earned (net of dividends) $1,768,522, substantially more than the $648,365 earned by the hedged portfolio. Because the sample is so short, it would be misleading to base any conclusions about the opportunity costs of hedging stock positions on these data. (What conclusions would be drawn had the sample ended on May 16, 1986?) Nevertheless, these data are consistent with the notion that, because hedging reduces risk, hedged portfolios should be expected to earn lower returns than unhedged portfolios.

The Estimated Hedge Ratio

The (tailed) hedge ratio for a one-day hedge developed in Chapter 5 equalled the relevant discount factor to the contract's maturity. This theoretical hedge ratio depends both on the contract's time to maturity and the interest rate. For a 9.0% interest rate, a one-day hedge placed with a three-month-to-expiration contract implies a theoretical hedge ratio equal to 0.978. The same one-day hedge placed using a futures contract having one day to expiration implies a theoretical hedge ratio of 1.00.

The estimated slope coefficient of 0.800 is significantly below either of these theoretical values. The theoretical hedge ratio rule was developed assuming an exact basis equals carry futures pricing environment. However, the actual pattern of mispricings between the futures and cash markets reveal actual S&P 500 futures returns to be too volatile relative to S&P 500 stock index returns.

Some insight into this issue can be derived from examining the components of the slope estimate. By definition,

$$b = \mathrm{Cov}(R^c, R^f)/\mathrm{Var}(R^f)$$
$$= \mathrm{Corr}(R^c, R^f)\{\mathrm{Std}(R^c)/\mathrm{Std}(R^f)\}$$

where Std(.) denotes standard deviation. Now, if fair basis equals carry pricing always held,

$$\text{Corr}(R^c, R^f) = 1$$

and

$$\text{Std}(R^f) = (1 + r n_t)\text{Std}(R^c)$$

so that

$$\text{Std}(R^c)/\text{Std}(R^f) = \text{Std}(R^c)/[(1 + r n_t)\text{Std}(R^c)]$$
$$= (1 + r n_t)^{-1}$$

The actual slope estimate of 0.800 indicates either that the correlation of cash and futures returns is less than perfect (i.e., $Corr(R^c, R^f) \neq 1$) and/or that the standard deviation of the futures return is greater than $(1 + r n_t)\text{Std}(R^c)$.

In fact, the low computed 0.800 slope occurs for both reasons. For this January 1985 to March 1986 sample of daily data, the estimated correlation coefficient equals 0.912 (<1.0). The standard deviation of cash returns equals 0.6903% per position, while the standard deviation of futures returns equals 0.7873%. The implied ratio of the standard deviation of cash returns to the standard deviation of futures returns equals 0.877 for these data. The estimated risk-minimizing hedge ratio is

$$b = \text{Corr}(R^c, R^f)\{\text{Std}(R^c)/\text{Std}(R^f)\}$$
$$= 0.912/0.877$$
$$= 0.800$$

Alternative Hedging Horizons

Hedge ratio choice, hedging effectiveness, and residual hedge return risk depend on the length of the hedging period. Regression analysis can be applied to guide hedging over any specific horizon. Table 6–3 presents estimates of the S&P 500 index return regression for one-week, two-week and four-week return data over the January 1985 to March 1986 sample period. These returns are based on Wednesday to Wednesday closing price data. The daily return results of Table 6.1 are reproduced here for comparison.

Estimates of the risk-minimizing hedge ratios for the one-week, two-week and four-week horizon hedges are much higher than the 0.800

Table 6–3.   Stock Index Futures Regression Parameter Estimates for Equation of the Form:

$$R^c = a + bR^f + e_t$$

Sample Period: January 3, 1985 – March 31, 1986. Daily, One-Week, Two-Week and Four-Week Returns (for non-overlapping data)

Return Horizon	Intercept (a)	Slope (b)	r^2	SER
Daily	.025	0.800 [0.020]	.83	.284
One-Week	.148	0.935 [0.028]	.95	.326
Two-Week	.227	0.984 [0.029]	.98	.328
Four-Week	.520	0.976 [0.043]	.98	.556

ratio found appropriate for one-day hedges. The hedge ratio for a one-week hedge is 0.935. For two-week horizon hedges, the risk-minimizing hedge ratio is 0.984. Finally, for four-week hedges, a hedge ratio of 0.976 minimized risk during the sample period.

Hedging effectiveness also varies with the horizon of the hedge. Recall that the regression's r^2 (the coefficient of determination) measures the fraction of the unhedged return's variance that could have been eliminated had the in-sample estimate of the risk-minimizing hedge ratio actually been used to hedge the position over the historical period. The estimated r^2 for each of the one-week, two-week and four-week regressions is larger than the .83 value found for the daily return regression. The r^2 for the one-week return regression equals .95, while both the two-week and four-week return regressions have r^2 values equal to .98.

Pitfalls in the Use of Regression Analysis

Regression analysis, while valuable in structuring hedge portfolios, should not be applied in an uncritical manner. There are problems with the application of the model in many cases. The most obvious relate to the assumed constancy of the regression model's parameters. In particular, there is no guarantee that the parameters of the joint distribution of cash and futures returns estimated from the historical data will be identical to those relevant for the current hedging problem.

Parameter Shifts Over Time

Table 6–4 compares estimates of the same daily stock return regression equation examined in Table 6–1 using calendar year subsamples starting on May 18, 1982 and ending on March 31, 1986. Note that the slope coefficient estimate rises substantially from its 1982 value of .66 to values near .80 in 1985 and 1986. Moreover, the rise in the regression's r^2 indicates that potential hedging effectiveness improved as the S&P 500 futures market matured.

Hedgers use regression analysis to develop a forecast of the future hedging period's risk-minimizing hedge ratio. In practice, the forecast may be seriously in error. For example, a portfolio manager hedging in 1983 using the 1982 regression results as a guide would have used about 13% fewer short contract positions than actually needed (i.e., 0.746/0.662) to minimize risk. Thus, to the extent that unexpected shifts in the regression slope parameter occur, hedgers will bear excess risk.

In contrast, the slope estimates for 1985 and 1986 are quite similar (0.809 and 0.778). Indeed, because a preliminary analysis showed that these slope estimates were not statistically different from each other, the combined January 3, 1985 to March 31, 1986 sample results (Table 6–1) were used in structuring the simulated hedging exercise of Table 6–2.

Such checks on the stability of estimated hedge ratios are important. In general, there is a trade-off in using a long calendar time period from which to draw the historical sample. On one hand, if the underlying regression parameters are identical for the entire period, a larger data sample will promote more accurate inferences about true parameter values. On the other hand, if the parameters actually do change in the period, estimates based partly on the older data will distort the hedge ratio actually appropriate to the more recent data.

All Hedges Are Not Created Equal

Careful selection of the sample period alone will not assure optimal estimation of the risk-minimizing hedge ratio. Recall that regression analysis treats all observations identically. In particular, the regression example underlying Table 6–1 above assumes that the joint distribution of daily cash and futures returns is the same on all days in the 15-month span of the January 1985 to March 1986 sample. There are good reasons to suspect that this assumption may be invalid.

Table 6–4. Stock Index Futures Regression Parameter Estimates for Equation of the Form:

$$R^c = a + bR^f + e_t$$

Calendar Year Subsamples of Daily Return Data

Subsample	Intercept (a)	Slope (b)	r^2	SER
1982*	.037	0.662 [0.029]	.77	.632
1983	.014	0.746 [0.023]	.81	.363
1984	.001	0.753 [0.023]	.81	.348
1985	.021	0.809 [0.024]	.83	.270
1986**	.040	0.778 [0.044]	.84	.340

*Less than a full year. Return data begins May 18, 1982
**Less than a full year. Return data ends March 31, 1986.

Table 6–5 presents estimates of the basic stock return regression equation for two new subsamples of the January 1985 to March 1986 daily data. The first subsample includes only observations for days on which the near futures contract was one month or less from its expiration date. The second subsample includes observations for days on which the near futures had more than one month left until expiration.

The estimated slope coefficient when the near futures is one month or less from expiration (0.877) is larger than the slope when the near futures has more than one month until expiration (0.779). This difference is statistically significant. A hedger could have improved the risk-reduction effectiveness of one-day S&P 500 return hedges by employing different hedge ratios depending on whether the near futures had one month or less until expiration.

For example, suppose that a $50,000,000 stock portfolio must be hedged for one day and that the current value of the near S&P 500 futures were $125,000. The guidance from the full sample slope estimate of 0.800 in Table 6-1 is to sell 320 contracts (= 0.800 × 400). However, the guidance from the slope estimates in Table 6-5 is to sell 351 (= 0.877 × 400) contracts if the futures has one month or less left to

Table 6–5. Stock Index Futures Regression Parameter Estimates for Equation of the Form:

$$R^c = a + bR^f + e_t$$

Subsamples of January 3, 1985 – March 31, 1986 Daily Return Data Based on Contract Time to Expiration

Subsample	Intercept (a)	Slope (b)	r^2	SER
One Month or Less to Expiration	.013	0.877 [0.041]	.81	.289
Between One and Three Months to Expiration	.034	0.779 [0.023]	.85	.274

expiration as of the start of the hedge or to sell 312 ($= 0.779 \times 400$) contracts if the futures has more than one month to expiration.

Expected Hedge Returns

Table 6–6 shows the results from another segregation of these daily stock return data. Here, two subsamples are formed based on the sign of the near futures contract's mispricing. Specifically, observations for days on which the futures was initially overpriced are segregated from the observations for days on which the futures was initially underpriced.

In contrast to the results from the previous sample splits, the estimated slope coefficients for the two subsamples are virtually identical. Thus, the fact that the futures is overpriced rather than underpriced on the day the hedge is placed has no effect on the risk-minimizing hedge ratio. However, there are important differences between the estimated intercepts from each subsample. The intercept (a) for the initially overpriced subsample (.131) is positive and large compared with that from the full sample regression of Table 6–1 (.025). The estimated intercept from the initially underpriced subsample ($-.079$) is negative and well below that from the full sample.

Recall that the intercept estimates the mean return on the risk-minimizing hedge. The difference between the intercept estimates reported in Table 6–6 documents that the average return on long stock-short futures hedges begun on days when the futures is overpriced is greater than that earned on hedges begun when the futures was

Table 6–6. Stock Index Futures Regression Parameter Estimates for Equation of the Form:

$$R^c = a + bR^f + e_t$$

Subsamples of January 3, 1985 – March 31, 1986 Daily Return Data Based on Sign Futures Contract's Initial Mispricing

Subsample	Intercept (a)	Slope (b)	r^2	SER
Initially Overpriced	.131	0.806 [0.025]	.87	.262
Initially Underpriced	−.079	0.795 [0.029]	.84	.254

underpriced. On average, the overpriced daily futures hedges gained about 0.13% for each position, whereas the underpriced futures hedges lost 0.08% for each position.

This finding—that the average return on a one-day long cash-short futures hedge depends on the sign of the futures' initial mispricing—makes sense. Overpriced futures will induce program traders to sell futures and buy stocks. Thus, over the course of the hedge's one-day holding period, some fraction of the initial overpricing should be eliminated. On average, the hedger who sold the initially overpriced futures will unwind her hedge by buying the contract back at closer to fair terms. The hedger's average return will consist of the fair return plus a positive mispricing reversal return generated by program trading pressures. Thus, long cash-short futures hedges begun on days when the futures is overpriced will be especially attractive. The hedger will benefit not only from the net transactions cost advantage of futures trading, but also from the expected rise in the basis. Note that the hedger is trading with, rather than against, the program traders.

In contrast, the average return on hedges begun on days when the futures is underpriced will be lower than that for initially overpriced days. In these cases, the long cash-short futures hedger sells underpriced futures and, on average, unwinds by buying contracts back at closer to fair terms. Here, the hedger is trading *against* the program traders. In fact, the hedger is providing these traders with their profits.

Nevertheless, the hedger may choose to bear the expected mispricing reversal loss, if this loss is small relative to the transactions cost advantage of the futures (over stock market trading). For one-day S&P 500 index futures hedges, the net transactions cost advantage of 0.6% or more will usually indicate that even "underpriced" futures transactions are beneficial. Underpricings greater than 0.6% in magnitude are rare occurrences.

Of course, during chaotic times, the liquidity offered by the futures market is sometimes worth the extra cost implied by trading at otherwise unattractive prices. Apparently, the risks associated with price changes in the face of possible cash market execution delays during the volatile October 1987 stock market crash period made apparently low futures prices acceptable for sellers.

Example 2: Non-index Stock Portfolio Return Cross-Hedges

Many practical uses of stock index futures hedges involve contracts entered to hedge the risk of a stock portfolio that is not index-weighted. For example, the head of an equity block trading desk might sell (or buy) S&P 500 index futures to hedge overnight exposure to a net long (or short) stock portfolio that contains significant positions in only two, five, or 10 companies. Or, a stock-picking portfolio manager might desire to hedge, over the next month, the market risk of a narrow portfolio concentrated in, say, pharmaceutical and leisure industry stocks.

Both hedging situations could be addressed through particular applications of regression analysis. First, the prospective hedger would construct a historical time series for the daily or monthly returns based on the value changes of the specific portfolio. Second, the hedge ratio appropriate for each case would be estimated by running a regression analysis. The specific cash portfolio's return would be used as the dependent variable and the S&P 500 futures return would be the independent variable. The regression output would be interpreted as before, and the same size adjustment, tailing, and rounding issues for turning the hedge ratio estimate into a trade would still apply.

Fortunately, there is a short-cut method for generating a reasonable estimate for the risk-minimizing hedge ratio that bypasses the need for specific new regressions for each particular non-indexed stock portfolio. This short-cut method exploits available estimates of stock return "betas."

Consider a particular non-indexed stock portfolio y, with returns denoted by R_t^y and a well-diversified index portfolio I, with returns denoted by R_t^I. The beta of portfolio y measured with respect to the well-diversified index portfolio I can be characterized by the slope of a regression of R_t^y on an intercept and R_t^I. Specifically, the portfolio y's beta (B) with respect to the index portfolio I is defined to equal the slope of the regression equation

$$R_t^y = A + BR_t^I + u_t^y$$

Here, u_t^y is the non-market related or idiosyncratic return component to R_t^y since a regression model restricts $Cov(u^y, R^I) = 0$.

Consider the S&P 500 index portfolio as the index portfolio against which to measure portfolio y's beta. Express the S&P 500 index return as the dependent variable in a regression using the S&P 500 index futures return as the independent variable. With R_t^I now denoting the cash S&P 500 index return, this regression equation (which was estimated for various holding period returns in Table 6.3) is

$$R_t^I = a + bR_t^f + e_t$$

By substitution, an expression for R_t^y in terms of R_t^f and a residual, e_t^y, is derived as

$$R_{\frac{y}{t}} = a^y + b^y R_t^f + e_t^y$$

where:

$$a^y = (A + Ba)$$

$$b^y = (Bb)$$

and

$$e_t^y = u_t^y + Be_t$$

As long as the portfolio's idiosyncratic risk term u_t^y is uncorrelated with R_t^f (as well as with R_t^I from above), this final R_t^y equation will satisfy the statistical assumptions of a regression.

Thus, the risk-minimizing hedge ratio for the arbitrary non-index portfolio y (Bb) can be generated without actually estimating the specific R_t^y on R_t^I regression: Simply multiply portfolio y's beta versus the S&P 500 (B) by the hedge ratio that would be appropriate to hedge the S&P 500 index itself with futures (b). An estimate of the average return on the hedge portfolio $(a^y = A + Ba)$ can also be generated.

The Step-by-Step Procedure

Suppose that a hedge of the weekly return of the $10.5 million 10-stock portfolio described in Table 6–7 is desired. Estimates of the beta of each of these 10 stocks with respect to the S&P 500 index might be computed in-house, or be purchased from a beta forecasting service. The beta for the 10-stock portfolio is computed as the value-weighted average of the individual stock betas; this portfolio beta equals 1.20.

Assume that this portfolio will be sold in one week. From the formula above, the hedge ratio that will minimize risk equals the portfolio's beta times the hedge ratio appropriate for hedging the one-week return risk of the cash S&P 500 index, using the S&P 500 stock index futures contract. In Table 6–3 above, the index hedge ratio was estimated to be 0.935 for such one-week hedges. Thus, the appropriate hedge ratio to hedge the weekly return risk of the specific 10-stock portfolio with the near S&P 500 futures contract is 1.12 (= 0.935 × 1.20).

Table 6–7. Hedging a Non-Index Portfolio with S&P 500 Futures

Stock	Shares Owned	Price Per Share	Dollar Value	% of Total	Stock Beta	Weighted Beta
1	10,000	86.75	$867,500	8.25%	0.90	0.07
2	19,000	41.00	779,000	7.41%	1.08	0.08
3	22,500	32.75	736,875	7.01%	0.85	0.06
4	14,000	76.50	1,071,000	10.19%	1.23	0.13
5	20,000	23.75	475,000	4.52%	1.10	0.05
6	32,000	54.00	1,728,000	16.44%	1.47	0.24
7	18,000	81.50	1,467,000	13.96%	1.22	0.17
8	20,000	68.25	1,365,000	12.99%	1.05	0.14
9	11,000	114.25	1,256,750	11.96%	1.60	0.19
10	17,000	45.00	765,000	7.28%	0.95	0.07
Totals			$10,511,125			1.20

Current S&P 500 Index = 268.45

Current Contract Size = $134,225 (= $500 × 268.45)

Index Hedge Ratio (b) = 0.935 (from Table 6-3, Weekly Hedge Results)

Portfolio's Minimum Risk Hedge Ratio = 1.20 × 0.935 = 1.12 (B × b)

Untailed Contracts Needed = 1.12 × ($10,511,125/$134,225) = 87.7

Tailed Position = 0.9987 × 87.7 = 87.6 ≃ 88 contracts.

To Hedge a One-Week Risk Exposure: SELL 88 contracts.

Suppose the S&P 500 index equals 268.45, so that the underlying stock value of the futures is $134,225 (= $500 × 268.45). To compute the "untailed" futures contract position, multiply the estimated hedge ratio (1.12) by the $10,511,125 market value of the 10-stock portfolio, and divide by the $134,225 value of the futures contract. Thus, the untailed position equals 87.7 contracts.

However, because this hedge lasts for more than one day, the position must be tailed. Multiply the untailed 87.7 contract position by the discount factor representing the initial six-day compounding period. At an assumed 8% interest rate, this present value factor equals 0.9987 (= [1 + (0.08 × 6/360)]$^{-1}$). The tailed position involves 87.6 (= 0.9987 × 87.7) contracts.

Of course, this answer must be rounded to reach a whole number of contracts. Thus, the hedge is initiated by selling 88 contracts. Because the hedging period is so short, the position's tail component is small enough to be wiped out due to the effect of rounding.

Summary

Empirical analysis often provides important insights into issues of hedge construction and performance. Regression analysis is an important statistical tool in this regard. This chapter has presented examples of how regression analysis might be used to guide hedging performance. Specific evidence from the stock index futures markets are examined.

Examples of how regression analysis might be misapplied in hedge ratio estimation are also provided. In particular, the evidence points to shifts in hedge ratio, hedging effectiveness, and expected hedge return estimates due to time-to-expiration, market mispricing and market maturity.

CHAPTER 7

Fixed-Income Hedging

"But the income is fixed. Why would I need to hedge?". . . .
(The unseasoned portfolio manager)

Futures contracts written on coupon-bearing Treasury notes and bonds compose the largest and most actively traded subgroup among all financial futures.[1] These contracts include the Treasury bond, 10-Year note and 5-Year note contracts of the CBOT, as well as the 5-Year and 2-Year note contracts of the FINEX. The bond contract, the most actively traded among all futures contracts, is by far the group's dominant member. However, the 10-Year note contract ranked fourth in year-end open interest, and seventh in annual trading volume among all financial futures contracts in 1988. Furthermore, it appears that the 5-Year contracts are developing a valuable market niche.

Arbitrage and Hedging

The specific terms of these Treasury futures—especially the delivery options extended to holders of short positions—were discussed in Chapters 2 and 4. The way in which the delivery options of Treasury futures alter the standard arbitrage pricing argument for these contracts was discussed in Chapter 4. This chapter explains how these Treasury bond and note contracts can be used to hedge the risks of cash market Treasury positions.

---

1. The accuracy of this statement depends on the criterion selected to measure size. It certainly is true using a "number of contracts" scale. However, the $1 million face Eurodollar contract represents 10 times the principal value of each of these $100,000 face Treasury bond and note contracts. Thus, on a "principal value" basis, the open interest of the Eurodollar contract alone dwarfs the Treasury bond and note group. Finally, in terms of "dollar risk exposure," the Treasuries climb back on top.

As usual, hedging involves both accurately identifying the cash position's risks and choosing the proper number of futures contracts. The hedger chooses the appropriate number of contracts after first translating the value risk of the futures into its cash market equivalent. This risk translation begins with the arbitrage trading process tying Treasury futures prices to cash market prices. The Treasury futures contract, bond or note, must be analyzed in terms of the risk characteristics of the deliverable cash market issues.

Since the basic price/yield relationship is central to fixed-income valuation and hedging analysis, this chapter begins with a quick review of bond pricing concepts.

The Price/Yield Translation

A coupon-bearing bond or note delivers a cash stream spread out over time. For a noncallable issue, the stream consists of periodic coupon payments and the return of its par value on the maturity date. The basic fixed-income valuation problem is to find the present value of that future income stream.

One way of summarizing a bond or note's income stream is through the issue's yield-to-maturity ("yield"). This yield is defined to be the discount rate at which the present value of the future payment stream equals the bond or note's current market value.

Consider a bond or note with a par value of M that pays a coupon of c every six months. This issue is assumed to have exactly N coupon periods left until its maturity date. The instant after this issue has paid its previous coupon, its annualized yield, R, is implicitly defined by the present value relation:

$$P = c/(1 + [R/2]) + c/(1 + [R/2])^2 + \cdots + (c + M)/(1 + [R/2])^N$$

Here, P refers to the issue's total market value. In the notation of Chapter 4, the bond or note's market value equals its flat price, B, plus its current accrued interest, A. Thus, $P = B + A$. On an ex-coupon date, the issue's accrued interest equals 0, so that $P = B$.

The market value/yield relationship on the same bond or note analyzed between coupon payment dates is calculated as follows:

$$P = (1 + [R/2])^{-w}\{c + c/(1 + [R/2])^1 + \cdots$$
$$+ (c + M)/(1 + [R/2])^{N-1}\}$$

or

$$P = c/(1 + [R/2])^w + c/(1 + [R/2])^{1+w} + \cdots$$
$$+ (c + M)/(1 + [R/2])^{N-1+w}$$

where w represents the fraction of the current coupon period remaining until the next coupon date.

The Price Value of a Basis Point

Table 7–1 presents examples of the market value increases induced by a decrease of one basis point in annualized yield-to-maturity (0.01 percentage points), for a variety of Treasury issues priced on Friday, September 23, 1988 for regular next business day settlement. Since accrued interest is predetermined, each issue's market value increase implies an equal rise in its flat price (quoted as a percentage of par value). This price change is termed the bond or note's "price value of a basis point" or "PVBP." For an increase of one basis point in yield, the issue's PVBP will measure the magnitude of the associated price decline.[2]

Duration

Duration is one of the most important concepts for fixed-income risk management. Duration is a measure of both effective futurity and of price elasticity with respect to gross yield. A bond or note's PVBP can also be expressed analytically in terms of its duration.

As developed by Macaulay in the 1930s, a fixed-income security's duration is a weighted average term-to-maturity of its stream of cash flows. The maturity of each individual cash flow (the number of periods remaining until it is received) is weighted by the fraction it contributes to the security's total present value. For example, on September 23, 1988, the 9% of May 1998 note (then, the "old" 10-year note) was priced at 100-02 to yield 8.987% for next business day (September 26) settlement. This issue has a term to maturity of 9.63 years. However, its duration equals 6.43 years (see calculation below).

This 6.43-year duration is more meaningful than the note's 9.63-year term to maturity as a measure of this note's true futurity, because term-to-maturity considers only the timing of the issue's final payment. Duration

---

2. The PVBPs in Table 7–1 are exact decimal values, whereas the bond values have been rounded to the nearest $\frac{1}{32}$.

Table 7-1. Price Increases of Selected Treasury Issues For One Basis Point Yield Fall. Pricing Date: 9/23/88. Settlement Date: 9/26/88.

Coupon Rate	Maturity (& Call-)	Yield	Price	Accrued	Initial Value	Final Value	PVBP	% Value Change
8.750	08/1993	8.715	100–02	2–26	102–28	102–29	.03923	3.81
9.000	11/1993	8.685	101–07	0–20	101–27	101–28	.04113	4.04
7.375	05/1996	8.944	91–14	2–22	94–04	94–06	.05152	5.47
7.250	11/1996	8.955	90–09	2–20	92–29	92–31	.05337	5.74
8.125	02/1998	8.998	94–17	0–30	95–15	95–17	.06026	6.31
9.000	05/1998	8.987	100–02	3–09	103–11	103–13	.06363	6.16
9.250	08/1998	8.962	101–27	1–02	102–29	102–31	.06550	6.37
11.625	11/2004	9.168	120–15	4–22	125–05	125–08	.09605	7.70
12.750	11/05–10	9.270	129–18	4–21	134–07	137–10	.10398	7.75
10.375	11/07–12	9.287	109–20	3–25	113–13	113–16	.09531	8.41
12.000	08/08–13	9.282	124–14	1–12	125–26	125–29	.10722	8.52
11.250	02/2015	9.151	120–24	1–09	122–01	122–05	.11623	9.52
7.250	05/2016	9.132	81–04	2–20	83–24	83–27	.08421	10.05
7.500	11/2016	9.125	83–20	2–23	86–09	86–12	.08667	10.04
8.750	05/2017	9.119	96–08	3–06	99–14	99–17	.09791	9.85
8.875	08/2017	9.114	97–18	1–00	98–18	98–21	.09928	10.07
9.125	05/2018	9.050	100–24	3–10	104–02	104–05	.10318	9.91

Note: PVBPs express the price change in decimals. Calculations for premium callable issues assume that these issues are called on the first possible call date. The calculations for discount callable issues assume that the issues will not be called.

also takes into account the size and timing of the coupon payments and their contribution to the issue's total present value. Intuitively, duration measures the life of a series of cash flows as the term-to-maturity of an equivalent zero coupon issue. Thus, the 6.43-year duration of the 9% of May 1998 Treasury note means that, on September 23, 1988, this issue had the same risk as a 6.43-year zero coupon note.

Macaulay's Duration Formula

The formula to calculate D, a bond or note's annualized Macaulay duration immediately after it has paid a coupon, is

$$D = 2(1/P)\{[c/(1 + [R/2])^1]1 + [c/(1 + [R/2])^2]2 + \cdots \\ + [(c + M)/(1 + [R/2])^N]N\}$$

where the timing index ($t = 1, 2, \ldots, N$) indicates the number of periods until each element in the remaining cash flow stream is received. As before, c represents the bond or note's semi-annual coupon (annual coupon divided by 2); M is its par value; N is the number of remaining coupons; R is the issue's annualized yield-to-maturity; and P is its current market value. Actually, Macaulay duration is a function of only three fundamental factors—(1) the amounts in the cash flow series, (2) the timing of those flows, and (3) yield—since P is implied by the first three through the basic price/yield translation.

If the bond or note in question is analyzed between coupon dates, its duration is calculated as

$$D = 2(1/P)\{[c/1 + [R/2]^w]w + [c/(1 + [R/2])^{1+w}](1 + w) + \cdots \\ + [(c + M)/(1 + [R/2])^{N-1+w}](N - 1 + w)\}$$

where w is the fraction of a semiannual period remaining until the next coupon date.

An Example. Table 7–2 presents the worksheet used to calculate the September 23, 1988 duration of the 9% of May 1998 Treasury note. The five columns in this table present: (1) the "maturity" of each individual cash flow expressed in semi-annual periods; (2) the amount of each cash flow; (3) the present value of each cash flow (discounted at the bond's yield); (4) the fractional weights applied to each maturity's cash flow; and (5) the individual weighted maturities of each cash flow. The sum of the elements of column (5) is the bond's Macaulay duration.

Table 7–2. Computing the Duration of the 9.00% of May 1998 Treasury Note as of September 23, 1988: Pricing at 100–02 to Yield 8.987%

Date	"Maturities" Periods (1)*	Cash Flow Amount (2)	Discount Factor (3)**	Present Value Weights (4)***	Weighted Maturities (5)
11/15/88	0.27	4.5	0.988	0.043	0.01
05/15/89	1.27	4.5	0.946	0.041	0.05
11/15/89	2.27	4.5	0.905	0.039	0.09
05/15/90	3.27	4.5	0.866	0.038	0.12
11/15/90	4.27	4.5	0.829	0.036	0.15
05/15/91	5.27	4.5	0.793	0.035	0.18
11/15/91	6.27	4.5	0.759	0.033	0.21
05/15/92	7.27	4.5	0.726	0.032	0.23
11/15/92	8.27	4.5	0.695	0.030	0.25
05/15/93	9.27	4.5	0.665	0.029	0.27
11/15/93	10.27	4.5	0.637	0.028	0.28
05/15/94	11.27	4.5	0.609	0.027	0.30
11/15/94	12.24	4.5	0.583	0.025	0.31
05/15/95	13.27	4.5	0.558	0.024	0.32
11/15/95	14.27	4.5	0.534	0.023	0.33
05/15/96	15.27	4.5	0.511	0.022	0.34
11/15/96	16.27	4.5	0.489	0.021	0.35
05/15/97	17.27	4.5	0.468	0.020	0.35
11/15/97	18.27	4.5	0.448	0.020	0.36
05/15/98	19.27	104.5	0.429	0.433	8.35

Duration: 12.87 Semiannual Periods,
or 6.43 Years.

Modified
Duration: 6.16 Years.

*Number of semiannual periods.

**$(1/[1 + (.08987/2)])^t$, where t is the number of semiannual periods from column (1).

***Column (2) times column (3) divided by the note's total market value (price plus accrued interest) of 103–11 (103.34375% of par).

A Convenient Duration Formula.

A convenient analytical expression exists for a bond or note's Macaulay duration. The formula computes Macaulay duration (in years) as a simple function of the issue's yield to maturity, R; its coupon rate, C ($= 2c/M$); the fraction of a year remaining until payment of the next coupon, z; and the total number of coupon payments remaining, N:

$$D = (1/R) + z - \frac{(1 + R/2) + (C - R)N/2}{C(1 + R/2)^N - (C - R)}$$

For the bond analyzed here, $R = 0.08987$; $C = 0.09$; $z = 0.135$; and $N = 20$. Thus, from the formula,

$$D = (1/0.08987) + 0.135$$
$$- \frac{(1 + [0.08987/2]) + (0.09 - 0.08987)[20/2]}{0.09(1 + [0.08987/2])^{20} - (0.09 - 0.08987)}$$

$$= 6.433 \text{years (or 12.87 semiannual periods)}$$

Duration as a Value Elasticity Measure. Duration also measures the bond's value elasticity with respect to a small change in its gross yield. The term "elasticity" refers to the percentage value change divided by the percentage change in gross yield. This elasticity formula can be expressed as

$$dP/P = -2Dd(R/2)/(1 + [R/2])$$

A more intuitive form of this formula expresses the market value effect of a small change in a bond's annualized yield:

$$dP = -\{D/(1 + [R/2])\}P\,dR$$

Furthermore, let

$$D^{\text{mod}} = D/(1 + [R/2])$$

be the bond's "modified duration." Thus, the market value change of a bond for a given small change in annualized yield equals the negative of the bond's modified duration times its current market value. Specifically,

$$dP = (-D^{\text{mod}}P)dR$$

Duration and PVBP. When the change in annualized yield equals one basis point ($dR = 0.0001$), the magnitude of the bond value change equals the bond or note's PVBP. Thus, define[3]

$$PVBP = 0.0001\{D/(1 + [R/2])\}P$$

---

3. Technically, this PVBP expression generates the price value of basis point change using the derivative of the value function with respect to the yield. This derivative changes as a function of the yield. An *arc* PVBP measure could be derived mechanically by using *t* differences of the price value functions after shifting the initial yield up and down by 0.5 basis points.

The PVBP of a Treasury Bond or Note Futures

Hedging the risk of a cash market Treasury position with Treasury bond or note futures contacts involves choosing the proper number of contracts. In turn, the choice of the appropriate number of contracts is made after first translating the value risk of the futures into its cash market equivalent. Such a translation can only be done by carefully considering the arbitrage trading process which ties Treasury futures prices to cash market prices. Thus, the Treasury futures contract, bond or note, must be analyzed in terms of the risk characteristics of the deliverable issues. Of course, this analysis is complicated by the possibility that the identity of the cheapest deliverable issue is not known with certainty in advance.

A Known CDI

Consider first the case in which the issue that will be the cheapest deliverable issue is known with certainty. Furthermore, assume that the optimal delivery date is predetermined and, for simplicity, assume that no coupon drop occurs during the holding period. Then, using a forward contract pricing approach to this single issue delivery case, the fair futures prices can be expressed as

$$F_{0,T} = (1/CF^{cdi})\{P_0^{cdi}(1 + r n_0) - A_T^{cdi}\}$$

where n_0 is the fraction of the 360-day year until the single delivery date and the superscript cdi denotes the particular Treasury issue certain to be the cheapest deliverable issue. At this futures price, basis equals carry.

The effect of a change in the yield of the CDI of the futures price can be expressed as

$$dF/dR = [dP_0^{cdi}/dR](1 + r n_0)/CF^{cdi} + [P_0^{cdi}/CF^{cdi}]n_0[dr/dR]$$
$$= -[10,000 PVBP_0^{cdi}(1 + r n_0)/CF^{cdi}] + P_0^{cdi}n_0[dr/dR]$$

where dr/dR is the change in the repo financing rate associated with the change in the CDI's yield. Finally, the PVBP of the futures, denoted $PVBP_0^{fut}$, is defined as

$$PVBP_0^{fut} = 0.0001[dF/dR]$$

or

$$PVBP_0^{fut} = \{[PVBP_0^{cdi}(1 + r n_0)/CF^{cdi}]$$
$$- [0.0001 P_0^{cdi}/CF^{cdi}]n_0[dr/dR]\}$$

Thus, ignoring the possibility of CDI identity switches, the PVBP of a Treasury futures is viewed as (1) the *PVBP* of the CDI multiplied by the CDI's financing factor and divided by a CDI's conversion factor; less (2) the impact of a one-basis point rise in the repo rate on the CDI's financing cost-to-delivery scaled by the change in the repo financing rate associated with the change in the bond's yield, $[dr/dR]$. Note how the futures contract's PVBP depends on the assumed relationship between the repo rate and CDI yield movements.

Calculating $PVBP_0^{fut}$

On Friday, September 23, 1988, the anticipated CDI for the December 1988 bond futures contract was the 7.25% of May 2016. Priced at 81-04 on this date to yield 9.132% for Monday, September 26 settlement, the 7.25% of May 2016 had a decimal PVBP of 0.08421 (i.e., 2.69 ticks). Furthermore, the repo financing rate for this specific bond was 7.45%; there was a 95-day financing period from September 26 settlement to December 30 (the assumed delivery day); and the conversion factor for December delivery of the 7.25% of May 2016 equalled 0.9171.

Since the December futures was priced at 87-30, the raw basis for the 7.25% of May 2016 equalled 15.3 ticks (81-04 − 0.9171 [87-30]). This issue's carry for the relevant 95-day holding period equalled 8.8 ticks (61.5 ticks of interest earnings less 52.7 ticks of financing). Basis after carry on this issue therefore equalled 6.5 ticks.

Fixed Repo Rates

As shown above, the $PVBP_0^{fut}$ computation must assume a value for dr/dR. The dependence of cash versus futures price movements on the financing rate was a major conclusion of Chapter 3. However, financing rates are uncertain and may be correlated with bond yields shifts.

Assume that the repo rate remains fixed regardless of the shift in CDI yield (i.e., $dr/dR = 0$). Then, substituting the appropriate values into the $PVBP_0^{fut}$ equation above, the September 23, 1988 PVBP of the December futures equalled 0.09363 (i.e., 3.00 ticks):

$$PVBP_0^{fut} = (1 + 0.0745[95/360])(0.08421/.9171)$$
$$= (0.0197)(0.09182)$$
$$= 0.09363$$

For a given one-basis point change in the yield of the 7.25% of May 2016, the futures would change by 3.00 ticks, whereas the cash issue itself would change by about 2.69 ticks. Thus, if the repo rate remains fixed, the bond futures should be about 1.11 times as volatile as the 7.25% of May 2016.

Parallel Repo Rate Shifts

Alternatively, if the repo rate changes by the full amount of the change in bond yield (i.e., $dr/dR = 1$), then the bond futures' PVBP will be smaller:

$$
\begin{aligned}
PVBP_0^{fut} &= \{0.09363 - [0.0001(83.75/.9171)](95/360)\} \\
&= 0.09363 - 0.00241 \\
&= 0.09122
\end{aligned}
$$

The effect of an equal basis point change in the repo rate is to reduce the price volatility of the futures contract. In this case, the bond futures is only about 1.08 times as volatile as the 7.25% of May 2016.

The Converted CDI PVBP

Another measure of the futures' PVBP is simply the ratio of the CDI's PVBP to its conversion factor. Here, this converted cash PVBP would equal

$$
\begin{aligned}
PVBP_0^{fut} &= PVBP^{cdi} CF^{cdi} \\
&= 0.08421/0.9171 \\
&= 0.9182
\end{aligned}
$$

From the forward pricing equation above, this $PVBP_0^{fut}$ measure is appropriate under the special case that

$$
dr/dR = D^{cdi}(r)
$$

Thus, if the duration of the CDI were 10.5 and the repo rate were 7.45% ($r = 0.0745$), the converted CDI PVBP measure would be an appropriate futures' PVBP measure as long as

$$
\begin{aligned}
dr/dR &= 10.5(0.0745) \\
&= 0.78
\end{aligned}
$$

Treasury Futures Hedges

Treasury futures contract hedges can be based on a simple rule that weights the futures contract position by relative cash/futures PVBPs. The rationale for such a weighting scheme is developed as follows: Let V_0 equal the date 0 value of the hedge portfolio consisting of X^i dollars in par value of bond i and N_0 bond futures contracts. (A positive value for X^i or N represents a long position; a negative value for X^i or N represents a short position.) As before, the initial date 0 total market value of bond i expressed as a percentage of par is donated by P_0^i. The futures price per dollar of par value is denoted by $F_{0,T}$.

Since a futures position is a pure bet, it has no initial value. Thus, at the inception of the hedge,

$$V_0 = P_0^i X^i$$

Recognizing that each Treasury bond contract is based on $100,000 in par value, the change in the value of the hedge on date 0 can be written as

$$dV_0 = dP_0^i X^i + dF_{0,T}(N_0 \, \$100,000)$$

Rather than concentrate on value changes directly, assume that bond yield riskiness is the fundamental concept. The associated value changes of the bond and futures positions can then be recovered through the respective PVBP translations. In particular, rewrite the hedge value change as

$$dV_0 = -(10,000)(PVBP_0^i X^i)dR_0^i$$

$$-(10,000)PVBP_0^{fut}(N_0 \, \$100,000)dR_0^{cdi}$$

where R^i and R^{cdi} refer to the yields of bond i and the date 0 CDI.

The PVBP-Weighted Hedge

Construct this hedge by taking the offsetting futures position that weights the par values of the cash and futures positions by their respective PBVPs. Such a rule can be expressed as

$$N_0 = -[PVBP_0^i/PVBP_0^{fut}](X^i/\$100,000)$$

and implies a hedge P&L of

$$dV_0 = -10,000PVBP_0^i X^i dR_0^i$$
$$+ 10,000PVBP_0^{fut}[PVBP_0^i/PVBP_0^{fut}]X^i dR_0^{cdi}$$

or

$$dV_0 = -10,000PVBP_0^i X^i[dR_0^i - dR_0^{cdi}]$$

Thus, the P&L riskiness of the PVBP-weighted hedge depends upon the relative basis point yield shifts between bond i and the (assumed known)

CDI underlying the pricing of the futures contract. Under the assumption that an "equal basis point change" best describes prospective yield shifts between bond i and the CDI, the simple PVBP-weighted hedge ratio would be the most appropriate hedge ratio choice.

PVBP Hedging: 2 Treasury Bond Hedging Examples

Example 1

On September 23, 1988, a Treasury portfolio manager decides to hedge a $20 million par value position in the current on-the-run long bond, the 9.125% of May 2018, by selling December 1988 Treasury bond futures contracts. On September 23, 1988, this bond was priced at 100-24 to yield 9.050%. The 9.125% of May 2018 had a modified duration of 9.91 years and a PVBP of 0.10318 (about 3.30 ticks).

The simple PVBP-weighted hedge will reflect the fact that the futures contract's price value of a basis point yield change is different from that of the 9.125% of May 2018. Assume that the repo rate is projected to remain fixed with respect to bond yield shifts (i.e., $dr/dR = 0$), so that the PVBP of the futures equals 0.09363. To calculate the appropriate bond futures position, substitute the respective PVBP values into the hedge equation above:

$$N_0 = -(0.10318/0.09363) \times (\$20,000,000/\$100,000)$$
$$= -(1.102) \times 200$$
$$= -220.4$$
$$= -220 \text{ contracts}$$

Thus, to hedge the bond position, the portfolio manager would sell 220 Treasury bond futures contracts. The decision to sell 220 contracts — representing 110% of the par value of the bond position to be hedged — reflects the fact that the 9.125% of May 2018's PVBP is about 1.1 times as large as that of the futures. The futures position must be scaled up in order to balance the dollar risk of the more volatile bond position. Furthermore, since the hedge is designed to protect portfolio value over the next instant in time (here, interpreted as one day), tailing is unnecessary.

In contrast, if the repo rate were assumed to change basis point for basis point with bond yields, the futures' PVBP would equal 0.09122 and the appropriate hedging decision would be to sell 226 December contracts.

Finally, if the simple converted cash PVBP formula is used, the futures' PVBP would equal 0.09182. Thus, the portfolio manager would sell 225 contracts to hedge the $20 million long bond position.

Factors Influencing PVBP Hedge Performance. How well should a PVBP-weighted hedge perform? In the final analysis, the hedge will work well only if the assumptions underlying its construction accurately reflect bond and bond futures pricing. The four main assumptions of the PVBP-weighted hedge are (1) that the relative PVBP weight itself is constant over the relevant range of yield moves; (2) that the calculation of the $PVBP_0^{fut}$ correctly incorporates the effects of repo rate changes; (3) that the identity of the cheapest deliverable issue does not change; (4) and that yields on both the Treasury issue to be hedged and the CDI move by exactly the same amount. Violations of all four assumptions occur in real markets. However, the hedge's results are most sensitive to violations of the final two assumptions.

Tables 7–3 and 7–4 provide some insight into the nature of PVBP-weighted Treasury futures hedge basis risk. Table 7–3 addresses the impact of both relative PVBP shifts and unexpected repo rate shifts on hedge returns. Table 7–4 reveals the effect of unequal shifts in the yield of the issue to be hedged versus the yield of the CDI. These hedge return impacts are illustrated using the September 23, 1988 bond futures hedge of 9.125% of May 2018 Treasury bond constructed above.

Table 7–3 investigates the impact of violations of the first three of the PVBP-weighted hedge's four main assumptions on the hedge's P&L. The logic of the experiment is as follows: First, yields on the bond held long (the 9.125% of May 2018) and the initial CDI (the 7.25% of May 2016) are shifted up and down by equal amounts. The value change of the 9.125% of May 2018 for each projected yield shift is readily calculated through the price/yield translation. Second, the new futures price associated with each projected bond price is calculated by repricing the CDI at the new yield level and using the forward pricing model to determine the fair futures prices.[4]

---

4. The new fair futures price assumes that the initial basis after carry value (see the 6.5 tick calculation in the section, "Calculating $PVBP_0^{fut}$") on the 7.25% of May 2016 does not change. For present purposes, this is a reasonable abstraction. The effects of market levels on this issue's basis after carry will be examined below. Furthermore, the three-point daily limit on the futures price move is ignored for the purposes of this table. The limit, when binding, would actually spread total futures gains or losses out over a number of days.

Table 7–3. Gauging The Hedge's Basis Risk: Curvature and Repo Rate Risk. PVBP-Weighted Hedge of 9.125% of May 2018 on September 23, 1988 Using December 1988 Treasury Bond Futures.

					If Repo Rate:		
		Remains Fixed			Changes by Equal Amount		
BP Yield Change	Bond Value Change	Futures Price Change	P&L of dr/dR = 0 Hedge (ticks)	P&L of dr/dR = 1 Hedge (ticks)	Futures Price Change	P&L of dr/dR = 0 Hedge (ticks)	P&L of dr/dR = 1 Hedge (ticks)
40	−4-00	−3-20	−0.4	3.1	−3-17	−3.7	−0.3
30	−3-00	−2-24	0.8	3.4	−2-21	−2.5	0.1
20	−2-01	−1-27	−0.1	1.7	−1-25	−2.3	−0.6
10	−1-01	0-30	0.0	0.9	0-29	−1.1	−0.2
5	0-16	0-15	0.5	1.0	0-15	0.5	1.0
0	0-00	0-00	0.0	0.0	0-00	0.0	0.0
−5	0-17	0-15	0.5	0.1	0-15	0.5	0.1
−10	1-01	0-30	0.0	−0.9	0-29	1.1	0.2
−20	2-03	1-29	−0.1	−1.9	1-27	2.1	0.3
−30	3-06	2-28	0.8	−2.0	2-26	3.0	0.3
−40	4-09	3-28	0.6	−3.1	3-25	3.9	0.3

Note: Price changes expressed in points and 32nds (ticks) of 100% of par value.

Since the futures price depends on the assumed response of the repo rate, two scenarios—a fixed repo case and an equal basis point repo shift case—are examined. Finally, hedge P&Ls are derived for PVBP-weighted hedges using the relevant futures contract PVBP measures where appropriate. Recall that the fixed-repo rate futures PVBP measure implied a hedge ratio of 1.10, whereas that for the variable-repo rate case equalled 1.13. In this way, Table 7–3 will reveal the repo-related basis risk impact of using the wrong futures PVBP measure.

First, analyze the hedge P&Ls for the cases in which the PVBP-measure used corresponds to the repo shift behavior observed. In particular, review the results of the $dr/dR = 0$ hedge where the repo rate remains fixed and those of the $dr/dR = 1$ hedge where the repo rate changes exactly match the parallel shifts assumed for both the 9.125% of May 2018 and the CDI. For yield shifts between –40 and +40 basis points, these hedge P&Ls are never more than one tick away from zero. These results are impressive, considering that the associated bond price changes span a range between −4-00 and 4-09.

Table 7–4. Gauging The Hedge's Basis Risk: Yield Slippage Effects For The Fixed-Repo Rate Case (Hedge Ratio = 1.10).

Basis Point Yield Shifts			9.125% 2018 Value Change	Futures Price Change	Hedge P&L (ticks)
9.125% 2018	7.25% 2016	Difference			
+5	+10	−5	−0–16	−0-30	17.0
5	9	−4	−0-16	−0-27	13.7
5	8	−3	−0-16	−0-24	10.4
5	7	−2	−0-16	−0-21	7.1
5	6	−1	−0-16	−0-18	3.8
5	5	0	−0-16	−0-15	0.5
5	4	1	−0-16	−0-12	−2.8
5	3	2	−0-16	−0-09	−6.1
5	2	3	−0-16	−0-06	−9.4
5	1	4	−0-16	−0-03	−12.7
5	0	5	−0-16	−0-00	−16.0
−5	0	−5	0-17	0-00	−17.0
−5	−1	−4	0-17	0-03	−13.7
−5	−2	−3	0-17	0-06	−10.4
−5	−3	−2	0-17	0-09	−7.1
−5	−4	−1	0-17	0-12	−3.8
−5	−5	0	0-17	0-15	−0.5
−5	−6	1	0-17	0-18	2.8
−5	−7	2	0-17	0-21	6.1
−5	−8	3	0-17	0-24	9.4
−5	−9	4	0-17	0-27	12.7
−5	−10	5	0-17	0–30	16.0

Note: Price changes are expressed in points and 32nds of 100% of par value. Hedge results are expressed in ticks.

However, even these "correct repo shift" hedges fail to work perfectly. On the one hand, rounding errors creep into the picture. The proper PVBP-weighted hedge is formulated based on exact decimal price/yield translations. However, (1) both cash and futures prices are quoted in discrete units (here, 32nds of 1% of par value) and (2) the fractional contract positions implied by the formulas cannot be transacted.

On the other hand, the proper PVBP-weighted futures position is not static, but changes with yield levels since bond prices are convex functions of yields. Technically speaking, some improvement in this hedge's performance could be attained by selling slightly more contracts as yields begin to rise, and buying back some contracts as yields begin to fall, as necessary to continuously match the proper PVBP weights. However, this dynamic reweighting effect implied by bond convexity is relatively minor since, in this instance, the PVBPs of both the bond to be hedged and the CDI change in a similar fashion.

Now consider both "incorrect repo shift" hedges. Note that the errors in these hedges over the same -40 to $+40$ basis point yield shift range are much larger than before and display a market direction bias. When a shifting repo hedge is placed ($dr/dR = 1$), but repo rates remain fixed, the futures price actually is more volatile than the hedge understands. Too many contracts (i.e., 226 instead of 220) are sold, and so the hedge's P&L has a net bearish profile.

Conversely, if a fixed repo hedge is entered ($dr/dR = 0$), but repo rates actually shift basis point for basis point with bond yields, the futures price actually is less volatile than the hedge would anticipate. Too few contracts (i.e., 220 instead of 226) are sold, and the resulting hedge's P&L has a net bullish profile.

The results in Table 7–3 are based on the assumption that both the 9.125% of May 2018 and the CDI (initially, the 7.25% of May 2016) exhibit equal basis point yield shifts. Table 7–4 examines the impact of relative yield shifts between these two issues. In particular, Table 7–4 focuses on the fixed-repo rate, correct $dr/dR = 0$ PVBP hedge of Table 7–3 for both the $+5$ and -5 basis point yield shift cases. However, Table 7–4 interprets the $+5$ and -5 basis point shift values to apply only to the 9.125% of May 2018 (the bond being hedged). Alternative yield shifts on the CDI—the 7.25% of May 2016— are then considered.

For the $+5$ basis point shift case, corresponding yield shifts for the CDI of between zero and $+10$ basis points are considered. Such a range implies relative bond-to-CDI yield shifts between $+5$ and -5 basis points. For the -5 basis points yield shift, CDI shifts between 0 and -10 are considered. This range also implies relative yield shifts between -5 and $+5$ basis points. Only in the cases where the CDI is presumed to shift by the same amount (either $+5$ or -5 basis points) will the hedge P&Ls correspond exactly to those of Table 7–3.

The results of Table 7–4 reveal PVBP-weighted hedge P&Ls to be dramatically affected by relative yield shifts between the hedged bond and the CDI underlying the futures. When the yield on the 9.125% of May 2018 falls relative to that on the CDI (indicated by negative values for the "Difference" variable in Table 7–4), the hedge benefits. Conversely, when the yield on the 9.125% of May 2018 rises relative to that on the CDI (indicated by positive values for the "Difference" variable in Table 7–4), the hedge suffers. The hedge P&L changes by about 3.3 ticks for every basis point of relative yield shift (reflecting the 9.125% of May 2018's PVBP of 0.10318).

Actual Hedge Results. Table 7–5 presents the results of this one-day hedge of the $20 million par value long position in the 9.125% of May 2018 implemented by selling 220 bond futures contracts at their 3:00 P.M. September 23 price of 87-30. The hedge is unwound at the 3:00 P.M. New York close of futures trading on September 26, 1988 for next day settlement. On the bond side of the hedge, an 11-tick drop in price produced a capital loss of $68,750, while one-day's accrued interest earnings totaled $4,959. thus, the bond side produced a net loss of $63,791.

The 14-tick drop in the bond futures price from 87-30 to 87-16 produced a gain of $96,250 on the 220 contract short futures position. Thus, the hedge's net P&L was a profit of $32,459. To put this hedge's gain into some perspective, one-day's riskless interest earnings on $20,812,500 (the bond portfolio's initial total market value) at an 8.0% rate would have been $4,625.

Example 2

Over the same weekend, another Treasury portfolio manager decides to hedge the risk of a $20 million par value position in the 12.75%

Table 7–5. A PVBP-Weighted Treasury Bond Hedge.

Position	September 23, 1988 Yield	Price	September 26, 1988 Yield	Price	Value Change
$20,000,000 Par 9.125% May 2018	9.050	100-24	9.083	100-13	−$68,750
			Gain in Accrued Interest: $4,959		
Short 220 Treasury Bond Futures Contracts		87-30		87-16	+$96,250
Combined Hedged Position					+$32,459

of November 2005-10 by selling December Treasury bond futures contracts. On September 23, 1988, this bond was priced at 129-18 percent of par value to yield 9.282% to its first call date. Furthermore, the 12.75% of November 2005-10 had a modified duration of 7.75% years and a PVBP of 0.10398 (about 3.33 ticks), assuming that the issue would be called in November 2005.[5]

To find the appropriate hedge position, substitute the applicable PVBP values for bond and bond futures into the formula below:

$$N_0 = -(0.10398/0.09363) \times (\$20,000,000/\$100,000)$$
$$= -(1.1094) \times 200$$
$$= -222.1 = -222 \text{ contracts}$$

To hedge the bond position, the portfolio manager would sell 222 Treasury bond futures contracts. The decision to sell 222 contracts — representing 111% of the par value of the bond position to be hedged — reflects the fact that the 12.75% of November 2005-10's PVBP is about 1.11 times as large as that of the futures.

Table 7–6 presents the results of this one-day hedge of the $20,000,000 par value long position in the 12.75% of November 2005-10. Again, the hedge is unwound at the 3:00 P.M. New York close of futures trading on September 26, 1988. On the bond side of the hedge,

Table 7–6. A PVBP-Weighted Treasury Bond Hedge.

Position	September 23, 1988 Yield	Price	September 26, 1988 Yield	Price	Value Change
$20,000,000 Par 12.75% of November 2005–10	9.270	129-18	9.324	129-00	−$112,500
			Gain in Accrued Interest:		$6,929
Short 222 Treasury Bond Futures Contracts		87-30		87-16	+$97,125
Combined Hedged Position					−$8,446

5. The true duration of this issue must account for the objective probability that the issue will not be called in 2005. No serious modeling of the call feature is attempted here.

the 18-tick drop in price from 129-18 to 129-00 produced a capital loss of $112,500, while one-day's accrued interest earnings totaled $6,929. Thus, the bond side produced a net loss of $105,571.

The 14-tick drop in the bond futures price from 87-30 to 87-16 produced a gain of $97,125 on the 222 contract short futures position. Thus, the hedge's net P&L shows a loss of $8,446. Again, to put this hedge's gain into some perspective, one-day's riskless interest earnings on $26,843,750 (the bond portfolio's initial total market value) at an 8.0% rate would have amounted to a gain of $5,965.

Yield Spread Risk

That both unusually high gains (Example 1) and outright losses (Example 2) can occur for hedges of different bond positions over the same hedging period should not be surprising. Under the specific assumptions concerning bond futures pricing, the PVBP-weighted hedge balances the dollar risk exposures of cash and futures positions only for equal basis point yield shifts on both the bond position held (i.e., the 9.125% of May 2018 or the 12.75% of November 2005-10) and the bond futures contract's cheapest deliverable issue (here, the 7.25% of May 2016). As illustrated in Table 7–4, when unequal yield movements between the bond being hedged and the CDI occur, the hedge position's P&L can be dramatically affected. The hedge gains when the yield on the side held long falls relative to the yield on the side held short. Conversely, the hedge loses when the yield on the side held long rises relative to the yield on the side held short.

The highly favorable performance of the first hedge can be traced to the fall in the yield spread between the 9.125% of May 2018 and the 7.25% of May 2016. Similarly, the poor performance of the second hedge was due to the rise in the yield spread between the 12.75% of November 2005-10 and the 7.25% May 2016.

On September 23, the yield on the 9.125% of May 2018 was 9.050%, while the yield on the 7.25% of May 2016 was 9.132%. Thus, the initial yield spread between the two bonds was −8.2 basis points. On September 26, the 9.125% of May 2018 was priced to yield 9.083 (a 3.3 basis point rise), while the 7.25% of May 2016 was priced to yield 9.180% (a 4.8 basis point rise). Thus, the yield spread between the two bonds fell 1.5 basis points to −9.7 basis points.

This 1.5 basis point fall in the yield spread between the 9.125% of May 2016 accounts for most of the unusually favorable performance of the hedge. Recall that the impact of this relative yield shift of the hedge's performance can be expresed as

$$dV_0 = -10,000 PVBP_0^i X^i [dR_0^i - dR_0^{cdi}]$$
$$= -0.10318[3.3 - 4.8]$$
$$= \$0.1548 \text{ per } \$100 \text{ of par value} = 4.95 \text{ ticks}$$

Thus, for the $20 million par value bond position considered above, the effect of this favorable relative yield shift was to increase the hedge's P&L by $30,960 (the total P&L was $32,459).

Similarly, between September 23 and September 26, the yield on the 12.75% of November 2005-10 rose 5.4 basis points, from 9.270% to 9.324%. Thus, the yield spread between this issue and the 7.25% of May 2016 (the CDI) rose 0.6 basis points.

The effect of this 0.6 basis point rise in the yield spread on the hedge in Example 2 can be quantified as

$$dV_0 = -10,000 PVBP_0^i X^i [dR_0^i - dR_0^{cdi}]$$
$$= -0.10398[5.4 - 4.8]$$
$$= -\$0.0634 \text{ per } \$100 \text{ of par value} = -2.03 \text{ ticks}$$

Thus, for the $20 million par value bond position considered above, the effect of this unfavorable relative yield shift was to decrease the hedge's P&L by $12,480 (the total P&L was −$8,446).

PVBP Hedging: A 10-Year Treasury Note Futures Example

On October 3, 1988, a portfolio manager decides to hedge the overnight risk of a $30 million par value position in the current on-the-run 10-year note, the 9.25% of August 1998, by selling December 10-Year Treasury not futures contracts. On October 3, 1988, this on-the-run note was priced at 102-22 to yield 8.833% for next day settlement, while the December 10-Year note futures was priced at 94-15.

Again, the first step in the hedging analysis is to characterize the risk of the futures in terms of the contract's CDI. On October 3, 1988, the cheapest deliverable note for December delivery was the 8.125% of February 1998. Furthermore, the 8.125% of February 1998 had a repo financing rate of 7.5%, a conversion factor for December delivery of 1.0079, an 87-day financing period until December 30 (the expected optimal delivery date), and a modified duration of 6.31 years and a PVBP of 0.060984 (1.95 ticks).

Using the formula presented above (assume $dr/dR = 0$), calculate the $PVBP_{0,T}^{fut}$ as

$$PVBP_{0,T}^{fut} = \{(1 + 0.075[87/360])/1.0079)\}0.060894$$
$$= 0.06151$$

The PVBP-weighted note futures hedge should reflect the fact that the induced futures contract's price change of a one-basis point yield shift is different from that for the 9.25% of August 1998. On this date, the PVBP of the 9.25% of August 1998 was 0.066135 (2.12 ticks).

Substituting the respective PVBP values calculated above and reconizing that each 10-Year Treasury note contract is based on $100,000 in par value, solve for the futures position:

$$N_0 = -(0.066135/0.061512) \times (\$30,000,000/\$100,000)$$
$$= -(1.075) \times 300$$
$$= -322.5 = -323 \text{ contracts}$$

Thus, to hedge the $30 million par value note position, the portfolio manager would sell 323 10-Year Treasury note futures contracts. The decision to sell 323 contracts—representing about 108% of the par value of the note position to be hedged—reflects the fact that the 9.25% of August 1998's PVBP is about 1.08 times as large as that of the futures.

Table 7–7 presents the results of this one-day hedge of the $30 million par value long position in the 9.25% of August 1998. Again, the hedge is unwound at the 3:00 P.M. New York close of futures trading on October 4, 1988. On the cash side of the hedge, the 6-tick drop in the note's price from 102-22 to 102-16 produced a capital loss of $56,250, while

Table 7–7. A PVBP-Weighted Treasury Note Hedge.

Position	October 3, 1988 Yield	October 3, 1988 Price	October 4, 1988 Yield	October 4, 1988 Price	Value Change
$20,000,000 Par 9.25% of August 1998	8.833%	102–22	8.861	102–16	−$56,250
			Gain in Accrued Interest:		+$7,541
Short 323 Treasury Bond Futures Contracts		94–15		94–09	+$60,563
Combined Hedged Position					+$11,854

one day of accrued interest earnings totaled $7,541. Thus, the cash side produced a net loss of $48,709.

The 6-tick drop in the 10-year note futures price from 94-15 to 94-09 produced a gain of $60,563 on the 323 contract short futures position. Thus, the hedge's net P&L was a profit of $11,854. To put this hedge's gain into some perspective, one-day's riskless interest earnings on $31,181,250 (the note position's initial total market value) at an 8.0% rate would have been $6,929.

Hedging a Treasury Portfolio

The PVBP-weighted futures hedging framework easily extends from single Treasury issue hedges to Treasury portfolio hedges. The extension is easy because the appropriate PVBP-weighted futures position to hedge the portfolio is just the sum of the positions that would be chosen to hedge each of the portfolio's constituent issues.

Table 7–8 presents an example constructing a PVBP-weighted bond futures hedge of a particular 10-bond Treasury portfolio using the same close-to-close September 23, 1988 to September 26, 1988 holding period used in the bond hedging example of Tables 7–3 and 7–4.

The computation of the total number of $100,000 face value futures contracts used to hedge a portfolio of 10 individual issues can be interpreted in either of two ways. The first approach views the portfolio as merely the sum of its individual bonds. Thus, the hedging problem is solved by (1) choosing the proper number of contracts to hedge each individual bond position and then by (2) adding up these individual futures positions to find the total number of contracts necessary to hedge the portfolio. Algebraically, solve for

$$N_0 = -[\sum_{i=1}^{10}(PVBP_0^i/PVBP_{0,T}^{fut})X^i]/100,000$$

In Table 7–6, the final column computes the number of December 1988 futures contracts necessary to hedge each bond position individually. As previously calculated, sell 222 contracts to hedge a $20 million par value position in the 12.75% of November 2005-10, and sell 220 to hedge a like amount of the 9.125% of May 2018. However, sell only 185 December contracts to hedge the 7.5% of November 2016. The sum of these individual entries—2,115 contracts—equals the PVBP-weighted hedge of the total portfolio.

Table 7-8. Constructing a 10-Issue Treasury Bond Portfolio Hedge
Price Date: September 23, 1988. Futures Price = 87-30. PVBP^{fut} = 0.09363.

Issue		Par Amount*	Yield	Price	Accrued	Market Value	% of Total Value	Modified Duration	PVBP	# fo Hedg
Coupon	Maturity									
11.625	11/2004	20	9.168	120-15	4-22	125-05	11.5	7.70	0.09605	20
12.750	11/05-10	20	9.270	129-18	4-21	134-07	12.3	7.75	0.10398	22
10.375	11/07-12	20	9.287	109-20	3-25	113-13	10.4	8.41	0.09531	20
12.000	8/08-13	20	9.282	124-14	1-12	125-26	11.5	8.52	0.10722	22
11.250	2/2015	20	9.151	120-24	1-09	122-01	11.2	9.52	0.11623	24
7.250	5/2016	20	9.132	81-04	2-20	83-24	7.7	10.05	0.08421	18
7.500	11/2016	20	9.125	83-20	2-23	86-09	7.9	10.04	0.08667	18
8.750	5/2017	20	9.119	96-08	3-06	99-14	9.1	9.85	0.09791	20
8.875	8/2017	20	9.114	97-18	1-00	98-18	9.0	10.07	0.09928	21
9.125	5/2018	20	9.050	100-24	3-10	104-02	9.5	9.91	0.10318	22
Totals/Averages		200*		108-29	0-12	109-09	100%	9.06	0.09900	2,11

Note: *Millions of dollars. Portfolio modified duration is a market value-weighted average of the modified duration of each individual issue. Portfolio PVBP is a par value-weighted average of the PVBP of each individual issue. Calculations for premium callable bonds assume tha bonds are called on the first possible call date. Individual contract positions may not add to sums due to rounding errors.

Alternatively, the portfolio's hedge can be constructed using portfolio analogs to the components of the single issue hedging problem. In particular, define the "portfolio PVBP" as a par value-weighted average of the individual issue PVBPs:

$$PVBP^p = \sum_{i=1}^{10} (X^i / X^p) PVBP^i$$

where $X^p = \sum_{i=1}^{10} X^i$. Then, the hedge position can be derived as

$$N_0 = -(PVBP_0^p / PVBP_{0,T}^{\text{fut}})(X^p / 100,000)$$

Here $\sum_{i=1}^{10} PVBP^i X^i$ can be interpreted as 100 times the portfolio's dollar value change for a one-basis point change in the yield on all issues.

Since there is $20 million of par value for each issue in the portfolio of Table 7–8, the portfolio PVBP is just the simple average of the 10 individual bond PVBPs. Thus, $PVBP_0^p = 0.09900$. The hedge position is

$$N_0 = -(0.09900/0.09363) \times (\$200,000,000/\$100,000)$$
$$= -2,115$$

Again, to hedge the portfolio, the portfolio manager should sell 2,115 December Treasury bond futures contracts.

The results of this hedge over the Friday close-to-Monday close hedging period are presented in Table 7–9. The loss of $856,250 on the bond portfolio is more than offset by the $924,437.50 gain on the 2,115 short futures position. The net P&L is a gain of $68,187.50. A close inspection of the results shows that the net favorable performance of this hedge can be attributed to the rather large relative yield increase of the 7.25% of May 2016 (the CDI) against two specific issues: the 11.625% of November 2004 and (as previewed in Table 7–5) the 9.125% of May 2018.

Managing Duration Gap Risk

Most fixed-income portfolio managers measure their portfolio yield risk exposure using the concept of duration or modified duration. Futures contracts can be used to manage portfolio risk as an alternative to cash market transactions: They are sold to shorten the duration of the portfolio, or purchased to lengthen the duration of the portfolio.

On September 23, 1988, the Treasury bond portfolio analyzed in Table 7–8 had a modified duration of 9.06 years. The hedge constructed in that example was designed to eliminate all portfolio yield risk (i.e., the portfolio modified duration was set equal to zero). However, suppose that the portfolio manager desires a somewhat less draconian yield risk adjustment. Assume that the actual investment strategy objective is to shorten the portfolio's modified duration to 7.5 years. What bond futures contract position would offset this current 1.56-year gap between actual (D^p) and desired (D^t) portfolio modified durations?

To answer this question, first express the 1.56-year modified duration gap in terms of a dollar risk exposure per basis point. Next, close the dollar risk exposure by choosing the offsetting futures position. In particular, the portfolio dollar risk associated with a modified duration gap, $[D^t - D^p]$, for a particular portfolio equals

Portfolio Risk Gap ($/BP) = $-0.0001[D^t - D^p]$(Portfolio Value)

For the portfolio of Tables 7–8 and 7–9, the 1.56-year modified duration gap implies a

$$\text{Portfolio Risk Gap } (\$/BP) = -0.0001[7.50 - 9.06](\$218,562,500)$$
$$= \$34,096$$

The futures position needed to close this gap must have a dollar risk exposure of $-\$34,096$ per basis point yield rise. The dollar risk exposure of a Treasury bond futures contract equals its PVBP multiplied by $1,000 (PVBP is measured per $100 of par value and the bond futures has a $100,000 par value):

$$\text{Risk of } N \text{ Bond Futures } (\$/BP) = -\$1,000 PVBP^{fut} N$$

In the example above, the associated $PVBP^{fut}$ equals 0.09363. Thus, to form a futures position with an approximate yield risk exposure of $34,096 per basis point rise, sell 364 December 1988 bond futures (364 = $34,096/[$1,000 (0.09363)]):

$$\text{Risk of Short 364 Contracts } (\$/BP) = -\$1,000(0.09363)(-364)$$
$$= \$34,081$$

By selling 364 Treasury bond futures contracts, the portfolio manager would reduce the portfolio's effective modified duration from 9.06 years to 7.50 years.

Table 7-9. Hedging a 10-Issue Treasury Bond Portfolio: Results
Start: September 23, 1988   Futures: Price = 87-30
Unwind: September 26, 1988   Futures: Price = 87-16 (Change: -14)
Initial $PVBP^{fut} = 0.09363$

Coupon	Issue Maturity	Par Amount	9/23/88 Yield	Value	9/26/88 Yield	Value	Position Value Changes (Ticks) Bonds	Futures	Hedge
11.625	11/2004	20	9.168	124-22	9.207	124-11	-11	14.35	+3.35
12.750	11/05-10	20	9.270	134-07	9.324	133-22	-17	15.54	-1.46
10.375	11/07-12	20	9.287	113-13	9.333	113-00	-13	14.28	+1.28
12.000	8/08-13	20	9.282	125-26	9.329	125-11	-15	16.03	+1.03
11.250	2/2015	20	9.151	122-01	9.202	121-15	-18	17.36	-0.64
7.250	5/2016	20	9.132	83-24	9.180	83-12	-12	12.60	+0.60
7.500	11/2016	20	9.125	86-11	9.175	85-30	-13	12.95	-0.05
8.750	5/2017	20	9.119	99-14	9.167	99-00	-14	14.63	+0.63
8.875	8/2017	20	9.114	98-18	9.161	98-04	-14	14.84	+0.84
9.125	5/2018	20	9.050	104-02	9.083	103-24	-10	15.40	+5.40
Totals							-137	+147.98	+10.98

Dollar Value Changes:
Bonds: 200 × -137 × $31.25   = -$856,250.00
Futures: 2,115 × 14 × $31.25   = $925,312.50
Hedge Portfolio: 200 × 10.98 × $31.25 = $ 69,062.50

To pose this modified duration gap problem more formally, solve for the futures position (N) that sets the hedge's value change equal to its target risk level:

$$-\$1,000 \, PVBP^{fut} N - 0.0001 D^p(\text{Portfolio Value}) =$$
$$-0.0001 D^t(\text{Portfolio Value})$$

The contract position that solves this condition is

$$N = -.0001[D^p - D^t](\text{Portfolio Value})/[1,000(PVBP^{fut})]$$

In the example above,

$$N = -[9.06 - 7.50](\$218,562,5000)0.0001/(0.09363 \times \$1,000)$$
$$= -364.2 \text{ contracts}$$
$$= 364 \text{ contracts short}$$

Of course, a full hedge is just a special case of this formulation where the target modified duration equals zero. To find the futures position which fully hedges the portfolio, solve for

$$N = -.0001[9.06 - 0](\$218,562,500)/[\$1,000(.09363)]$$
$$-2,114.9 \text{ contracts} = 2,115 \text{ contracts short}$$

Given the portfolio's modified duration and the futures contract's PVBP, this 2,115 short contract position is solved immediately.[6]

---

6. Some analysts view the hedging solution by assigning a modified duration value to the futures contract. This could be done mechanically here by defining the modified duration of the futures to be 10,000 times the $PVBP^{fut}$, divided by the futures price. Similarly, the value of a futures could be defined to be the futures price (as a percent of par) multiplied by the contract's $100,000 par value. Using both definitions, and making the appropriate algebraic manipulations, the hedge position could be viewed as filling the modified duration gap with the futures:

$$N = -[D^p - D^t] \times \text{Portfolio Value}/\{[10,000 PVBP^{fut}/F] \times [F \, \$1,000]\}$$

Above, the modified duration of the futures would be devined to equal $10,000 \times (0.09363/87.9375) = 10.647$ years. The solution would be

$$N = -[9.06 - 7.50] \times \$218,562,500/(10.647 \times \$87,937.5)$$
$$= -364.2 \text{ contracts} \sim 364 \text{ contracts short}$$

The $PVBP^{fut}$ approach is preferred over this "futures duration" interpretation because the futures' percentage value change is somewhat ad hoc (a futures contract has no initial value). In contrast, the cash flow from the futures contract (which $PVBP^{fut}$ indexes) is a clear and meaningful financial concept.

The Yield Volatility-Weighted Hedge

The simple PVBP-weighted hedging rule implemented in the examples above implicitly assumes that equal basis point changes reflect the true structure of changes in Treasury yields. Instead, suppose that a more general linear relationship satisfying the assumptions of the regression model can be postulated:

$$(R_t^i - R_0^i) = a + b(R_t^{cdi} - R_0^{cdi}) + e_t$$

where a is the intercept, b is the slope coefficient and e_t is the regression's residual. Now, the number of futures contracts that would balance the risks of the bond position would be

$$N_0 = -[PVBP_0^i/PVBP_{0,T}^{fut}]bX^i$$

where b, the slope coefficient, may differ from unity. Furthermore, the relative volatility weighted hedge's P&L would equal

$$V_t - V_0 = -10,000PVBP_0^iX^i(R_t^i - R_0^i)$$

$$-10,000PVBP_{0,T}^{fut}\{[PVBP_0^i/PVBP_{0,T}^{fut}]bX^i\}(R_t^{cdi} - R_0^{cdi})$$

or

$$V_t - V_0 = -10,000PVBP_0^iX^i[(R_t^i - R_0^i) - b(R_t^{cdi} - R_0^{cdi})]$$

or

$$V_t - V_0 = -10,000PVBP_0^iX^i[a + e_t]$$

If $b \neq 1$, the volatility-weighted hedge will have a lower P&L variance than the simple PVBP-weighted alternative.

CDI Identity Shifts and Hedge Performance

Treasury futures risk analysis typically proceeds under the assumption that the identity of the CDI will not change. However, as discussed in Chapter 4, the CBOT's conversion factor system of premiums and discounts contains yield-related biases, so that market movements can cause CDI identity switches. Such CDI identity uncertainty has important implications for hedge ratio selection and hedging effectiveness.

Ignoring the possibility of a CDI identity switch can be costly. For example, during late January and early February 1989, the probability that one of the high coupon, callable issues such as the 12% of

August 2008-13, the 10.375% of November 2007-12 and the 12.5% of August 2009-14 would replace the 7.25% of May 2016 as the CDI for March 1989 Treasury bond futures contract deliveries increased from under 30% to about 50%. This dramatic rise in the high coupon, callables' delivery probability was caused by a combination of a general market rally and a widening of yield spreads between these issues and the 7.25% of May 2016.

During this period, issues like the 12% of August 2008-13 and the 7.25% of May 2016 were nearly equally cheap to deliver against the March contract in converted forward price terms. However, the yield risk characteristics of these two issues are quite dissimilar. Thus, hedges constructed using standard static single-issue analyses under the assumption that the 7.25% would be the CDI were quite different than those which assumed that the CDI was the 12% of August 2008-13.

Consider hedging a Treasury position with the March 1989 bond futures contract on January 20, 1989. Using the constant repo rate formula for the futures' PVBP, the PVBP of the March futures would be 0.0970 if the 7.25% of May 2016 were used as the base CDI. However, if the 12% of August 2008-13 were used as the base CDI, the futures PVBP would be only 0.0797.

Suppose that a $100 million par value long position in a bond with a PVBP of 0.1000 needs to be hedged. The hedging guidance from the standard single-issue futures PVBP approach implies 1,031 March contracts (i.e., $[0.1000/0.0970] \times 1,000$) if the futures is risk-weighted off the 7.25% of May 2016, but 1,255 March contracts (i.e., $[0.1000/0.0797] \times 1,000$) if the futures is risk-weighted off the 12% of November 2008-13. Thus, the latter calculation is 22% higher than the former.

By definition, a single-issue futures' PVBP measure focuses solely on the issue currently flagged by the specific identification rule (such as "minimum converted forward price" or "minimum basis after carry"). When the rule flags a new issue, the futures' risk-weighting abruptly shifts its focus to the newly identified bond. Given the "at-the-money" switching situation during late January/early February 1989, a continued rally would have signaled a switch to the 12% of August 2008-13, whereas a market decline would have indicated a switch back to the 7.25% of May 2016. Thus, with the right kind of volatility within a narrow trading range, the single-issue futures risk-weighting would have generated a series of 22% shifts in the bond contract's PVBP.

Such sharp shifts in the PVBP of the futures contract do not make sense. The crux of the problem is that the single-issue approach *reacts to*, but does not *anticipate*, changes in bond deliverability. Thus, the single-issue futures risk-weighting approach ignores an important dimension of the effect of delivery option value on futures price risk.

Ignoring the switching possibility until after the fact accentuates certain option-like biases in the hedging performances of single-issue weighted hedges.

- If the 7.25% of May 2016 (a low coupon issue) were currently the likely deliverable:

  a. A *short* futures position weighted solely off the 7.25% of May 2016 to hedge a long cash position will perform *favorably* in a rally as the market begins to price in delivery of the high coupon issues. The position benefits from the market rally since the futures will tend to lag the converted price 7.25% of May 2016. By overweighting the risk of the futures, this position has too few short contracts if the market trades up. However, should the market trade down, the futures converge to the 7.25% of May 2016 weighting so that the position is floored. The result is a *long* call option-like bias in the position's payoff profile.

  b. Conversely, a *long* futures position weighted off the 7.25% of May 2016 to hedge a short cash position will perform *unfavorably* in a rally. Again, by overweighting the risk of the futures, this position is holding too few contracts long if the market trades up since the market begins to price in delivery of the high coupon issues. However, the position is hedged should the market trade down. The result is a *short* call option-like bias in the position's payoff profile.

- If the 12% of August 2008-13 (a high coupon issue) were currently the likely deliverable and switching between the 13% of August 2008-13 and the 7.25% of May 2016 is considered:

  a. A *short* futures position weighted solely off of the 12% of August 2008-13 to hedge a long cash position will perform *favorably* in a bear market as delivery of the low coupon issues becomes more likely. The position benefits in a bear market since the futures, now more closely linked to the higher-converted PVBP 7.25% of May 2016, will tend to underperform the converted price of the 12% of August 2008-13. By underweighting the risk of the futures, this position has too many short contracts if the market trades down. However, should the market trade up, the position is hedged since the weighting of the futures will converge to that of the 12% of August 2008-13. The result is a *long* put option-like bias in the position's payoff profile.

b. Conversely, a *long* futures position weighted solely off the 12% of August 2008-13 to hedge a short cash position will perform *unfavorably* in a bear market. The position has too many long contracts in a down market where delivery of the low coupon issues is becoming more probable. However, should the market trade up, the position is hedged since the weighting of the futures will converge to that of the 12% of August 2008-13. The result is a *short* put option-like bias in the position's payoff profile.

• Finally, a deliverability switch from the 12% of August 2008-13 to an even lower risk-weighted issue like the 14% of November 2006-11 would again generate a call option bias to hedges weighted off the 12% of August 2008-13 (see the 7.25% to 12% switch case above).

Intuitively, the solution to the hedging problem is to use an option pricing approach and view the risk of the contract as a weighted average of the risk implied by each possible individual CDI. The weights would reflect the probabilities that each individual issue would be the ultimate CDI.

Since there are sometimes 30 or so deliverable issues, the problem sketched above is most easily addressed through simulation methods. However, simplifying the problem to a two-bond scenario (e.g., the 7.25% of May 2016 versus the 12% of August 2008-13) with a single known delivery date permits a simple closed-form solution using the Margrabe [1978] exchange option model. Margrabe's model, suitably adjusted, provides valuable insights for both pricing the quality option and solving the futures contract PVBP calculation problem.

A Two-Bond Margrabe Framework.

The Margrabe exchange option model can be tailored to handle the Treasury bond futures quality delivery option. The tailored problem's assumptions would be as follows:

1. Only two issues, Bond 1 (say, the 7.25% of May 2016) and Bond 2 (say, the 12% of August 2008-13) are potential cheapest deliverable issues.

2. The returns on these bonds follow a bivariate geometric Wiener process.

3. The appropriate volatility parameter (the standard deviation of the difference in the returns on the two bonds) is known and constant.

4. The exchange option's expiration date, date T, is the futures contract's single delivery date. The single delivery date is also the contract's last trading date.

The Pricing Formula. Under the assumptions above, the delivery date's final futures price converges to the lower of the two bonds' converted prices. Following the logic of Chapter 4, the bond with the lower converted date T forward price on date 0 is indicated as the most likely deliverable issue. For discussion purposes, normalize on this situation by viewing the problem of the Bond 1 long basis trader who, on date T, will have the option of delivering either Bond 1 (the issue held) or selling out Bond 1 in favor of acquiring and delivering Bond 2.

On date 0, this Bond 1 basis trader must value the option to exchange $1/CF^2$ units of Bond 2 for $1/CF^1$ units of Bond 1 on date T. Using the notation of Chapter 4, the *per contract* final date T payoff, $G_{T,T}$, to the long Bond 1 basis trader can be described by the terminal payoff:

$$G_{T,T} = \text{Maximum}\{0, (B_T^1/CF^1) - (B_T^2/CF^2)\}$$

The Margrabe-inspired solution to the value of this exchange option as of date 0, $G_{0,T}$, is

$$G_{0,T} = [1/(1 + rn_0)]\{[FP_{0,T}^1/CF^1]N(d) - [FP_{0,T}^2/CF^2]N(d - Sn_0'^{.5})\}$$

where:

$FP_{0,T}^i$ = the date 0 forward price of bond i for date T settlement

n'_0 = the fraction of a year until delivery:

$d = [\log([FP_{0,T}^1/CF^1]/[FP_{0,T}^2/CF^2]) + (S/2)n'_0]/Sn_0'^{.5}$;

S = the standard deviation of the return of Bond 1 minus the return of Bond 2; and

$N(.)$ = the cumulative normal distribution function.

The basic futures pricing formula from the model equals;

$$F_{0,T} = FP_0^1 - G_{0,T}(1 + rn_0)$$

This formula views the (cum-delivery option) futures as the equivalent of a forward contract on $1/CF^1$ units of Bond 1 minus an option to exchange $1/CF^2$ units of Bond 2 for $1/CF^1$ units of Bond 1.

The futures price discount from the converted forward price of Bond 1, $G_{0,T}(1 + rn_0)$, multiplied by the conversion factor of Bond 1 equals the model basis after carry for Bond 1:

$$\text{Bond 1 Basis After Carry} = CF^1 G_{0,T}(1 + rn_0)$$

After some substitutions and rearrangements, an alternative expression for the model futures price is obtained:

$$F_{0,T} = \{1 - N(d)\}FP^1_{0,T}/CF^1 + N(d - Sn_0'^{.5})FP^2_{0,T}/CF^2$$

In this light, the theoretical futures price is a special weighted-average of the converted forward prices of the two possible deliveralbe bonds.

Example.   On January 20, 1989, the forward price (for March 31, 1989 settlement) of the 7.25% of May 2016 was 83-05, while that of the 12% of August 2008-13 was 126-01. The March 1989 conversion factor of the 7.25% of May 2016 was 0.9175, so that its converted forward price was 90-20. The March 1989 conversion factor of the 12% of August 2008-13 was 1.3893, so that its converted forward price was 90-23.[7] In terms of the model inputs, $n_0' = 0.192 (= 70/365)$ and, using $S = 0.022$ as the volatility input, $d = -0.08920$. Then, $N(d) = 0.46446$ and $N(d - Sn_0'^{.5}) = 0.46063$. With these imputs, the model futures price equals 90-10:

$$F_{0,T} = \{1 - 0.46446\}(90.625) + 0.46063(90.71875)$$
$$= 90.32109$$
$$= 90\text{-}10$$

The futures price's discount from the converted forward price of the 7.25% of May 2016 equals 10 ticks:

$$G_{0,T}(1 + rn_0) = 0.46446(90.625) - 0.46063(90.71875)$$
$$= 0.304$$
$$= 10 \text{ticks}$$

Finally, the model basis after carry on the 7.25% of May 2016 equals nine ticks ($= 0.9175 \times 10$).

---

7. Thus, in converted forward price terms, the 7.25% was three ticks cheaper to deliver than the 12%.

Hedging Guidance

Suppose that Bond 1 initially has the lowest converted forward price. Using the constant repo rate measure of the BVBP of the futures, the single-issue futures' PVBP would be calculated as

$$PVBP_0^{fut} = (1 + r\,n_0)PVBP^1/CF^1$$

This $PVBP_0^{fut}$ is appropriate for a contract written on Bond 1 with no delivery options attached. In the example above, if the repo rate were 8.75%, the single-issue futures' PVBP would equal:

$$\begin{aligned}PVBP_0^{fut_1} &= (1 + [0.0875(70/360)])[0.0875/0.9175]\\ &= 1.017[0.0954]\\ &= 0.0970\end{aligned}$$

However, this futures risk measure ignores the possibility that the 12% of August 2008-13 might become the deliverable March 1989 bond. The corresponding single-issue futures' PVBP value using this 12% bond equals 0.0797 ($= 1.017\,[0.1089/1.3893]$). The two-bond pricing model can be used to suggest an alternative futures' PVBP.

A Simple Weighted-Average Futures' PVBP

As conventionally interpreted to apply to parallel basis point shifts, the model suggests a simple measure of the PVBP of the futures:

$$PVBP_0^{fut} = \{1 - N(d)\}PVBP_0^{fut_1} + N(d - S\,n_0'^{.5})PVBP_0^{fut_2}$$

The suggestion is to view the $PVBP^{fut}$ as a weighted-average of the standard solutions appropriate when each individual bond is the CDI and there is no possibility of a switch. The weights reflect the risk-neutral probability that Bond 2 will become the date T CDI.

For example, if the converted forward price of Bond 1 were such lower than that of Bond 2, $N(d)$ and $N(d - S\,n_0'^{.5})$ would be relatively close to zero, the option to swap for and deliver Bond 2 would be low in value, and the weighted-average $PVBP_0^{fut}$ would tend toward the static Bond 1 CDI solution.

On the other hand, if the converted forward price of Bond 1 were much higher than that of Bond 2, $N(d - S\,n_0'^{.5})$ would be relatively close to one, the option to swap for and deliver Bond 2 would be high in vlaue, and the weighted-average $PVBP_0^{fut}$ would tend toward the static Bond 2 CDI solution.

If the converted forward prices of Bonds 1 and 2 were equal, $N(d)$ and $N(d - Sn_0'^{.5})$ would be close to 0.5, the option to swap for and deliver Bond 2 would be "at-the-money." Here the weighted-average $PVBP_0^{fut}$ solution would approximately be a simple average of the two individual static CDI solutions.

Finally, any other intermediate case would be handled in a similar fashion, using the appropriate risk-neutral probability weighting. Of course, the significance of the weighted-average hedge ratio solution is that the weights shift over time in response to changes in the probability that it will be optimal to deliver each bond.

In the January 20, 1989 example above, the suggested futures' weighted-average PVBP would equal:

$$PVBP_0^{fut} = \{1 - 0.46446\}[0.0970] + 0.46063[0.0797]$$
$$= 0.0887$$

Finally, the hedger should tailor the weighted-average measure to reflect the expected movement in term repo rates. Table 7–10 presents a matrix of futures' PVBP measures suggested by alternative repo shift assumptions.

Table 7–10. **Alternative Futures' PVBP Measures for March 1989 Contract Price Date: January 20, 1989.**

Assumed CDI	Constant Repo	Converted Cash PVBP	Parallel Shift Repo
If 7.25% of May 2016	0.0970	0.0954	0.0952
If 12% of August 2008–13	0.0797	0.0784	0.0779
Weighted-Average (Weightings: 0.536/0.461)	0.0887	0.0873	0.0869

Historical Application

Figure 7.1 plots both the model's delivery probability weight for the 12% of August 2008-13, $N(d - Sn_0'^{.5})$, and the March 1989 futures price over the interesting January 11, 1989 to February 17, 1989 period.[9]

---

9. In computing the model delivery probability, each day's implied standard deviation of the difference in the returns of the 7.25% of May 2016 and the 12% of August 2008-13 is used as the S input. This implied value equates the model and market futures prices.

Figure 7–1. Deliverability and Market Levels.

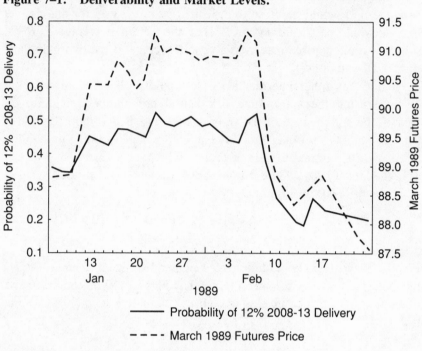

Note how the 12%'s delivery probability weight rose sharply from 34% to the 50% range as the market rallied into 90 and 91 handles. With the sudden bearish break in the market on February 9th and 10th, the probability of the 12% of August 2008-13 becoming the March 1989 CDI fell dramatically.

Figure 7–2 presents a comparison of the futures' PVBPs implied by the single-bond CDI approach for the 7.25% of May 2016 and the 12% of August 2008-12, as well as that for the two-bond weighted-average solution. The converted cash bond PVBP measure is chosen for illustrative purposes. In mid-January, the increased probability of the 12% of August 2008-13's delivery against the March contract drives the weighted-average futures' *PVBP* away from the 7.25% of May 2016 single-issue value implied by the 12% of August 2008-13. As illustrated in Figure 7–1, the probability of the 12% of August 2008-13 being the March 1989 CDI drops sharply beginning February 9. As a result, the weighted-average futures' PVBP shifts toward the single-issue PVBP answer implied by the 7.25% of May 2016.

Figure 7–2. A Probability-Weighted Futures' PVBP.

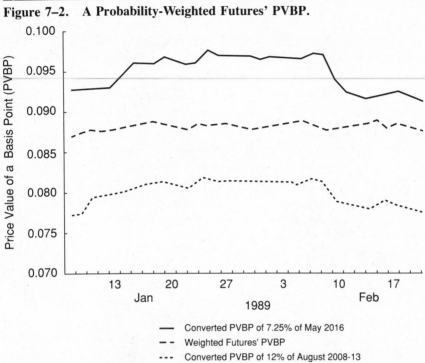

Note that the two-bond weighted-average futures' PVBP is less volatile than either of the single-issue measures. Each single- issue converted PVBP rises and falls with movements in the futures price level. However, market level fluctuations also change the weights mixing the two converted PVBPs. Thus, while the market rally between January 9 and February 7 raises the converted PVBPs of both the 7.25% (from 0.0926 to 0.0970) and the 12% (from 0.0769 to 0.0795), the rise in the 12%'s delivery weighting from about 35% to about 50% remixes the weighted-average from the high 7.25% value to the much lower 12%'s value. This reweighting tends to offset the effects of the rises in the individual issue converted PVBPs. Thus, the weighted-average futures' PVBP measure rises by a smaller proportion (from 0.0871 to only 0.0882).

Simulation Models

The two-bond Margrabe exchange option model provides a first approach that is easy to implement in handling CDI uncertainty for both basis pricing and futures risk-weighting. However, the two-deliverable issue and single delivery date assumptions are unnecessarily constricting. Cheng [1985] applies the framework to pricing the bond futures delivery option for up to three deliverable issues. Hemler [1988] provides extensions for the n-deliverable bond case. However, these single date approaches are unable to address the full range of timing and quality options given to the short position under the terms of Treasury bond and note futures contracts.

Simulation analysis is one practicable solution to a complete analysis of Treasury contract delivery options. Kane and Marcus [1986] use simulation analysis to suggest a blended futures' PVBP defined as the $PVBP^{fut}$ of each deliverable issue weighted by the probabilities of each individual issue becoming the final CDI. Within their simulations, Kane and Marcus show that such a blended $PVBP^{fut}$ would outperform the naive "no CDI switch" approaches.

Summary

This chapter has focused on hedging with Treasury bond and note futures. A variety of factors affect PVBP-weighted Treasury futures hedge performance: bond and note convexity, repo rate shifts, relative yield shifts, and CDI identity uncertainty. The convexity issue is the most easily managed, especially since available contract markets now span important points in the maturity structure (i.e., two-year, five-year, 10-year and the bond). Repo rate uncertainty is less manageable, but clear choices exist. CDI indentity uncertainty has important implications for hedge ratio selection. The impact of CDI identity switching can be modelled either analytically (under simplifying assumptions) or through simulation methods. Relative yield risk is what remains after hedges are implemented. This risk can be controlled to some extent through yield volatility weighted hedges.

CHAPTER 8

Regulatory Concerns: The Volatility of 1986, the Crash of 1987, and the Trading Scandals of 1988–89

"Wait 'till next year.". . . . (Cub fan/Local)

With the appearance of isolated episodes of wild intraday stock price volatility in 1986 and early 1987, the stock market crash of October 1987, and the U.S. Justice Department's investigation of trading abuses in 1988 and 1989, financial futures markets have been placed under growing scrutiny. Current regulatory concerns are properly focused upon a number of questions. Does financial futures trading have adverse effects on the underlying cash markets? What was the role of the stock index futures markets during the 1987 stock market crash? Do the current organization of open-outcry pit trading and certain dual trading practices foster an environment in which public orders are systematically abused? Is futures trading fair? This chapter presents a brief overview of these current market structure and regulatory issues. Since questions regarding the effects of stock index futures trading on the stock market have been central to the recent controversies, the discussion begins with an analysis of this issue.

Effects of Futures Trading on Cash Securities Markets: A Case Study of Stock Index Futures[1]

Even before the October 1987 stock market crash, traders, investors and the market regulators voiced concerns about the possible adverse effects of index futures trading. In particular, the cash stock market impact of program trading has become an important issue in contract design and market regulation. The concern centers on whether program trading has increased stock market price volatility. Excess price volatility is undesirable because investors may have to buy or sell stocks at artificial prices, thus creating windfall gains and losses in a market where the gains and losses from the "fundamentals" are variable enough. Such excess volatility is also undesirable since it decreases the informational content of stock prices.

Stock index futures program trading has two profound effects on the cash market for stocks. The first concerns the role of the index futures market in the "price discovery" process. The second concerns the distortion of the natural order flow to the floor of the stock exchanges caused by program trader activity.

Price Discovery Effects

Program traders do cause pressures on cash market prices. However, in a broad sense, such price pressures generated by arbitrage trading only bring the cash market in line with the valuation reflected by the previous movement in the futures.

One useful way to view the effects of stock index futures arbitragers concerns the sequence of events surrounding the decision of a previously bullish portfolio manager to turn bearish on the stock market. However, assume that the portfolio manager still believes that his individual stock "picks" will outperform the market over time. Consequently, he keeps

---

1. This section draws in part from Merrick (1987).

his portfolio intact, but sells S&P 500 futures contracts of equivalent value to hedge his position against market risk. Since no sell order on the cash side is entered, only the futures market is initially affected by the portfolio manager's change of heart: In order to find buyers to absorb this new futures contract sell order, the index futures price is nudged down a bit.

If prices were initially in their fair basis equals carry relation, now they are slightly misaligned. Index futures are cheap relative to the basket of actual index stocks. This is the signal for the arbitrager to act. He buys the underpriced futures contract and sells a basket of stocks carefully selected to mimic the value change of the S&P 500 index. The arbitrager's orders put some upward pressure on the index futures price and (at last) downward pressure on the prices of the stocks composing his basket.

In the "bearish portfolio manager" example above, cash market selling by program traders directly leads to the cash index decline. However, in this instance, the true source of the cash market fall was the previous weakness in the futures price. The futures market "discovered" the new bearish sentiments of the investing public. Arbitragers ensured that this "bad news" was transmitted to the cash markets in individual stocks. The *net* results of the portfolio manager's shift to bearish sentiments are lower futures prices *and* lower cash stock prices.

In effect, the portfolio manager made the sell decision, but delegated responsibility for the actual stock market sales to the arbitrager. The "fee" collected by the arbitrager consists of the spread implicit in the initially underpriced futures. The portfolio manager was willing to pay this fee (that is, sell the futures at less than fair value) because the implied transactions costs of accepting this "low" futures price were lower than his direct transactions costs of selling out and then subsequently rebuilding his cash stock portfolio. Also, the futures sale is accomplished almost immediately, whereas the liquidation of a large portfolio might take some time.

Through implicitly delegating his cash market sales to the arbitrager, the portfolio manager shifts the burden of selling a large complex stock portfolio to an agent who has come to specialize in such sales (or purchases). Thus, one can interpret the advent of stock index futures, and the arbitragers themselves, as responses to the institutional investor's desire to develop low-cost ways to acquire or liquidate large portfolio holdings. In fact, the term "program trading" as applied to futures/

cash index arbitragers makes perfect sense in this regard, since investment houses servicing large-scale portfolio restructurings for institutional investors traditionally referred to their services as "doing a program" long before the advent of index futures trading. For the case of arbitrage in futures, however, the stock portfolio involved is always the index-based basket or a reasonable facsimile.

The Economic Role of Arbitragers

Arbitragers seek to profit from misaligned relative prices. This last statement might seem to mean that "arbitragers make easy money at the expense of true investors." However, such an interpretation would be misleading. First, the arbitrage process itself is costly. Arbitrage firms must invest heavily in communication, trade evaluation, and trade execution systems. Second, the trades themselves are not completely without risk. For some trades, the cash positions assembled by the arbitrager do not always track the futures returns perfectly. For example, stock index futures program traders accept both tracking risk and execution risk. Tracking risk is incurred, since program traders typically use a subset of the entire index portfolio to create their stock baskets. Program traders must accept execution risk because, while futures positions can be changed almost immediately, stock orders may actually be executed only after some delay. Both tracking risk and execution risk mean that unfavorable basis slippages may occur.

Most important, it can be argued that basis market arbitragers actually help true investors. By working to bring about fair intermarket relative pricing, arbitragers allow speculators and hedgers to open and close futures positions at prices that are fairer relative to the underlying cash market than those they would have attained without arbitrage trade price pressures. Thus, arbitragers help reduce some of the excess uncertainty that users of futures markets bear. Furthermore, arbitrage trading adds to market liquidity. Additional liquidity in a market benefits all market users. In particular, it lowers total transactions costs by shrinking the bid-ask spread and allows larger orders to be placed with shorter time delay.

Stock Market Congestion Effects

Program traders change the way orders flow to the floor of the stock exchanges. The most well-known distortionary effect of program trading is that associated with contract expiration days: the so-called "Triple Witching Hour" congestion effect. Design changes in the final settlement procedures of the major index futures contracts have mitigated the expiration day problem to a large extent.

The Triple Witching Hour Phenomenon.   Prior to the June 1987 expirations, the Triple Witching Hour occurred at 4:00 P.M. New York time on the quarterly expiration Fridays of the stock index futures contracts. On these days, three instruments—stock index futures, stock index options, and options on individual stocks—expired at the close of trading on the New York Stock Exchange.

Taken at face value, contract expirations would not appear to be such dramatic events. After all, trade in the various commodity and other financial futures contracts has occurred for years, and individual contract expirations have come and gone with very little public attention. However, the cash settlement design of the stock index futures (and index options) contracts presents special problems related to the expiration date unwinding of positions previously accumulated by arbitragers.

Recall that arbitragers hold offsetting positions in stocks and index futures. Their return is hedged perfectly if they liquidate their stock basket at the moment of the future's expiration, since the futures price is marked to the value of the cash stock index at that time. Thus, the planned expiration day strategy of the arbitrager was to submit "market-on-close" orders to the specialist trading each stock held in the stock basket. On expiration days when the net (long or short) aggregate stock position of arbitragers was large, order imbalances appeared in each specialist's book at the market's close, which produced unusual temporary price swings in one direction or the other. The imbalance occurred because the index futures are settled in cash, not through delivery of the securities.

In brief, at market close on expiration day, arbitragers supplied or demanded an abnormal quantity of stocks, but nothing in the futures settlement process provided an automatic mechanism to generate offsetting stock orders to absorb the disturbance.

Congestion effects in the cash markets of the index component stocks during the last hour of trading on index futures expiration days have been documented. Specifically, for 1983–1985 data, Stoll and Whaley (1986) find that NYSE volume in the last hour of trading is approximately double the last-hour volume of non-expiration Fridays; that last-hour cash market return volatility for index component stocks is significantly higher than for non-expiration days; and that abnormal price reversals occur on the morning following these quarterly expirations.

Possible NYSE price distortion effects are of particular interest. Stoll and Whaley's specific estimates of shifts in volatility and return reversals associated with index futures expiration days are intriguing. They estimate the standard deviation of S&P 500 index portfolio returns over the last hour of trading to be 0.23% per day when neither S&P 500 index futures nor S&P 100 index options expire, but 0.64% per day on S&P 500 index futures expiration days. Furthermore, the increase in stock return volatility on expiration days seemed to be associated with only those stocks that might be part of an arbitrage program unwinding. In particular, Stoll and Whaley report that the return volatility of NYSE stocks which are not part of the S&P 500 index shows no corresponding expiration day increase.

Return reversals are characteristic of a congested market. An abnormal price rise caused by temporary buying pressure, or an abnormal price fall caused by temporary selling pressure, would tend to be ameliorated by a price change in the opposite direction. Stoll and Whaley estimate that the S&P 500 index portfolio has a mean return reversal in the last hour of trading of 0.38% for expiration days. In contrast, no reversal takes place on non-expiration days. Furthermore, they found no evidence of expiration day-associated return reversals for non–S&P 500 stocks.

Table 8–1 presents updated evidence on expiration day return reversal effects as reported by Stoll (1988) for the June 1984 to June 1987 contract expirations. For each contract expiration, S&P 500 index returns over the last hour of trading on the expiration Friday and the first half-hour of trading on the following Monday are calculated. A reversal is said to occur if the sign of the Monday return is opposite that of the Friday return. Reversals are measured by giving the Monday return a positive sign if the Monday versus Friday return sign switch occurs; otherwise, the Monday return is given a negative sign. The average reversal for the entire period is 0.28%.

The magnitude of the average reversal accompanying index futures expiration days have been likened to the temporary cash market distortions of "block" trades in individual stocks. However, it is clear from the extreme reversals that took place on September 20, 1985 (1.401%) and June 20, 1986 (0.784%), that expiration day market congestion may not be so easily dismissed.

Table 8–1. Price Effects of S&P 500 Index Futures Friday Expirations.

Date	S&P 500 Index Values			% Returns		
	−60 Minutes	Settlement*	+30 Minutes	t	$t+1$	% Reversal
6/15/84	149.78	149.03	148.81	−0.501	−0.148	−0.148
9/21/84	167.79	165.67	165.99	−1.263	0.193	0.193
12/21/84	165.04	165.51	165.98	0.285	0.284	−0.284
3/15/85	178.27	176.53	177.03	−0.976	0.283	0.283
6/21/85	187.74	189.61	187.93	0.996	−0.886	0.886
9/20/85	183.11	182.05	184.60	−0.579	1.401	1.401
12/20/85	211.10	210.94	209.96	−0.076	−0.465	−0.465
Average	177.55	177.05	177.19	−0.302	0.095	0.267
3/21/86	235.96	233.34	234.82	−1.110	0.634	0.634
6/20/86	244.89	247.58	245.64	1.098	−0.784	0.784
9/19/86	231.00	232.21	233.01	0.524	0.345	−0.345
12/19/86	245.95	249.73	248.72	1.537	−0.404	0.404
3/20/87	296.62	298.17	297.81	0.523	−0.121	0.121
6/19/87	304.80	306.16	305.70	0.446	−0.150	0.150
Average	259.87	261.20	260.95	0.503	−0.080	0.291
Grand Avg.	215.54	215.89	215.85	0.069	0.014	0.278

Note: *Index close until 3/20/87. Index opening value thereafter. (A special opening value is calculated).
Source: Stoll (1988).

Procedural Reforms

Procedural reforms to lessen the stock price impact of contract expirations became a major issue in light of the evidence of expiration day congestion. A major change effective with the June 1987 contracts for the S&P 500 and NYSE index futures shifted the expiration of these contracts from the cash market's close to its open. This change has helped reduce excess expiration day volatility, since it effectively expands the amount of time that NYSE specialists have to assemble large orders to offset any imbalances created by arbitragers. First, arbitragers must submit their market-on-open unwinding orders prior to 9:00 A.M. on expiration day. Second, at 9:00 A.M., the New York Stock Exchange will announce any buy or sell order imbalances of 50,000 shares or more in 50 selected "blue chip" stocks. Third, as on any other day, the specialists are able to advertise unusual excess demand or supply situations by indicating the expected opening price prior to the actual opening of trading.

Finally, as on any other day, each specialist retains the prerogative to delay the opening of trading for stocks faced with unusual pricing patterns. In turn, potential buyers or sellers of the stock, given extra time and more complete information about the nature of net arbitrager activity, find it easier to respond to perceived imbalances with offsetting orders.

Index futures contract expirations typically have been "uneventful" since the adoption of the settlement at open procedure. The new procedures certainly are part of the reason for the calmer expirations. However, it is also true that program traders have become much more sophisticated about the optimal trading strategies. In particular, program traders now pay more attention to opportunities to unwind their positions (when the original mispricing reverses sign) or roll them into the next contract month (if the deferred expiration month is sufficiently mispriced), prior to the near contract's expiration day. Simulations of the optimal early program unwinding and/or rollover strategy of a hypothetical S&P 500 index futures program trader show that both the existence and direction of expiration day effects can be forecast more accurately by considering such unwinding or rolling opportunities.[2] Of course, NYSE specialists need no academic research to confirm their own observations

---

2. See Merrick (1989).

that index futures arbitrage-related program trading has changed the way buy and sell orders flow to the floor of the exchange.

Program Traders and Stock Market Order Flow

It is natural to think that program traders distort stock market order flow to some degree or another almost every day. This more general distortion problem is fundamentally caused by the fact that program traders aggregate orders in conjunction with unrelated technological advances in routing orders directly to the specialist's rings via electronic mail.

Consider the effects of generally bearish news on NYSE order flow with and without stock index futures markets and futures-related program trading. In the no-futures case, the bearish news would cause large institutional investors to begin unloading some portion of their stock portfolios. Sell orders would go out directly to the floor of the exchange, or perhaps with an intermediate stop at the block trading desks of brokerage houses. While a broad sell off of the market may take place, each individual sell order comes at a slightly different moment in time. These differences in response times reflect variation across investors in the exact meaning of the bearish news, the position change approval process, and the mechanics of placing orders. Thus, while the specialists are sure to face a sea of sell orders, the placement of these sell orders would resemble a sequence of small to medium sized waves.

The advent of stock index futures trading does not change the fact that bearish (as well as bullish) news frequently hits the market. However, the availability of stock index futures trading does mean that the investor response to bearish news is somewhat different. Exploiting the lower trading costs of futures, a good deal of the selling is diverted to the futures pits instead of going directly to the exchange. Again, because of differences in the response time of individual investors, the futures sell orders reach the pits at different moments in time. The futures marketmakers—the locals—provide liquidity to these sell orders. At some point, however, the sell pressure depresses the futures price enough that index arbitragers begin their sell programs, buying the depressed futures and sending sell orders to the floors of the NYSE and other stock exchanges.

While sell orders still reach the stock specialists' rings, they take a very different form. Program traders all watch exactly the same signal— the cash-futures basis after carry. Program traders all use the same electronic mail system to transmit their NYSE orders directly to the specialists' rings—the NYSE's Designated Order Turnaround ("Super DOT") system. Thus, while each program trader may be acting independently, as a group, they are relatively homogeneous. The program-generated sell orders that they transmit hit the floor of the NYSE in large waves. In some cases, especially on pre-June 1987 expiration days and on some of the wilder trading days of 1986 and 1987, the programs (both to sell and to buy) that hit the specialists must have seemed like tidal waves. A Securities and Exchange Commission study of the volatility experienced on September 11 and 12, 1986, exonerates program trading as a cause of the specific declines. Nevertheless, the SEC study concludes that "index-related futures trading was instrumental in the rapid transmission of changed investor perceptions to individual stock prices, and may have condensed the time period in which the decline occurred."[3]

Index Futures and the Stock Market Crash

Between the stock market's close on Tuesday, October 13, 1987 and the close of trading on Monday, October 19, 1987, the Dow Jones Industrial Average fell 30.6% in value, from 2,505 to 1,738. Most of the downward move occurred between Friday, October 16 and the close of trading on "Black Monday," when the Dow fell 508 points (22.6%). Table 8–2 presents a daily record of closing prices of the Dow, the S&P 500 index, the December S&P 500 index futures contract, and the index-futures basis.

Table 8–2. Crash Week Closing Stock Indexes and S&P 500 Futures Prices

	Date	DJIA	S&P 500	DEC 87 Futures Price	Basis
Tuesday,	Oct. 13	2,505	314.52	315.65	−1.13
Wednesday,	Oct. 14	2,412	305.23	305.00	0.23
Thursday,	Oct. 15	2,355	298.08	298.25	−0.17
Friday,	Oct. 16	2,246	282.70	282.25	0.45
Monday,	Oct. 19	1,738	224.84	201.50	23.34
Tuesday,	Oct. 20	1,841	236.83	216.25	20.58

3. See the SEC study, "The Role of Index-Related Trading in the Market Decline of September 11 and 12, 1986." See also Stoll and Whaley (1988).

Various fundamental factors have been viewed as triggers for the crash. The crash was preceded by an unexpectedly high merchandise trade deficit, a sharp increase in interest rates and Treasury bond yields, and Congressional proposals to eliminate tax benefits associated with the leveraged buyouts and tax profits from "greenmail."[4]

While the exact cause may not ever be completely understood, the role played by stock index futures markets and futures trading strategies during the crash poses an important public policy question. Of particular interest are the impacts of arbitrage-related program trading, and of a dynamic hedging strategy known as "portfolio insurance." Index arbitrage program trading has been previously discussed. A brief overview of portfolio insurance is now necessary.

Portfolio Insurance

Portfolio insurance (referred to by some as "portfolio protection") is a dynamic hedging strategy designed to assure a particular floor value for a portfolio at some specific future date, while simultaneously capturing some portion of the upside potential available to an unhedged position.[5] The strategy is a variant of stop-loss trading. Under a stop-loss strategy, the investor swaps completely out of 100%-invested position in the risky security into a riskless interest-bearing asset, should prices fall below a critical stop-out level. However, in contrast to the in-or-out stop-loss strategy, the portfolio insurance strategy employs a continuously changing risky security/riskless asset mix.

The particular rule to determine the proportion of the portfolio invested in the risky security is based on an option-replicating dynamic trading strategy. This type of strategy underlies the option pricing approach first developed by Black and Scholes (1973). Indeed, the intent of the strategy is to provide an option-like payoff. A synthetic put option position is added to the underlying long position in the risky security.

The theoretical risky security/riskless asset mix changes with the probability of the risky security's price finishing above a predetermined critical level. As this probability rises, the proportion that should be invested in the risky security increases. To finance additional purchases

---

4. See *The Report of the Presidential Task Force on Market Mechanisms*, and discussions within Kemphius, Kormendi, and Watson (1989).

5. Versions of "perpetual" portfolio insurance do exist.

of the risky security, an equal dollar amount of the riskless asset is sold. Conversely, as the probability of the risky security's price finishing above the critical level falls, the proportion that should be invested in the risky security decreases. As the position in the risky security is decreased, an equal dollar amount of the riskless asset is purchased.

The probability of the risky security's price finishing above the critical level is an increasing function of its current price.[6] As the risky security's price rises, the portfolio insurer needs to purchase more of the risky security. Conversely, as its price falls, the portfolio insurer needs to sell some of the risky security. Furthermore, the strategy requires continuous portfolio shifts in response to price changes. Thus, if prices suddenly jump up or break sharply down, the portfolio insurer will find himself underhedged or overhedged.

Note that portfolio insurance is a "buy on strength, sell on weakness" strategy. Thus, a key assumption underlying the plan is that the risky security's market is liquid enough to absorb the necessary readjustments without adverse price effects. Finally, to minimize transactions and liquidity costs, portfolio insurance plans typically emphasize futures trading.

Estimates of the value of pension assets (both equities and fixed-income securities) under formal portfolio insurance at the time of the crash ranged from $60 billion to $100 billion. With a five-year bull market in equities seemingly still on course, portfolio insurance seemed to be a prudent way of participating in a continuing stock market rally, while simultaneously limiting losses in a down market. It is likely that such portfolio insurance programs induced institutional investors to carry more stock exposure than they would have traditionally held. That is, the promise of the portfolio value floor attainable through dynamic hedging probably displaced (to some extent) the traditional static hedging method of stock/bond/bills diversification. This excess equity exposure on the part of pension funds could have been as much as $30 billion.[7]

The paradox, of course, is that the growing acceptance of the portfolio insurance paradigm by large institutional investors undermined the strat-

---

6. This probability also depends upon the "strike price" (critical floor level), the time left until the policy's expiration, the short-term interest rate and the volatility of the return on the risky security.

7. See a conjecture made within the *Preliminary and Final Reports of the Committee of Inquiry Convened by the Chicago Mercantile Exchange*.

egy's ability to match its promised performance. A strategy that would work for any single portfolio manager employing it in isolation would not work for a large group of managers employing it simultaneously. A "buy on strength, sell on weakness" strategy is destabilizing in nature. To be implemented successfully, the market must supply liquidity through the appearance of "value investors" willing to sell on strength and buy on weakness. However, such value investors were in short supply on Black Monday and marketmakers of both the stock and futures exchanges were unable to provide the necessary liquidity.

The Report of the Presidential Task Force on Market Mechanisms (the *Brady Report*) examined data on trading flows throughout the crash period. Tables 8–3 and 8–4 present day-by-day estimates of large trader sales and purchases of S&P 500 index futures contracts broken down by trader type. The identified categories list portfolio insurers, index arbitragers, options traders, locals, other pension fund managers, trading-oriented investors, foreign investors, mutual funds, and other financial institutions.

These data reveal how portfolio insurers were forced to sell huge quantities of contracts as the market tumbled on October 14, 16, and 19. On October 19, portfolio insurers were net sellers of 33,482 contracts (i.e., 34,446 contracts sold minus 964 contracts purchased). The dollar value of net contract sales by portfolio insurers on Black Monday topped $3.9 billion.[8] Large-scale selling by portfolio insurers continued through October 20, indicating that these insurers were not fully adjusted to their (moving) target equity exposure by this date.

Index Arbitrage Activity

In contrast, index arbitragers were net buyers of contracts throughout the crash period. Driven by selling pressure from portfolio insurers, the December S&P 500 index futures contract became underpriced relative to the cash index beginning about 2:30 P.M. on Friday, October 16 (see Table 8–2 for a review of closing price data). This underpricing continued for most of the following week. Taking the index at face value, the futures opened on Monday, October 19 more than 20 index points below its basis equals carry level. Late that afternoon, the futures

---

8. See the *Brady Report*.

Table 8–3. S&P 500 Index Futures Contract Sales by Large Traders (Sales in Number of Contracts)

Sales	Oct 14	Oct 15	Oct 16	Oct 19	Oct 20
Portfolio Insurers	3,460	6,413	14,627	34,446	26,146
Index Arbitragers	700	2,700	2,700	1,100	285
Options	3,589	6,618	9,643	7,667	5,890
Locals	47,426	49,773	48,847	46,753	25,214
Other Pension	238	1,122	1,615	5,387	4,770
Trading-oriented Investors	12,906	13,587	23,246	22,098	25,651
Foreign Investors	2,575	2,927	3,301	4,212	3,050
Mutual Funds	300	19	77	160	375
Other Financial	317	720	1,705	4,478	2,808
Published Total	109,740	124,810	135,344	162,022	126,562
Contracts Accounted For	71,511	83,879	105,761	126,301	94,189
Percent Accounted For	65	67	78	78	74

Source: the *Brady Report*

Table 8–4. S&P 500 Index Futures Contract Purchases by Large Traders (Purchases in Number of Contracts)

Sales	Oct 14	Oct 15	Oct 16	Oct 19	Oct 20
Portfolio Insurers	461	1,136	751	964	4,682
Index Arbitragers	8,500	4,750	11,750	13,500	1,100
Options	3,848	5,725	8,639	7,804	5,049
Locals	47,272	49,911	49,098	48,487	24,945
Other Pension	582	504	2,029	3,816	9,931
Trading-oriented Investors	9,673	14,823	25,043	38,482	37,149
Foreign Investors	1,553	1,972	3,051	5,199	3,874
Mutual Funds	0	179	505	1,217	473
Other Financial	1,006	378	867	2,727	4,793
Published Total	109,740	124,810	135,344	162,022	126,562
Contracts Accounted For	72,895	79,378	101,733	122,196	91,996
Percent Accounted For	66	64	75	75	73

Source: the *Brady Report*

traded as much as 30 index points below its fair value. Compare these 20 and 30 points discounts with a maximum closing price discount of about four points for the period between May 1982 and March 1986 reported in Merrick (1988).

However, exact measurement of the true degree of underpricing over the crash week is problematic because of stale prices in the cash index due to late openings and periodic halts of trading in individual stocks. The cash index is measured using the latest transactions price for each component stock. For stocks that had not yet opened, the previous day's last trading price is used.[9] Thus, the opening 20-point discount on October 19 was largely illusory. Nevertheless, even after adjustments are made for the staleness of index prices, underpricing throughout the crash week was the norm.[10]

Using the *Brady Report* data, program traders were net buyers of 12,400 futures contracts on October 19, and transmitted about $1.45 billion in selling activity back to the stock market.[11] The 14,600 contract gross level of trading (purchases plus sales) by index arbitragers was about 11.8% of the trading represented of publicly accounted-for volume. As a percentage of trading, arbitrage activity on October 19 was less than that generated by the 9,200 contracts traded by index arbitragers on October 14, which by any account, had been a much calmer day.

Arbitragers suffered the same cash market order execution problems as other traders selling stocks during the crash. The execution risks of the index arbitrage program trade were huge, since transactions were backed up on the NYSE's DOT system. Buying the underpriced futures contracts (with instant execution) and selling the stock side after some delay (even if only 10 or 15 minutes) is not a get rich quick scheme during a crash. Furthermore, beginning Tuesday, October 20, NYSE member firms were barred from using the DOT system to execute program trades. As the *Brady Report* emphasized, the breakdown in the arbitrage process meant that potential smoothing influences in each market could not be effectively transmitted to the other: The cash and futures markets became decoupled. This decoupling became dramatically clear when the CME suspended trading on Tuesday, between 12:15 P.M. and 1:04 P.M.

---

9. At the opening of trading on Thursday, October 22, the measured futures' discount was an unfathomable 60 index points ($30,000 per contract). Again, the index at the opening of trading (as opposed to the index of opening prices) contained many prices from the previous afternoon.

10. See Harris (1987).

11. See the *Brady Report*.

Aftermath of the Crash

A main theme of the *Brady Report* is that the stock, index futures, and index options markets constitute "one market." This thinking is easily understandable, given both the arbitrage linkages usually in place, and the dependence of hedgers like portfolio insurers on the futures market as an important source of market liquidity. Along these lines, the *Brady Report* recommended that a set of "circuit breakers" be adopted and that crisis coordination between futures and stock exchanges be improved. Two price limit rules were in place on the CME as of early 1989. First, there was a 15-point daily price limit (down from a 30-point limit instituted after the crash). Second, there was a special 5-point limit for the opening of trading set to trigger a 10-minute trading halt, and an additional 30-minute halt should the futures fall by 12 points for the day.

The NYSE also will change its trading rules for a major market drop. First, after a 96-point fall in the Dow, program trading orders will be routed into a special Super DOT file, and may be held for five minutes. Second, should the Dow fall 250 points for the day, a one-hour NYSE trading halt will be called. Third, a second NYSE trading halt will be called if the Dow trades down 400 points. This second halt will last two hours. Whatever the psychological effects of these trading halts, the specialists' jobs will be made easier. Specialists will be able to use these halts to advertise order imbalances and search for a marketclearing price (as is done at each morning's opening).

The Trading Scandals

The open-outcry auction process has been central to futures trading in the United States for over one hundred years. Given the growth and successes of futures markets over this period, the industry has typically been protective of this mode of trading versus alternatives such as a specialist system or an automated auction or order-matching system. Nevertheless, first-time visitors to the floor of a futures exchange, typically amazed at the environment of organized chaos, usually leave asking, "How can such a system work?" As indicated by their in-depth undercover investigations of the pits in 1988 and 1989, the U.S. Attorney's Office and the Federal Bureau of Investigation became intrigued by similar questions.

The federal investigations were initiated amid investor complaints of irregularities in order execution by futures brokers. A study by the

General Accounting Office lists the following major abuses that the Commodity Futures Trading Commission (CFTC) and exchanges attempt to detect:[12]

- Prearranged trading: agreeing to some aspect of a transaction before it is openly executed on the exchange floor.

- Accommodation trading: entering transactions to assist another floor participant in accomplishing improper trading objectives.

- Trading ahead of customer orders ("front-running"): trading for one's personal account or an account in which one has an interest, while having in hand any executable customer order in that contract.

- Bucketing: failure to introduce an order to the marketplace, traditionally occurring when a broker noncompetitively takes the other side of a customer order, to the detriment of the customer or other members.

- Wash trading: entering or purporting to enter into transactions to provide the appearance of trading activity without resulting in a change in market position.

- Curb trading: trading after the official close of trading.

- Cuffing: delaying the filling of customer orders to benefit another member.

- Cross-trading: matching customer orders without offering them competitively.

The physical organization of open-outcry trading, where exact time-sequencing of all trades is not known ex post, makes it difficult for surveillance systems to detect all rules violations. Trades executed during volatile market periods are especially susceptible to abuse. A customer would have little proof of abusive treatment as long as her particular trade was executed within the price range occurring around the time of the execution. Precise sequencing of trades is impossible, since current procedures require that trade executions be reported in time brackets of one minute. Furthermore, floor traders may make errors in recording or reporting such data, especially during "fast" markets.[13]

---

12. General Accounting Office, 1989, "Chicago Futures Market: Initial Observations on Trade Practice Abuses," (March): GAO/GGD-89-58.

13. Until January 14, 1986, time sequencing was even more difficult to establish since trades were reported within 30-minute brackets.

Dual trading—the practice of floor brokers trading for themselves as well as customers—is among the most controversial of pit trading practices. Critics of this practice maintain that it invites front-running. The exchanges have typically defended this practice, arguing that brokers who trade on their own account add to market liquidity and consequently lower customer trading costs. However, in 1987, the CME banned dual trading on the top step of its S&P 500 index futures pit (a valued physical trading position which facilitates reception of off-the-floor order flow).

Finally, the recent trading practices investigations have reinforced interest in electronic trading systems. One pure computerized trading system already exists (the Swiss Options and Futures Exchange: SOFEX). Furthermore, both the CME and the CBOT plan to introduce computerized trading systems. The CME's system (GLOBEX) is designed as an off-hour order matching trading system. The CBT's system (Aurora) is designed as an electronic auction market. Both systems hold the potential to extend U.S. exchanges into a 24-hour market.[14]

Concluding Comments

The 1980s have been a decade filled with both growth and turmoil for futures exchanges and their financial futures products. Primarily because of the increase in stock volatility and the crash, topics such as the effects of derivative contract trading on the underlying cash markets, and the market effects of dynamic trading strategies such as portfolio insurance—while always of academic and practitioner interest—have found their way into public policy debate. However, the case for regulatory actions to restructure cash and futures markets in a major way must be carefully argued. Any structural changes truly necessary to smooth out sources of friction and inconsistency within the overall stock market trading system and to reform futures pit trading practices in general are inevitable, if for no other reason than that international market forces will demand them.

---

14. As of mid-1989, talks between the CME and the CBOT continued concerning a possible joint computerized trading effort.

References

Arak, M. and L. Goodman, 1987, "Treasury Bond Futures: Valuing the Delivery Options," *Journal of Futures Markets*, 7 (June): 269–286.

Black, D., 1986, "Success and Failure of Futures Contracts: Theory and Evidence," *Monograph Series in Finance and Economics*, No. 1986-1, Salomon Brothers Center for the Study of Financial Institutions, New York University.

Black, F. and M. Scholes, 1973, "The Pricing of Options and Corporate Liabilities," *Journal Of Political Economy*, 81 (May/June): 637–654.

Boyle, P., 1989, "The Quality Option and Timing Option in Futures Contracts," *Journal of Finance*, 64 (March): 101–113.

Cheng, S., 1987, *Multi-asset Contingent Claims in a Stochastic Interest Rate Environment*. Ph.D. Dissertation, Stanford University.

Cox, J., J. Ingersoll, and S. Ross, 1981, "The Relation Between Forward Prices and Futures Prices," *Journal of Financial Economics*, 9 (December): 321–346.

"Delivery Strategies and the Royal Flush Option in the Treasury Bond and Note Futures Markets," 1988, Derivative Products Research Group, Shearson Lehman Hutton, Inc.

Ederington, L., 1979, "The Hedging Performance of the New Futures Markets," *Journal of Finance*, 34: 157–170.

Figlewski, S., 1984, "Hedging Performance and Basis Risk in Stock Index Futures," *Journal of Finance*, 39 (July): 657–669.

Figlewski, S., J. Merrick, and K. John, 1986, *Hedging With Financial Futures For Institutional Investors*, Ballinger (Cambridge).

Garbade, K., and W. Silber, 1983, "Cash Settlement of Futures Contracts: An Economic Analysis," *Journal of Futures Markets*, 3 (Winter): 451–472.

Garbade, K., and W. Silber, 1983, "Futures Contracts on Commodities with Multiple Varieties: An Analysis of Premiums and Discounts," *Journal of Business*, 56(3): 249–272.

Gay, G., and S. Manaster, 1984, "The Quality Option Implicit in Futures Contracts," *Journal of Financial Economics*, 13 (September): 353–370.

Gay, G., and S. Manaster, 1986, "Implicit Delivery Options and Optimal Delivery Strategies for Financial Futures Contracts," *Journal of Financial Economics*, 16 (May): 41–72.

Gay, G., and S. Manaster, 1989, "Equilibrium Futures Prices in the Presence of Implicit Delivery Options: Theory and Application to the T-bond Futures Contract," Unpublished Working Paper.

General Accounting Office, 1989, "Chicago Futures Market: Initial Observations on Trade Practice Abuses," (March): GAO/GGD-89-58.

Harris, L., 1987, "Nonsynchronous Trading and the S&P 500 Stock-Futures Basis in October 1987," Unpublished working paper, University of Southern California, December.

Hegde, S., 1987, "Coupon and Maturity Characteristics of the Cheapest-to-Deliver Bonds in the Treasury Bond Futures Contract," *Financial Analysts Journal*, (April): 70–76.

Hemler, Michael L., 1988, "The Quality Delivery Option in Treasury Bond Futures Contracts," Fuqua School of Business, Duke University, Working Paper 88-106, August.

Hieronymous, T., 1971, *The Economics of Futures Trading*, Commodity Research Bureau (New York).

Hill, J., and T. Schneeweis, 1982, "Risk Reduction Potential of Financial Futures," in G. Gay and R. Kolb (eds.), *Interest Rate Futures: Concepts and Issues*, Prentice-Hall (Englewood Cliffs, N.J.).

Jarrow, R., and G. Oldfield, 1981, "Forward Contracts and Futures Contracts," *Journal of Financial Economics*, 9: 373–382.

Jonas, S., 1986, "The Basis Book," Institutional Financial Futures Group, Shearson Lehman Hutton (January).

Kamara, A., and A. Siegel, 1987, "Optimal Hedging in Futures Markets with Multiple Delivery Specifications," *Journal of Finance*, 42 (September): 1007–1021.

Kamphius, R., R. Kormendi, and J. Watson (eds.), 1989, *Black Monday and the Future of Financial Markets*, Irwin (Homewood, Ill.), for the Mid America Institute for Public Policy Research, Inc.

Kane, A., and A. Marcus, 1986, "The Quality Option in the Treasury Bond Futures Market: An Empirical Assessment," *Journal of Futures Markets*, 6 (Summer 1986), 231–48.

Kane, A., and A. Marcus, 1986, "Valuation and Optimal Exercise of the Wild Card Option in the Treasury Bond Futures Market," *Journal of Finance*, 41 (March) 195–207.

Kilcollin, T., 1982, "Difference Systems in Financial Futures," *Journal of Finance*, 37 (December): 1183–1197.

Leibowitz, M., 1981, "The Analysis of Value and Volatility in Financial Futures," *Monograph Series in Finance and Economics*, No. 1981-3, Salomon Brothers Center for the Study of Financial Institutions, New York University.

Margrabe, W., 1978, "The Value of an Option to Exchange One Asset for Another," *Journal of Finance*, 33 (March): 177–186.

Merrick, J., 1987, "Fact and Fantasy about Stock Index Futures Program Trading," Federal Reserve Bank of Philadelphia *Business Review*, (September/October): 13–25.

Merrick, J., 1988, "Hedging With Mispriced Futures," *Journal of Financial and Quantitative Analysis*, 23 (December): 451–464.

Merrick, J., 1989, "Early Unwindings and Rollovers of Stock Index Futures Arbitrage Programs: Analysis and Implications for Predicting Expiration Day Effects," *Journal of Futures Markets*, 9 (April): 101-111.

Merrick, J., and S. Figlewski, 1984, "An Introduction to Financial Futures," Salomon Brothers Center for the Study of Financial Institutions, New York University.

Pitts, M., and R. Kopprash, 1984, "Reducing Inter-Temporal Risk in Financial Futures Hedging," *Journal of Futures Markets*, 4 (Spring): 1-13.

Preliminary and Final Reports of the Committee of Inquiry Convened by the Chicago Mercantile Exchange, 1988, Chicago Mercantile Exchange (Chicago, Illinois).

Richard, S., and M. Sundaresan, 1981, "A Continuous Time Model of Forward Prices and Futures Prices in a Multigood Economy," *Journal of Financial Economics*, 9 (December): 347–371.

Report of the Presidential Task Force on Market Mechanisms, 1988, U.S. Government Printing Office (Washington, D.C.).

"The Role of Index-Related Trading in the Market Decline of September 11 and 12, 1986," Securities and Exchange Commission.

Rolfo, J., 1980, "Optimal Hedging Under Price and Quantity Uncertainy: The Case of a Cocoa Producer," *Journal of Political Economy*, 88 (February)

Silber, W., 1982, "The Economic Role of Futures Trading," in *Futures Markets: Their Economic Role*, American Enterprise Institute (Washington, D.C.).

Silber, W., 1984, "Marketmaker Behavior in an Auction Market: An Analysis of Scalpers in Futures Markets," *Journal of Finance*, 39 (September): 937–953.

Stoll, H., 1988, "Index Futures, Program Trading, and Stock Market Procedures," *Journal of Futures Markets*, (August): 391–412.

Stoll, H., and R. Whaley, 1986, "Expiration Day Effects of Index Options and Futures," *Monograph Series in Finance and Economics*, N. 1986-3, Salomon Brothers Center for the Study of Financial Institutions, New York University.

Stoll, H., and R. Whaley, 1988, "Volatility and Futures: Message Versus Messenger," *Journal of Portfolio Management*, (Winter): 20-22.

Toevs, A., and D. Jacob, 1986, "Futures and Alternative Hedge Ratio Methodologies," *Journal of Portfolio Management*, (Spring).

Wang, G., E. Moriarty, R. Michalski, and J. Jordan, 1989, "Empirical Analysis of the Liquidity of the S&P 500 Index Futures Market During the October 1987 Market Break," Commodity Futures Trading Commission (February, revised).

Working, H., 1962, "New Concepts Concerning Futures Markets and Prices," *American Economic Review*, 52 (May): 431–459.

Index

About the Author

John J. Merrick, Jr. is a Vice-President at Shearson Lehman Hutton Inc. His work at Shearson focuses on financial futures research, portfolio management, and trading and client support.

Prior to joining Wall Street, he was an Associate Professor of Finance at New York University's Graduate School of Business Administration, where he taught courses on financial futures and options markets. He has also served as a visiting scholar in the research department of the Federal Reserve Bank of Philadelphia.

Dr. Merrick has published papers on futures and options hedging and arbitrage strategies in a variety of professional and academic journals, and collaborated with Stephen Figlewski and Kose John on *Hedging with Financial Futures for Institutional Investors*, (Ballinger, 1986).

He holds a Ph.D. in Economics from Brown University.

The Institutional Investor Series in Finance

The Institutional Investor Series in Finance has been developed specifically to bring you—the finance professional—the latest thinking and developments in investments and corporate finance. As new challenges arise in this fast-paced arena, you can count on this series to provide you with the information you need to gain the competitive edge.

Institutional Investor is the leading communications company serving the global financial community and publisher of the magazine of the same name. Institutional Investor has won 36 major awards for distinguished financial journalism—including the prestigious National Magazine Award for the best reporting of any magazine in the United States. More than 560,000 financial executives in 170 countries read Institutional Investor publications each month. Thousands more attend Institutional Investor's worldwide conferences and seminars each year.